Showing Up Naked

Peeling Away the Layers to Your Authentic Self

Erica Boucher

Copyright © 2011, 2019 Erica Boucher

All rights reserved.

No part of this book may be used or reproduced in any manner whatsoever without written permission from the author or publisher except in the case of brief quotations embodied in critical articles or reviews.

ISBN: 978-0-9849081-0-3

Published by Earth Harmony Publishing, Orlando, Florida

For Information Address:
Earth Harmony Publishing
7330 Cherry Laurel Drive
Orlando, Florida 32835

The author can be reached at erica@ericaboucher.com, www.ericaboucher.com.

Printed in the United States of America

Design, Composition, and Layout by Erica Boucher & Martin "Wolf" Murphy

DEDICATION

To God. And to my parents.
Thank you for giving me Life.

What a beautiful co-creation.

Acknowledgments

I'd like to thank the many people who have influenced me and my work, and therefore this book, over the past 12 years. Some had a very direct affect on me and my growth both personally and professionally. Sometimes that growth came in the form of disappointment, heartbreak, pain and conflict…and for that I am eternally grateful. These are the ones that so often had the biggest impact, and inspired the greatest evolutionary growth spurts within me. Thank you, thank you, thank you for being such an important part of this life experience for me.

Then there are those who, without which, I would never have been able to carry this vision through to completion. I am blessed with a beautiful network of friends and family who do a wonderful job of spurring me on, always encouraging me to keep writing, to keep sharing, to keep going. A body of work such as this, that has taken me over a decade to complete, could never have been done without the love and support of countless others. Sometimes that support came directly, through words and acts of encouragement. Other times it was a simple, off-hand comment made by another that would inspire an entire section of this book.

Throughout this book I share stories and examples inspired by friends, family and the many people with whom I've worked to help support the understanding of the material. In each and every case it is with reverence, appreciation, respect and gratitude for what they taught me, and while I always protect the anonymity of others, I can only hope that for those who find themselves somewhere in this book, that they realize the spirit with which I share.

This book is a thank you to Life, and to everyone who shares in it with me. With that being said, I would like to specifically thank my parents, who loved, challenged and supported me in all the right ways to make me who I am today. Everything about our experience together has been perfect. Thank you for believing in me Mauro Diez, Mark Miller, Sonya Savage, Christine Dalton, Sherry Evans, Marsha Defacci, David O'Donnell, Harley & Sue Bessire, Rave Mehta, Laura Larmay, Kristen Manieri, Krista Berman, Brian Burgess. Thank you to my ex-husband, Steve, for everything we shared together. I have no regrets, and I wouldn't change a thing about our experience together. It was exactly what it was supposed to be. A very specific thank you to Martin Murphy (Wolf) for your editing, layout and design work, not to mention the hours upon hours of stimulating conversation we shared around this material. This would not have been possible without you.

Thank you to all past and future Empath Yoga graduates for answering the call within you to spread love and light through your work with others.

This list goes on and on, and since I can't possibly include everyone, I simply say thank you to everyone who has been a part of my journey in any way. You know who you are.

Table of Contents

Introduction 1

SECTION I: WAKING UP 14

Chapter 1: The Journey Back Home 16
    So How Did We Get So Lost? 19
    The "I Am" Presence 19
    The Social Condition 20
    The Social Mask 22
    So Now What? 24
    Become Your Own Best Friend 25
    So What is True? 27
    The Birth of Fear 28
    The "I Am" Presence 30
    An Empath Yoga Perspective on Easy Pose 33

Chapter 2: Touch Your Soul 34
    There is Nothing to Fix 34
    Awakening From the Dream 34
    Love vs. Fear 38
    Returning to Love 39
    Spend Time Alone 41
    Silence the Critic 43
    When it Becomes Dangerous 44
    Watch Your Language 46
    Choose Love 49
    Be Gentle 50
    Touch Your Soul 52
    An Empath Yoga Perspective on Child's Pose 55

Chapter 3: From I to We 56
    ego vs. Ego 57
    The Illusion of Separation 58
    The Nature of Cooperation 59
    Look Again 61
    We Are All Connected 63
    The Universal One Mind 64
    Unconditional Love 67
    An Empath Yoga Perspective on Cat Pose 69
    An Empath Yoga Perspective on Cow Pose 70

Chapter 4: The Internal Compass ... 72
- You Have a Purpose ... 73
- Dreams ... 75
- Values ... 77
- What Do You Want? ... 80
- Vision ... 81
- Co-Creating With Spirit ... 84
- An Empath Yoga Perspective on Boat Pose ... 87

SECTION II: EMOTIONAL EMPOWERMENT ... 88

Chapter 5: Feel Your Way to Real ... 92
- Uncomfortably Numb ... 94
- The Body is the Subconscious Mind ... 95
- The Body Doesn't Lie ... 96
- Developing a Bodily Sense ... 97
- Meditation ... 100
- Learning to Label Your Feelings ... 101
- Our Feelings As Guideposts ... 104
- An Empath Yoga Perspective on Crescent Moon ... 107

Chapter 6: Coming Alive Again ... 108
- Compulsive Behaviors ... 109
- Breathe ... 112
- Breathe Into the Center of It ... 113
- Develop Trust in Yourself ... 115
- Emotional Energy as Fuel For Our Live ... 116
- Cathartic Emotional Release ... 116
- Move ... 117
- Create ... 118
- Expanding and Contracting ... 118
- An Empath Yoga Perspective on Downward Facing Dog ... 123
- An Empath Yoga Perspective on Supported Fish ... 124

Chapter 7: Forgiveness: The Correction of an Error ... 126
- Effects of Unforgiving Minds ... 128
- Acceptance ... 130
- Compassion ... 130
- Willingness is a Key Ingredient ... 134
- Grieving ... 137
- Self-Forgiveness ... 138
- A Story of Forgiveness ... 139
- An Empath Yoga Perspective on Triangle Pose ... 145

Chapter 8: Letting Go 146
    Clearing the Clutter 146
    What's Your Story 150
    What Are You Addicted To? 153
    Creating Space 155
    Feeling Stuck? 156
    There is Beauty in Death 158
    An Empath Yoga Perspective on Savasana 164

SECTION III: BEING IN RELATIONSHIP 166

Chapter 9: Deep Listening 169
    A Lesson in Listening 176
    Over-Empathizing 178
    Deep Listening to Ourselves 179
    Wise Decisions Don't Come From Your Head 181
    Deep Listening to Life 184
    An Empath Yoga Perspective on Seated Forward Bend 188

Chapter 10: Keeping it Real 190
    The Frame of Reference 192
    What is Real? 195
    The Power of Our Thoughts 199
    Think For Yourself 202
    When Does Positive Thinking Become Dangerous? 204
    It's Time to Wake Up 206
    An Empath Yoga Perspective on Five-Pointed Star 209
    An Empath Yoga Perspective on Warrior I & II 210

Chapter 11: The Gift of Conflict 212
    The Mirror 216
    Humility 217
    Self-Love 218
    Sometimes It's Not About You 218
    The Win-Win 220
    Become Defenseless 222
    Judgment vs. Discernment 226
    Setting Boundaries 227
    Compassion 229
    An Empath Yoga Perspective on Plank Pose 231

Chapter 12: Being Fully Expressed 232
    Becoming Fully Expressed In Our Relationships 233
    Speaking Your Truth 233
    Finding Center in Self 235
    We Teach People How to Treat Us 236
    The Power of Our Words...................................... 239
    Becoming Fully Expressed In Our Lives 242
    Becoming Bigger Than the Fear 242
    Stop Making Excuses 245
    Gratitude 247
    Choice 250
    Courage 252
    Non-Attachment 253
    Trust... 253
    Fill Out Your Spirit 255
    You Are the Channel 256
    Your Life is Your Canvas..................................... 257
    An Empath Yoga Perspective on Tadasana 261

*"A life which is not examined
is not worth living."*

—*Plato*

Introduction

I'll never forget the day, now more than 20 years ago, when something inside of me finally let go. I was in my late twenties, a graduate of a prestigious college, and working in a corporate environment in which I felt completely out of place—miserable, really. I was married with a comfortable home, a nice car, trendy clothing, and lots of friends. I had everything I was always told I would need in order to be happy. And yet I wasn't happy. Participation in numerous leadership training programs did little more than build me up so I could get better at playing the corporate game. Something deeper was missing. One day, after working so hard to get somewhere and feeling like I was spinning my wheels, I finally had enough.

That day, as I drove home from work, I put my hands on my steering wheel, looked up at the sky, and prayed, honestly prayed, for the first time in my life, to a God I wasn't even sure existed. "Δ God, I give up. I don't know what I'm supposed to be doing here. If you exist, and if I have a purpose on this Earth, please show me because I obviously don't have a clue." I realize now looking back that I was letting go, admitting to myself and to life how much I didn't know. Although born and raised Catholic, I was never a religious person, and that direct, heartfelt communication was the most honest, sincere conversation with God I had ever had.

I started searching for a meaningful job that would allow me to feel passionate and alive and purposeful. So when I was offered the opportunity to work at a shelter for homeless families—at a hefty cut in pay—my hesitation lasted only briefly. My responsibility was to create a comprehensive rehabilitation program for homeless adults. I was given very little direction—just instructed to create a four-week program that would teach life and leadership skills to homeless adults to help break their cycle of dependency. This greatly appealed to me, for up to that time I felt my career, and my life, lacked creativity and inspiration. Finally, I could sink my teeth into something exciting and meaningful.

I spent my first three months behind closed doors brainstorming about what to teach, in what order, and to what end. I ventured outside of my office only to interview guests at the shelter for insight into what they thought would be most useful to them. I toyed with the idea of teaching typing skills, showing them how to use a register, and other marketable skills. I had almost complete creative license to teach them the skills I believed would most benefit them. In the end, with some coaxing by the executive director and program manager, I streamlined my approach. My objectives became to boost their self-esteem, motivate and inspire change, and open the door to a new way of life.

On January 3, 2000, the first 120-hour Adult Leadership Program was launched. I walked into a room with 13 homeless adults who had just been informed they would be required to attend this program before looking for a job. Most of them were angry and resentful—both for being homeless and jobless, and for being forced" to attend a program that would only delay their goal of leaving the shelter. I spent the first hour overcoming my own self-doubts about a program that had yet to be taught—all the while accepting everything from grumbled complaints to angry outbursts. After hearing them out and validating their concerns, I offered another way to perceive the situation—as a tremendous opportunity to get to know themselves and some of the habitual patterns of behavior that may have contributed to their current situation.

By the first break (a mere hour later) the faces looking back at me were much more open and interested. Somehow, by acknowledging their concerns, standing my ground, and making the argument to give it a chance, I got through to them. From that moment on we were a room of fully-invested adults.

The program met for four weeks, five days a week, from 9 a.m. until 4 p.m. We started by exploring questions like, "Who am I?" and "Why am I here?" We wrote in journals, engaged in small group discussions, read excerpts from books, and watched movie clips as I sought creative ways to motivate and inspire them to be more conscious of the lives they were living. Everything became an opportunity to learn, and I sought volunteers and guest speakers who could offer a fresh perspective. Looking back, I realize my primary goal was to raise their self-esteem. It seems they got that, and much more.

A month after our aggressive and even hostile first morning together, we were all excited and motivated about completing the program, and we chose to celebrate with a graduation ceremony. Everyone dressed up in their new duds (which we all picked out together through the clothing provided by another local non-profit organization) and looked fantastic. The local newspaper came out to take pictures, and there was a story aired on the evening news. One by one, each participant came up to receive their certificate of completion and share how the program affected them. There wasn't a dry eye in the house, which was quite literally filled to overflowing. Something truly amazing had happened in that classroom.

For most, it was the first time anyone had invested any time or energy in *them*, to truly listen to and see them, and their hearts were full and open. We bonded, we saw each other, we accepted each other, and we knew and accepted ourselves on a deeper level than ever before. It was a beautiful experience.

I was shocked and amazed by the success of the program, and felt incredibly humbled by the students' and their families' gratitude. I'll never forget Rodney, the muscle-bound, 6'4" black man who was the most disgruntled that first morning, as he stood in front of the room during graduation, tears streaming unabashedly down his face as he expressed his appreciation. Hearts had been opened wide in four short weeks, and the love that came pouring out was something to behold.

Exhibiting the generosity of the human spirit, this small group of homeless men and women had gathered their pennies, along with the help of their friends and families, and gifted me with flowers, homemade cards and poems written and read aloud. I was humbled, for I knew that something magical had happened during our time together, and I couldn't take responsibility for it. I was as surprised as everyone else at the depth of emotional healing that had occurred, and knew I had been nothing more than a facilitator. Somehow the sum total of everyone and everything coming together had resulted in magic—a miracle really—and I was as surprised and grateful as everyone else. So much so that when the next program began the following Monday, I decided to participate in every exercise and assignment right along with the participants. I became both the teacher and the student.

This is when I fell in love with people—and myself—and my whole life changed. I realized I was carrying around much of the same pain they did. Even though I was educated, supported by friends and family, and appeared to have my life together, I, too, held a deep-seated belief that I was alone in this world. For me, too, a pervading sense of guilt lay just beneath the surface, and I spent much of my life looking outside of myself for validation, acceptance and love.

It was while working with these incredible men and women that I realized that regardless of our background or where we come from, regardless of our education level, the clothing we wear, or the material possessions we have, *we are all the same.* The questions that led me to this were the same questions with which they struggled. Who am I? And why am I here? Over the course of the next two years, I became personally invested in the coursework, and every month had a new group of men and women enthusiastically embarking on the journey with me.

Word got out. The program was a success. So successful that new arrivals at the shelter would tell me that they couldn't wait for the next class to begin. People in the surrounding community sought the opportunity for themselves or family members to participate, and those seeking to break addiction, overcome depression, or improve self-esteem found us. Other agencies started hiring me to offer similar workshops at various abuse and recovery shelters throughout Central Florida.

Right around this time I started writing, and my first article, titled *The Search for the Authentic Self,* was published in a local magazine. A college graduate with a degree in Communication, I always loved my writing assignments the most, but I had no idea if I was good enough to write for publication—and even if I could get published, would anybody read it? I decided to write the same way I taught, straight from the heart. More than a dozen phone calls resulted from that article from individuals commenting on the impact it had on them, and I realized that what I learned through my experience wasn't just applicable to me and the homeless, abused, or addicted, it seemed to resonate with everyone, from all walks of life.

With great humility and gratitude, I realized I had stumbled upon something, falling right into a niche that I didn't even know existed, and it happened only after I completely let go of my agenda and started listening to my heart.

After two years at the shelter, life was sending me signs that it was time to move on. I had no idea what that was going to look like, but what I did know was that I would always work with people on that deep, honest, heartfelt level. I felt like I had been given a gift and now had a responsibility to share what I learned.

Again I prayed, asking for guidance and direction. Meanwhile, I was taking yoga classes at a nearby studio, and even had a volunteer come and teach at the shelter. One day at the end of a yoga class, I realized a sense of open, peaceful surrender that was similar to what I and my students had found after learning to let go of outdated beliefs, emotional holding patterns, and old story lines. Seeing this as an opportunity to continue working with people on a very real, honest level while I figured out what I was going to do next, I researched the right program and shortly thereafter completed my first yoga training.

I planned to begin graduate school to seek licensure as a mental health counselor, and the yoga would be something I did on the side to support that process. The graduate program, while the best in the state of Florida, wasn't a fit, and I knew it on the first night of class. At the urging of a friend I finished the semester, only to get even more clarity with each passing day that the approach—with a strong focus on categorizing, labeling, and diagnosing—was too clinical for me. The work I enjoyed doing with people went deeper than that.

Meanwhile, in my yoga classes, students were having emotional releases as they opened up their bodies and freed themselves of stuck energy that had been accumulating inside of them, in some cases for a lifetime. With each new opening an opportunity for awareness presented itself, and it was just a matter of time before what I learned with the homeless made its way into my yoga classes. Still, the decision to withdraw from graduate school wasn't an easy one for me, even though it felt right. My ego struggled with that change in plans, telling me people wouldn't understand my decision, and that I needed that piece of paper in order to establish credibility.

And again I was left with a space I wasn't sure how to fill. While dining out one day, I again asked life to show me what was next, knowing my journey wasn't finished. As I headed to the car only moments later, I passed a vacant store-front in the quaint downtown Orlando suburb of Thornton Park. The sign read, "For Rent," and as I peered inside at the open space and beautiful, natural pine wood floors, I thought, *this would be a great space for a yoga studio*. In that moment the thought was born, and three months later I opened Yoga for Transformation and became a business owner for the first time. This came with its own lessons and growing pains, many of which I still work with to this day, but suddenly I had a forum and a space within which to do my work.

Yoga classes grew slowly and steadily, but at that point it was still the personal development work I loved most. When I eventually offered my first 12-week program titled *The Search for the Authentic Self*, I had a full house.

While the program took place at my studio, it didn't include yoga. The truth is, while I thankfully attracted some wonderful instructors to teach with me, I still hadn't come into my own as a yoga instructor, and was humbled by how little I understood the body. Before long, this would become enough of a pebble in my shoe to motivate me to attend massage school, where I would eventually specialize in a unique combination of yoga and massage introduced to me as Yogassage. With my massage license came confidence in understanding the body and how it works, along with the legal permission to touch people beyond a simple adjustment during a yoga posture.

In my second yoga training, I deepened my level of awareness and understanding of emotional energy as it processes through the body, and how the breath and movement—combined with attention and intention—are part of a powerful healing combination. Although I was already developing a following for my ability to create and hold a safe and healing space, it was around this time I really started to come into my own as a yoga instructor.

Eventually the desire to lighten my load emerged, and while business was good at the studio and growing every day, I wasn't enjoying the administrative details of running it. That inner guidance system I was learning to trust was communicating with me again, and it was time for my work to shape-shift. After three years, I closed the studio and started doing even deeper work with individuals, couples, and small groups. My communication, life coaching, yoga, and massage backgrounds were all coming together in the most organic way in response to the needs of the people who were seeking me out. Finding and addressing those places where energy was stuck in the body—and in the mind—became almost automatic, as my ability to listen to the words people used and observe how they were holding themselves in their bodies deepened.

Men and women from all walks of life—from doctors, lawyers, and CEOs to college kids, young adults and full time moms—sought me out for support with addictions, insomnia, anxiety, depression, grief and loss, low self-esteem and more. It was around this time I organized my first yoga retreat in Costa Rica, and I called it *Yoga & the Search for the Authentic Self*. The retreat was a success and drew people from all over the United States and Canada.

For years I had been becoming increasingly aware of the power of the mind, and while meditation had been coming in and out of my life for years, the untapped, raw power of the human mind still fascinated me. It was this fascination that inspired me to seek training and certification in hypnotherapy. My teacher was also a yogi, with a belief system similar to my own, and was an expert hypnotherapist with more than 10 years' experience.

I immersed myself in an intensive experiential training that allowed me to bring my understanding of the human body and emotion together with a deep appreciation and reverence for the power of the human mind. This training took me deep into the conscious and subconscious mind, and explained how beliefs are formed and the mind programmed. My already natural affinity towards meditation, guided imagery and visualization techniques was strengthened. I received new tools for unlocking suppressed memories, healing deep-seated childhood wounds, and breaking habits to which we are otherwise enslaved.

Within days of completing my training, I was on a plane headed for the Philippines where I had volunteered to assist in the development of an experimental, integrative health program at a hospital high up in the mountains. Both in the hospital and throughout the community, I led yoga classes and healing meditations. High up in the secluded mountain province of this third-world country I found men and women who were thirsty for an experience unlike anything they had ever experienced. Many of them had never even heard of yoga. Still, the classes became popular quickly, and we outgrew our first two locations within the first couple of weeks.

Not wanting to return home and leave the community without a yoga instructor, I decided to test the yoga training program I had recently started to develop. It would be a pilot program, but certainly enough to educate and train a couple of local women so they could teach classes after I was gone. We picked a date a few weeks out, and I worked diligently to bring *The Search for the Authentic Self* and yoga together into one powerful program I called Empath Yoga.

Through it all, I stayed in constant communication with my growing database of yoga, massage and life coaching clients over the years. When I shared in one of my blogs my plan to facilitate an Empath Yoga training in Sagada, I never expected to receive so many responses from people expressing interest.

Unbeknownst to me at the time, all my labor pains up to that point were culminating, and I was giving birth to Empath Yoga right there in the mountains of the Philippines. Men and women flew across the world from the U.S. and China to join us, and along with Filipinos, it was a healthy group of 12 that participated in that first ever training. The healing that took place, the bonds that were formed, and the transformations that occurred within all of us brought me back to the powerful work with the homeless. Although the material had been expanded upon, tweaked, tried, and tested over the course of several years, much of the material was exactly the same. It was yet another reminder that underneath it all...*we are all the same.*

> ***"The same heart beats***
> ***in every human breast."***
>
> —*Matthew Arnold*

Inspired by this surprising and yet not-so-surprising turn of events, I returned to the United States to an eager group of individuals waiting for an Empath Yoga experience of their own. Suddenly, Empath Yoga was on the map.

While I never set out to do this work, I am deeply humbled and grateful for the gift that I've been given. And that same inner guidance that so effortlessly brought me to this place in my life is nudging me again, telling me it is time to share what I've learned.

Through it all, in the background of my entire professional journey, was a tremendous amount of personal growth, and through a divorce, bankruptcy, and various relationships that came and went, I was being challenged to live as authentically as I could, and apply the tools and knowledge picked up along the way. Just like the awkward phases that come with learning—be it an instrument, dance, or yoga—it wasn't always pretty. I played the wrong string, tripped over my own good intentions, and fell out of balance more times than I care to admit.

Yet each experience offered me a gift, if I was willing to see it. First I had to learn, and still to this day must choose to remember, that this is why I'm here. This is a human journey. And I, just like everyone else, am doing the best I can.

The Search for the Authentic Self, now known as *Showing Up Naked: Peeling Away the Layers to Your Authentic Self,* along with Empath Yoga, is a culmination of more than 12 years of my own personal evolution, the experiences of others with whom this was shared, and how the ripple effects of this work can have an impact on all of humanity.

This book is different in that it fills in what I believe to be a gaping hole in many of the self-help books out there today. While we've come a long way on our journey as human beings—as evidenced by the popularity of books and documentaries about the power of the mind, positive-thinking and self-leadership—there's a critical element that seems to be missing. Where we used to be led almost entirely by fear, we are now pushed solely to be positive, allowing only room for that which feels "good" to be acknowledged in our lives. But this does not allow for a deep, rich inner life of self-honesty and authenticity.

Everyone has an opinion, and they're often willing to share it with great conviction. Choosing to live an authentic life isn't always easy, and I find myself having to sift through not only old, outdated beliefs of my own—many of which have been passed down to me from generations past—but also through the beliefs of nearly everyone with whom I interact.

When everyone around us is claiming to know the truth with a capital "T," it can be challenging to find the space, and the humility, to realize that it's something we must be willing to explore for ourselves.

I've been warned not to talk about the spiritual aspect of my journey and how my own beliefs have evolved along the way, as this may conflict with someone else's previously established beliefs. But to tell my story and leave out such a relevant piece would be inauthentic. It would be like making a chocolate cake without the chocolate, changing the very nature of what it is by removing the key ingredient.

I'm grateful for the differing opinions and suggestions of others, as they've required me to step back from any agenda I may have had and give this very sensitive topic further consideration. Careful reflection on this landed me back in the place I was when I gripped the steering wheel that day, when I finally admitted to myself, and to life, that *I don't know.* In the end, I concluded that only those who have already decided to open their minds would be inclined to read this book.

It's not my intention to garner a legion of robotic followers now dependent on me for guidance and direction. That's exactly the point of this work. It wasn't until I started to look at what rang true for me—sometimes in spite of the well-meaning intentions of others—that I found peace.

Mine was and continues to be a search for authenticity, not popularity, and I share with you here with great humility what I know to be true for me. It's my hope *not* that the words you're about to read teach you what to think, but rather inspire you to think *for yourself,* free from the guilt of questioning outdated teachings, the interpretations and expectations of others, and anything that even closely resembles blind faith.

There have been many lessons along the way, and I share here what has allowed me to make sense of things in my own life, as well as the lives of hundreds of others with whom I've worked and grown through the years. These are the tried and true learnings which time and time again have proven themselves to be of value and worth in my tireless search for authenticity. These principles have survived years of experiential application, and the study of various different disciplines has only served to strengthen my belief in them. They are *for me,* now, inarguable truths, having become such an integral part of my thinking that the very lens through which I view and experience the world has shifted to accommodate them.

I invite you to read this book with an open mind, and explore for yourself what is real. In the end, take what fits and discard the rest.

At the conclusion of each chapter I include a yoga pose or two for your consideration. Whether you are brand new to yoga or a seasoned student of this ancient art, it is my hope that these offer a different perspective on how you can "live your yoga," and take the practice off the mat and into your life. Although I include these, as well as introduce some basic yoga principles throughout the following chapters, this isn't a book about yoga, nor was it written for yogis. This is a book about self-honesty, love, and living an intuitive, authentic life.

I am passionate about the material presented in each chapter of this book, and as I wrote it was my intention that each one be powerful enough to stand alone. However, it became apparent that some themes would be repeated often and in different ways, both out of necessity and to help clarify a point. Because the concepts in this book are so closely intertwined, and since repetition is the mother of all learning, there will be some consistent threads present throughout the book to help deepen your understanding.

I recommend reading through the material first and allowing yourself to simply be with the words and mental imagery it conjures up, letting old holding patterns in the mind and body start loosening their grip on you. Then read through it again, participating in the exercises and journal-writing processes along the way as you absorb the material on an even deeper level. Many say they refer back to this book time and time again, and that no matter what seems to be

"We are meant to midwife dreams for one another...Success occurs in clusters."
—Julia Cameron

happening in their lives at that particular time, it is always relevant, and helps give them the perspective that they need. It is my hope that this book be a continued resource for you for many years to come.

This book was always intended to be a companion workbook; to support the process I take people through in my 12-week SUN program. So you may find that in order to take what you learn in this book beyond a mere intellectual understanding, and to really integrate it into your life and change your experience, it's worth taking that deeper dive with me. To say that the experience is life-changing is not an overstatement. This includes weekly live, small-group coaching with me, or private coaching for those who prefer more personalized support. You'll also gain access to a growing community of like-minded others who've embarked upon this journey right alongside you.

Visit www.showingupnaked.com or www.ericaboucher.com to find out more about working with me, my upcoming courses, trainings, and yoga travel.

This is a soul's journey, and there's no reason why you have to go it alone.

"We are meant to midwife dreams for one another...Success occurs in clusters."
—Julia Cameron

au•then•tic [aw-then-tik]:
not false or copied; genuine; real

The word "Authentic" etymologically derives from the Greek, *autos* "self" + *hentes* "doer, being." So it actually deeply means the self or individual doing and being. Or more simply, being yourself.

I
Waking Up

(If You Prefer Smoke)   ADYASHANTI

If you prefer smoke over fire
then get up now and leave.
For I do not intend to perfume
your mind's clothing
with more sooty knowledge.

No, I have something else in mind.

Today I hold a flame in my left hand
and a sword in my right.
There will be no damage control today.

For God is in a mood
to plunder your riches and
fling you nakedly
into such breathtaking poverty
that all that will be left of you

will be a tendency to shine.

So don't just sit around this flame
choking on your mind.
For this is no campfire song
to mindlessly mantra yourself to sleep with.

Jump now into the space
between thoughts
and exit this dream
before I burn the damn place down.

Chapter 1

The Journey Back Home

*"Though we seem to be sleeping,
there is an inner wakefulness
that directs the dream,
and that will eventually startle us back
to the truth of who we are."*

—*Rumi*

It's time for us to stop: to stop doing, pushing, forcing, struggling and trying so hard. For many, life has become a struggle, and we are exhausted before our day even begins. In a world where everything is speeding up and technology has kindly stepped in to make our lives run more smoothly, we've simply expanded what's required of us and become overloaded with responsibilities. Multi-tasking is considered a natural by-product of success, and those that have convinced themselves they are truly happy are the ones that are able to do it all with a smile on their faces.

But while we are focusing on filling our roles as employees or business owners, parents, spouses, caretakers to our parents, responsible neighbors, involved community members, politically proactive persons and homeowners, there is little if any time left for the most important relationship we will ever have in this lifetime: the one we have with ourselves.

So it's no wonder anti-depressant usage is at an all time high, alcoholism is still a prevalent disease, obesity has become the norm, and marriages have as much a chance of failing as they do of surviving. As life around us has reached warped speed, it is easier to clamor for a quick fix, a way to self-medicate, an opportunity to numb out, than it is to simply stop, breathe, and check in with ourselves. In a time and place where slowing down or stopping is judged lazy, weak, and unproductive, the innate desire to do just that has become shrouded in guilt. We think to ourselves, why should I be the one that needs to step back and re-evaluate the quality of my life when everyone else seems to be doing just fine?

And that's the biggest misconception of all. Everyone else is not doing just fine. We've just learned to keep going…to wake up, put on the social mask, and go through the motions.

I used to see an aesthetician who loved the opportunity to bounce some of her life questions off of me. As soon as the doors closed behind us, she would start sharing and asking questions. One day she admitted that it wasn't until her daughter went to bed at night that she could finally sit and relax. But instead of enjoying that time, she would reach for a glass of wine, and wouldn't stop until she had finished the entire bottle, or more. This was a woman that functioned well at work and appeared to be happily married and fulfilled by her life. "What do you think that's about?" she asked me. I looked her in the eyes and said very pointedly, "There's something you're not willing to look at, and whatever that is, it's trying really hard to get your attention." After listening intently she said, "Okay, but what do you think that is?" Again looking into her eyes I said, "I don't know, maybe there's something you aren't being honest with yourself about." With that, her eyes filled with tears, and she said, "Wow, there's obviously something to that," as she wiped her eyes. I suggested she take time to herself to sit and reflect, without the wine, and write in her journal about everything and anything that came up for her.

When you start to become more self-aware and look around you at others standing in line at the grocery store, sitting in traffic, at colleagues, friends, and neighbors going about their lives, you begin to see that the vast majority of them are on automatic pilot, too. While pumping gas, they are thinking about an interaction with the boss the day before; while mowing the lawn, they are reliving last night's fight with the spouse; while driving home from work, they are stressing over where the money is going to come from to pay this month's bills. Have you ever arrived at your destination only to realize you have no recollection of the drive?

> *"Give up the search for something to happen and fall in love, fall intimately in love with the gift of presence in 'what is.'"*
>
> —Tony Parons

So distracted are we by the thoughts, worries, and fears filling every crease and crevice of our minds that we have lost touch with the present moment. For the most part, inner peace and happiness are fleeting feelings, often closely linked to some external event in our lives.

I have a vivid memory of a moment from my childhood. I was about four years old, standing in my front yard next to some bushes. I used to pull off the leaves and break them open so I could smell their scent. On this day there were ladybugs on some of the leaves. Reaching out with my tiny little girl hand, I let the ladybug climb onto my finger and then placed her in my palm. I felt so connected to this living thing innocently tickling my skin that I was compelled to look up at the sky. I noticed the expanse of blue, the puffy clouds floating by, and the sound of the wind rustling through the trees and blowing my hair from my shoulders before looking back down at my new friend lounging in my hand. In that moment, I felt a connection to life. Now, over 30 years later, that image is still firmly embedded in my mind, so much so that I can remember the sights, smells, sounds, and sensations of it. That moment has become timeless—still a part of me today, only because I was so completely in it.

> **EXERCISE:** In your journal, write about any early, vivid childhood memories you have that are etched in your mind, perhaps also because you were so completely in it. Were there any moments when you felt a connection to all of life?

I too have allowed myself to be pulled from my center more than once, and have floundered about looking for peace and connectedness outside of myself, feeling angry and disappointed when it doesn't present itself, or when it does but then evaporates into thin air. Quick fixes never last. And true peace and lasting happiness will never be found outside of ourselves.

Why then do we keep moving so fast, like hamsters on a wheel, trying to get somewhere that doesn't exist out there, but can only be found inside? Maybe it's because most of us haven't been shown what a deep, connected relationship with ourselves looks like. We lack in role models who show us what it is to be grounded, self-assured, and comfortable in our own skins. Instead, we are bombarded with messages telling us we are not enough, and images showing us to strive to have more and to do more. We haven't been taught how to be at peace, or how to stay there. Most of us move through life thinking of peace as an elusive ideal, a concept that is not truly obtainable in any kind of real and lasting way.

For many of us, that's when we turn to compulsive behaviors as a way to fill a gaping hole we feel inside. Some—apparently more and more, according to the growing obesity rate in this country—use food as a way to try to fill the emptiness. Others self-medicate with alcohol, shop their way into debt, or move from one sexual partner to the next looking for that lasting distraction from their own thoughts. If none of these behaviors work, there's always a doctor willing to prescribe antidepressants in an attempt to put a smile back on your face.

"How can one awaken? How can one escape sleep? These questions are the most important, the most vital that can ever confront a man."

—Gurdjieff

So How Did We Get So Lost?

How is it that a book such as this creates enough curiosity inside that we reach for it in search of some nugget, some kernel of truth to help make sense of our lives? Let us retrace our steps.

From pure potential—unmanifest, raw potential—a spark of energy is created, and we are conceived. It is called the miracle of life for a reason. Suddenly there is a presence; we are that presence. A presence of pure light, pure love, pure truth…pure being.

Gestating inside of a safe, warm, and loving womb, what starts as pure spirit and energy develops and slowly wraps itself in a body; a body that will become a vessel for this energy. Eventually, with our birth, our sojourn into the physical world begins. It takes some time to get used to the skin we are in. From pure, limitless potential we now must make a home inside of, and get comfortable in, these bodies in which we now dwell. And so begins the human journey.

The "I Am" Presence

We are born, and without an intellectual construct with which to make sense of the world, we are simply in it. We respond to our most basic needs and communicate with emotion. When we are hungry, uncomfortable, or in need of human touch, we cry. When we are feeling happy and secure and loved, we smile, or giggle, or laugh. In those early stages of our lives, we are very tuned into our basic needs.

The Journey Back Home   19

As young children we are not consumed with fear, or worried about tomorrow, or obsessing about yesterday. As children we only know the present. We don't over-think anything, or feel the need to rationalize away our wants and needs.

The Social Condition

Then something happens. In an effort to mold us into socially acceptable human beings, we are told what to do, believe, and think. We receive these messages not only from our parents, but from siblings, other relatives, neighbors, religious leaders, teachers, and the media. In the process of having our reality molded for us, we are even told who we are, accepting a self-concept almost entirely constructed by others. Since our concept of Self was to such a large extent created *for* and not *by* us, it is often misaligned with the deepest core truth of who we are. For so many, the simple "I Am" presence that we are gets buried.

Although it was necessary for us to be parented and guided into appropriate behaviors in order to learn to function effectively in society, it is not necessary for the pendulum to swing so far in that direction that we lose our sense of Self: our individuality. Nor is it socially healthy for us to be left to our own devices, without boundaries or guidance to help us navigate our way through the years that most powerfully shape our lives. But like any tightrope that we walk, it is so easy to overcompensate and lean too heavily to one side. As with everything else in life, balance is about finding that place in the middle—somewhere between childlike innocence and adult responsibility.

One of my clients lost her mother when she was only four years old. Left with no older siblings to care for her, and an alcoholic father clueless as to how to raise a little girl, she became quite a handful as she waited for someone to show her boundaries. Although her father remarried, she never felt close to her stepmother, and suffered a blow to her self-esteem every time she was called "incorrigible" by her new mom, her step-sisters, and eventually others as her label caught on. When she heard that word bandied about throughout her life, the message she got was that she was a bad girl—uncontrollable, and unlovable. The more she got that kind of feedback, the more she cried out to be seen. To others, she was misbehaving, but what she really needed was to feel and be loved. Since that was the message she was receiving from everyone around her, she accepted that as the truth of who she was, and her behavior worsened. At that tender age, she had no conceptual framework to help her understand that those labels were being doled out by individuals with their own limited understanding and warped perception.

Another client was born into a family that valued assertiveness and direct communication. That behavior was recognized and applauded, but tweaked so that it was also respectful and appropriate. She is now confident and unwavering in her role as a strong leader in the corporate world. With few negative associations linked to her role as a powerful, assertive woman, she rarely second-guesses herself, does not hesitate to have her voice heard, and does not deny herself the right to be fully expressed.

The messages don't always have to be so obviously cruel in order to be damaging. I know a woman whose tastes have always appeared to me to be simple but classic. Rather than changing with the trends, she has a timeless quality about her. I watch in amazement as her sister teasingly and regularly calls her "plain Jane." I have seen the fleeting hurt expression she quickly masks as she takes that message in. Now well into her fifties, I can't help but wonder how many times she has heard it, and how much it shaped her identity, perhaps even robbing her of a desire to explore her creative side for fear of the attention her early attempts might draw.

The intentions of others aren't necessarily malicious, but result from a lack of awareness. Surely we, too, have labeled another in an effort to know where to place them in our lives. In a world where name-calling and judgment is so often modeled by the very leaders in whom we put our faith, we learn to think in black and white about how things should be, allowing very little room for grey. Ironically, it is this tendency toward judgment that has created our greatest limitations.

Sometimes we've been gifted with labels that are positive, that don't usually leave us feeling conflicted. I remember hearing my mother tell someone that I made friends easily, and had a real outgoing personality. As I grew up she commented on how much she admired my gumption on more than one occasion. There have been times in my life I was paralyzed by shyness and insecurity when faced with an unfamiliar group of people, or struggled with what to talk about when meeting somebody new. Then my mother's words would play in the recesses of my mind, and I would step forward, hand outstretched, to make my new friend…because it seems that's what I do, and that's who I am.

Just as that positive, reinforcing label had an impact on my self-concept and self-esteem, so, too, do the negative words I have been saddled with throughout my life. Regardless of whether the messages are positive or negative, they still leave a lasting impression on our developing young minds. These messages and labels from our childhood lead to a self-concept almost entirely defined by others, with no real understanding of who we are at our very core. Before we discover who we truly are, our truth gets written over by the "truths" of others.

> **EXERCISE: BEGIN PEELING AWAY THE LAYERS** On a blank piece of paper list those people that contributed to your self-concept, positively or negatively, throughout your lifetime. Don't forget teachers, neighbors, religious leaders, encounters with strangers, the media and other relevant entities. Then on a fresh sheet of paper, answer the following question: What are some of the messages that I have been receiving throughout my life? How much of what they told me was true? Was it always true, or did it become true?

The Social Mask

Somewhere along the way, the message we receive, whether it is stated or implied, is that who and what we are intrinsically is not enough. Beliefs are born about life and our place in it. We start out as a blank slate, and through the messages we receive from others, and assumptions we make, often erroneously, about what things mean, we develop a belief system from which we function and interpret life. Eventually we move around inside of our lives behind a mask that we create to fit in, and so begins the disconnect from our deepest, truest, most authentic core selves.

"We tell lies when we are afraid…afraid of what we don't know, afraid of what others will think, afraid of what will be found out about us. But every time we tell a lie, the thing that we fear grows."

—Tad Williams

Until we are willing to look at the beliefs from which we are operating and acknowledge how many of them are false, we will be stuck. It is like going through our closet and rifling through our clothing to remove those items that no longer fit or that we really never did care for. Every time we do this, we realize how much has been taking up space unnecessarily.

Without an understanding of how we have been conditioned, many of us simply entered automatic pilot mode, following a road map that was drawn out for us. Although on some level we may question whether or not this is the road we want to take, it has been mapped out and modeled by people we love and trust. We begin rationalizing the lives we find ourselves living and numbing ourselves to that subtle, nagging voice inside that keeps trying to call us back to our Selves.

I know a man who listened to his mother's urgings that he become an attorney when he grew up. Although he loved to express himself through art, he had never been encouraged to find out for himself who he was and what he wanted to do with his life, so he behaved according to her wishes and graduated at the top of his class. Years later, a successful law practice under his belt, he struggled with unhappiness. It took him quite some time to realize he didn't want to wear a suit every day, or work in an office, or litigate for a living. After years of going through the motions because he didn't know what else to do, he began to evolve his career, and his life, bringing them closer and closer into alignment with who he truly is.

This internal conflict creates discomfort, and often we avoid going within and practicing complete and total self-honesty because most of us aren't even sure where the road begins, or how to get back to it. As we move further and further away from our truth, we go further and further into our heads, intellectualizing our lives away to avoid having to feel any of the emotions that are churning beneath the surface.

For some it takes an event that forces them to stop and regroup—be it a divorce, an illness, an accident, or loss of a loved one—something that brings them to their knees and humbles them enough to open to the possibility of another way of being in this world. Others hit rock bottom after succumbing to addiction or compulsive behaviors that result from a complete and total disconnection from their

> *"Being inauthentic is the biggest cause of stress."*
>
> —Robert Holden, PhD

Self. As a result of giving up personal responsibility for their lives, they wreak enough damage that their eyes are finally opened, leaving them stunned at what they have created.

And still others are just unsettled enough, just exhausted enough from a never-ending search for a peace and happiness that vanishes almost as soon as it arrives, that they start asking the right questions.

So Now What?

See this as a time to start over. Live in alignment with your deepest core values. Discover your truth and let your days, and those quiet moments, be guided by an internal compass. What better time to start answering the questions: Who am I? And what do I have to offer this life?

Like a gardener approaching a neglected, abandoned landscape, you must begin by clearing away the brush and the overgrowth. As you pull the weeds, be sure to go after the roots and till the soil in preparation for, and as part of, your journey back to yourself.

Any true journey inward begins with the question, "Who am I?" When I asked a participant in one of my self-awareness workshops to answer this question for herself, she fidgeted in her seat and became very frustrated and agitated before grumbling, "I don't know!" My response was, "Doesn't that bother you?" She looked at me with a rather puzzled expression before I saw something register on her face. She was coming to realize that she didn't know who she was and that, at 73 years of age, perhaps it was time to find out.

When we wake up, sift through all of the messages of others, and get in touch with who we are, we start seeing things for what feels like the first time. This is what is meant by the terms "awakening" and "enlightenment." It's as if a light has suddenly been turned on, and we can see things we weren't able to see before.

After a lifetime of moving through life virtually asleep, it's time to answer that most important question about yourself, for yourself.

"What ought a man be? Well, my short answer is 'himself.'"
—Henrik Ibsen

Become Your Own Best Friend

Seek to know yourself better. If your best friend shared her fears, her perceived failings and insecurities with you, you would be quick to support her, to reassure her, to boost her back up. Do this for yourself.

It is very important to create and hold a space within which you can do this work, and all of the reflection and excavation you will be doing during the course of this book. Take a moment now and visually wrap yourself in a protective bubble of safety, filling it with unconditional love, respect, and non-judgmental compassion and support toward yourself. From this moment on, give yourself permission to shine the light of understanding on your experience, rather than allowing self-recrimination at what you find.

This is not an exercise that can be done by talking with friends or focusing externally on some project. The very work itself is the decision to go within and to simply sit and be with what comes up. This is how we become comfortable in our own skin again, by moving through the layers of our experience to find our way back to our center, making contact once again with our very core.

Consider gifting yourself with time every day; waking up 30 minutes earlier, taking solitary lunch breaks, or ending your evenings by creating some quiet, uninterrupted space in which to do your deep inner work. Give yourself permission to be alone with yourself and your thoughts. You will become capable of observing your Self-talk, and over time patterns in your thinking will begin to reveal themselves.

It is possible to become your own best friend, holding yourself gently with compassion, patience, understanding and love while making the inward journey. In truth, that's the only way to explore successfully. Failure to give yourself the support and encouragement you need throughout this process will cause you to stall or get stuck and stop moving forward altogether. Let your new mantra be, *it's not right, it's not wrong, it just is.*

In order to excavate our way back to our deepest, most authentic selves, we must begin by undoing all of the defining done by others, peeling away the layers of labels and judgment. We do this not in an angry, belligerent way, but with a curious attitude, choosing to know

"Knowledge is power. Consequently, self knowledge is self empowerment."

—Bruce Lipton

ourselves from a depth and with an openness that is unfaltering... unchallengeable. When we know who we are and we stand in our truth, there is no stronger, more confident, more authentic way to be. Without the messages of others outlining our world and defining who we are, we can navigate our way back to a core sense of self that is unshakable.

The next step in navigating your way through this journey is by journaling your way back to yourself. In her popular book, "The Artist's Way," Julia Cameron proposes that our creative energy is closely linked to emotions which get bottled up inside. She suggests a stream-of-consciousness style of journaling, no less than three pages every day, as a way of letting that energy flow again. In this book, I include dozens of journaling exercises that, if you embrace them fully, are designed to assist you on your journey. I cannot express adamantly enough the value of quiet reflection and journaling as powerful tools for gaining self-awareness.

Spend the next several weeks getting in touch with your Self. Use your journal. Reflect on why you make the choices that you make and why you have the beliefs about yourself that you have. Go on an information-gathering search as you start to observe yourself, your reactions, your thoughts, your relationships, and any patterns that you recognize. Become reacquainted with yourself. The process is quite simple, but it takes tremendous courage and a willingness to be completely honest with your Self.

> **EXERCISE: WHO AM I?** Using your journal, take your time answering the question, "Who am I?" Admit all that you accept as good about you, your strengths, your accomplishments, and positive habits. Then be willing to accept those "negative" traits and habits that you may have denied for so long. These are the things we so vehemently defend when confronted by others. In my workshops I sometimes refer to this as "The Good, The Bad, and The Ugly" exercise, for that was what I called it when I first did it myself nearly 20 years ago. My journal started with an acknowledgement of those aspects of myself that I knew existed inside of me, but that maybe

got little or no recognition from others. After thoroughly covering all of what I considered to be my positive traits, I decided to go a layer even deeper with the exercise, and start acknowledging those things about myself that I wasn't so proud of. That's when things started to get real, but I stayed gentle with myself and saw it merely as a private opportunity for me to get honest with myself about everything. There was a part of me that knew, even back then, that if I couldn't love and accept those "negative" aspects of myself, I would be stuck in a place of denial. And I was finally at a place in my life where I was ready to move beyond that once and for all. There is no light without shadow. To really appreciate the benefits of this exercise, you must be willing to be completely honest with yourself about all aspects of yourself, and be willing to own them. It is very difficult to come to a place of complete honesty, but when you have the courage to go to that place, you are on your way to finding an inner strength that can only emerge from a strong, solid core which is your authentic self.

"It always comes back to the same necessity: go deep enough and there is a bedrock of truth, however hard."

—May Sarton

So What is True?

One can only surmise, since you've picked up this book, that you were ready for some answers, attracted by the promise that there would be some guidance, some support, some sort of hope in finding your way back to truth…to *your* truth. In the search for our authentic selves, we ultimately come face to face with the knowledge that we have been a product of our cultural environment. Our sense of self is almost entirely created by others, our identify defined by the world outside.

We have inherited a world, passed down from generation to generation, that was taught *what* to think rather than *how* to think. We live in a system of rules and expectations to which we have all agreed because we didn't know we had a choice. It's time to wake up and realize that there is another choice.

"A man's doubts and fears are his worst enemies."

—William Wrigley

The Birth of Fear

If there were one word to define the predominant thought system to which the masses have been subjected, it would be fear. And it is the same fear that has kept men and women from questioning that construct. Until we wake up and realize that it's the construct that is flawed, we operate under the subconscious belief that *we* are flawed.

Unless you are experiencing the same love, joy, wonder, and connection now that you did as a child, unless you are in a place of peace and love with your life, then somewhere inside the recesses of your mind, regardless of how it got there, is a thought that is blocking you from that experience. The way back is to free ourselves from the thought that we are flawed.

This deep-seated thought is widespread—an epidemic apparently—evidenced by the hundreds of men and women with whom I have worked over the last 20 years. Many have asked, when about to embark on this journey of self discovery, "What if I start looking and I find something really bad? What if I'm so bad, so ugly, so horrible deep down inside that nobody could ever love me?"

As children, our minds are wide open, and like sponges we absorb everything we hear, witness, and experience as if it is absolute truth. We don't even begin to develop a filter for what's coming in to our impressionable young minds until somewhere between the ages of seven and eleven. Up until that time, our entire construct of the world is being defined by everyone around us.

We've all been subject to social conditioning. Unfortunately, for most of us, embedded somewhere deep in our subconscious minds, deep in our social conditioning, is the belief that there is something wrong with us. While being molded and shaped in an attempt to prepare us for what we needed to be successful in the world, in society, the underlying message many of us received is that who and what we were naturally was not enough. Children take things literally, and when they hear "you're bad" often enough, they start to believe it.

My cousin's six-year-old son, Joey, recently asked, "Mom, how come I feel guilty all the time?" At a loss for words, she asked, "Well…are you sure you haven't done something wrong… maybe something you forgot about?" Shaking his head, he insisted, "No, I thought about it, and I can't think of anything… so how come I feel guilty?"

She didn't have an answer for him, for how do you explain to a six-year-old something that we as adults are still trying to understand? I remember feeling the way Joey described as a child, and looking back now, I can't help but wonder at what age I bought into the guilt and shame.

I remember, as a young adult, listening to a taped lecture by best-selling author and speaker Marianne Williamson, where she said, "You are lovable not because of what you do. You are lovable because of who you are." I had to replay that part of the tape over and over again, as it was so out of sync with the belief that was already in place. It wasn't because I didn't believe it, but because I knew that I would need to hear it several times before that realization could stick.

Most of us are drawn to babies and little children. They remind us of all that is pure and innocent and loving. Their hearts are open; they feel unadulterated love and joy. Unadulterated: untainted by the social conditioning and fear to which we as adults have been subjected. The thought that they are not connected to everything has not yet been planted in their minds.

We, too, were once those innocent, unconditionally loving and lovable bundles of light and joy. Truth is, *we still are.*

Before we learned that we were anything but love, we knew we were connected to everything. We were in awe of life, of nature, of every bug, animal, living creature, as well as rock, shell, and blade of grass. Everything was a curiosity, and we wanted to explore and experience all of it. And just like most of our parents, and many of their parents before them, we forgot something that was beautiful and rich and true: We forgot our natural innocence.

In order to experience the peace, joy, love, wonder and connection we once felt as children, we must free ourselves of perhaps the biggest mistake we ever made: buying into the false belief that there is something wrong with us.

The "I Am" Presence

In the journey back to our deepest, truest, most authentic, naked selves, we have to be willing to look at our constructs. And the concept of God, the idea of God, is way too big to skirt around. If we are peeling away the layers to our most authentic, naked selves, that means we have to be willing to look at everything, to peel away everything. We will be left with the very essence of who and what we are—free of the construct, free of anger, free of guilt, free of resentment, free of righteousness, free of judgment, free of everything. That's what naked means.

Even the writing of this book went through a process of getting naked as, draft by draft, I went deeper. With each pass peeling away another layer, feeling a little bit safer, a little bit braver as I got closer and closer to the heart of the message. This section of the book was the most challenging to write, because any talk of God is an emotional minefield. Wars have been fought in the name of God. It has become a hot topic, one that is often best avoided.

I once read an interview with actor Kevin Bacon. When asked if he believed in God he replied, "I believe in love and I believe in nature." Then he went on to share his dismay at what people have been willing to do throughout history, and to this day, in the name of God.

There was a moment when I was working at the homeless shelter, right around the time I started falling in love with people—when I started to see past the story, past any judgments or preconceived ideas I had about each of those individuals, and I started to really see and feel their essence, I fell in love with them. I saw myself in them. Simultaneously, I was falling in love with myself. I was understanding human nature. And I remember having a moment where I was walking from the main building over to the school and I stopped. I could feel the breeze and hear the sound of the wind in the trees.

"Your own self-realization is the greatest service you can render the world."
—Ramana Maharsh

I could feel the warmth of the sun on my skin and smell nature all around me. It was a moment, as I looked around and up, when I suddenly felt my connection to everything again. I knew I was connected to everything. When I realized my connection again, the doorway was through love. It was when I opened my heart in love again—with myself and with people and with nature—that I found my connection to life again, that I found my connection with God. As I was developing my relationship with myself, as I found myself, I found God. I realized my relationship with myself *is* my relationship with God.

The way back to the simple I Am presence that we are is to remember what we knew as children...that we are all connected, one with everything—each other, nature...*Life*.

You can study human anatomy and physiology, gaining an intimate understanding of its inner workings. You can dissect the body and examine it. You can explore this vessel we are in all the way down to a cellular level, peering intently through a microscope to see what it is we are made of, but you will never find the human spirit there, or anything you could point to and identify as Love. Yet even though we cannot identify and locate it within the human body, we do not question its existence. It's the most potent, powerful force in the universe.

It's time to stop looking, researching, and attempting to analyze under a microscope something we will never find. The fact that we will never find it doesn't mean it doesn't exist, only, thankfully, that there is something out there more intelligent than us.

The human spirit is a presence, an energy felt in and around and through us. There is another presence—an energy felt in and around and through everything. And whether you want to refer to this omnipresence as God, energy, spirit, consciousness, nature, life, Source, the universe, or Love—it is an intangible something that we cannot touch or see.

There is a level upon which we already know this. Beyond the thinking mind, behind the cognitive intellect, there is a presence. There is life...an energy vibrating.

"Awareness is the greatest alchemy there is. Just go on becoming more and more aware, and you will find your life changing for the better in every possible dimension. It will bring great fulfillment."

—OSHO

This is an invitation to develop your relationship with that. And again, whether you want to call that part of yourself, that changeless inner core of yourself, Energy, the "I Am" presence, Spirit, Truth, Love…or God, it is the most important relationship you will ever have. Your relationship with yourself is your relationship with Spirit.

Humility is the opening through which we let an awareness of spirit in. It is available to us only when we let go of the search. It is found in our experience—of each other, and of life—which is why Spirit, God, Nature, Life, Mother Earth, the Universe and Love are used interchangeably throughout this book. It's all the same thing… or non-thing. It's a source—an energy—an ever-presence. It's found in the space between things, and in the things themselves. It's found in the space between matter, and in matter itself.

Love is what we are. As babies, as small children, we knew this. We knew we were connected to everything and that we were loved. The light you see in their eyes, the peace and joy that radiates from within, comes from an intrinsic knowing of who they are that has nothing to do with intellect. The fact they have not yet developed an intellect is what makes it so easy for them to Know.

> **EXERCISE:** Journal about your relationship with Spirit. Start with Dear God (or Love, or Spirit, or Life, or Nature—whatever you want to call it), and see what comes. Take plenty of time with this. Afterward, go back and read what you wrote. Notice (without judgment) how far outside of yourself you put that energy.

An Empath Yoga Perspective

Easy Pose **Find your center**

In Easy Pose, sit tall, and relax into your body. Let your lower body ground you, connecting you to the Earth below as your heart opens to the sky above. Close your eyes and turn your focus inward, eliminating about 95% of the external distractions.

Breathe deep, rich, full breaths, allowing each breath to cleanse you, to nourish you, to nurture you. Feel every breath you take as act of self-love. Empty your mind, immersing yourself deeply into the moment, and relax everything around the breath. Let the breath be your anchor into the moment. Find your center here.

Chapter 2

Touch Your Soul

*"Since life is our most precious gift,
let us be certain it is dedicated
to the liberation of the human mind and spirit...
beginning with our own"*

—Maya Angelou

There is Nothing to Fix

So many people, after we start working together, report a sense of relief. Relief at the realization that there is nothing to fix… that there is nothing wrong with them and that the only thing they need to do is love themselves. It's a revelation for so many who bought into a belief a long time ago that there was something wrong with them.

It is by lifting the veil that has been clouding our minds, by letting go of any story or belief that would have us turn against ourselves, and choosing instead to see ourselves through the eyes of unconditional love and acceptance, that we return to our natural state of wonder and awe at the gift of life.

Awakening From the Dream

The movie *The Matrix* struck such a cord with people because it created a ripple in the collective dream we were all having…for many making them question the paradigm within which they had been so blindly operating. Fear is the collective dream, the conditioned way of experiencing the world. Statistics show that at least 75% of all illnesses are stress-related, which is another way of saying fear-related. Fear has become integrated into our social condition.

Love is the way we came into the world. It heals, bonds, unites, makes everything come alive. It's in everything and everyone. Love is energy. The "I Am" presence. *This is what you are.*

This is why we love being in love. Because when we are in love we are closest to God…to Source. Anything seems possible. Our field of possibilities opens up. We expand.

In order to love—to truly love—we must start with ourselves. We must remember that above all else, we are a conduit for that love. We are that love. And while fear-based thinking may block our awareness of this, that doesn't make it any less true.

"The essence of your being is Love."
—Gerald Jampolski

There comes a point when you know this. Where it resonates on a core level. When every part of your being remembers, you realign with your basic Truth with a capital "T," as when I was a girl holding that lady bug in my hand, or as the woman working at the homeless shelter walking to the classroom that day. Those were both moments of Knowing. It wasn't an intellectual experience, nor was it contrived or planned. It came from a spontaneous cellular-level understanding. In both cases time stopped, and I was no longer merely a body. I was in ecstatic union with everything. It didn't feel like a realization as much as a memory. I had entered into a realm of pure being. And it felt…familiar.

Leading up to that experience, I had been reading books like *Love is Letting Go of Fear* by Gerald Jampolski, *A Return to Love* by Marianne Williamson, and even *A Course in Miracles*, which is a psychological training for the mind that teaches that Love is what is real, and everything else is the illusion. The more I thought about Love, the more I looked for Love. I started to see it in everyone, like a light shining inside. It was brighter in some, but when I focused on it, I realized it was present in everyone.

"Love is the only alchemy that transforms people. It should be the only religion too… So become absolutely loving. Don't allow any corner in your heart for anything else except love. When one is loveful, one is godful."

—OSHO

Then I started to believe in Love. And I discovered the light I was seeing in people was the same light, the same essence I saw every time I looked into a baby's eyes or observed a toddler playing. It was a light of innocence...of love.

> *"Teach only love, for that is what you are."*
> —*Gerald Jampolski*

So I started teaching about Love and writing about Love, encouraging everyone to look for Love within themselves and others. And every time they, and I, did, the light that shone within got brighter. The more we looked for love, the more we found love, the more we experienced love, and the brighter our light became. Like the day I was standing in class teaching and I felt it in and all around me, only to have students approach me afterward to tell me they were seeing with their eyes what I was feeling inside. I knew exactly what they were describing, because I was seeing the same thing happening within them! They, and I, were starting to believe.

A thought takes place in the mind. When you think a thought (positive or negative) often enough, it starts to become a part of you, and takes residence in your body as a belief (true or false). When it is a positive and true belief, your mind and your body come into alignment, and that is when you Know. At the point of Knowing, it is no longer an intellectual process. It is a re-alignment with Truth.

I once ran into one of my students several years after I worked with her at the shelter. I was happy to see her, and she looked genuinely happy. She had a job, an apartment, and a boyfriend. We sat and chatted for a while, and eventually I asked her if she thought the experience she had while in the program had a lasting affect on her. She said, "Oh yes, it totally changed my life!"

It wasn't until years later, while in my hypnotherapy training, that I understood why the program had such a lasting affect on her. The conscious mind is the analytical, thinking mind. It is the intellect. And it's where the social mask was developed in an attempt to keep people from seeing into us, because just beyond the conscious mind is the subconscious, where all of our core beliefs, memories, and emotions are stored. Beyond the subconscious mind is the superconscious—a place that has nothing to do with the future or the past. It is a realm of Knowing…of Truth. It is not subject to the conditioning and programming of the physical world. It is timeless wisdom, the doorway to Source, the simple energy and presence we've been talking about here. It is our changeless inner core. And the way to the Superconscious, to Absolute Truth, is through the subconscious. And one of the ways we access the subconscious is through consistency and repetition.

> *"The mind is everything.*
> *What you think you become."*
> —*Buddha*

I once had a telephone conversation with a friend who challenged me on my belief that love is the basic underlying truth of life. Wondering how I could satisfy his intellectual curiosity about something that I experienced on a level of Knowing, I decided to have a conversation with his mind. I explained that through my hypnotherapy training, I know that once the mind is programmed with a belief it is there until replaced by another one. And the mind is conditioned to look for and find whatever it is we focus on. "If I focus on fear," I said, "my mind will find proof of its existence everywhere. If I focus on Love, my mind will find proof of that everywhere. Why wouldn't I train my mind to look for Love's presence everywhere?" I asked. He fell silent. "Are you still there?" I asked, wondering if the call had been dropped. "Yeah…I'm thinking." He replied.

And that's where it begins. We have to start thinking for ourselves again. We have been taught to believe in fear. It is time to re-educate our minds.

> *"When in doubt, pray.*
> *When in prayer, doubt."*
> —*Unitarian Universalist*

Always remember, the map is not the terrain. Move from a paradigm, a construct, a map of the world that was handed down to us

> *"To be disenchanted, to be dispirited, is to be diseased."*
>
> —Frank Natale

and was based largely on fear, and an over-buying into of the human drama—to a new map, a new construct, a new paradigm based on pure love, pure light, as your ultimate reality.

This is where some get stuck. Not wanting to be misled, disillusioned or made a fool of again, they are hesitant to jump on the Love bandwagon. Many become skeptical of everything, and choose to believe in nothing that cannot be proven to them. Believing in nothing is a choice. But if you choose to believe in nothing, that is what you will experience. Nothing is…empty. It's a choice that leads to a life of mere existence. There is no magic. There is no connection. Love is relegated to a mere concept in a far recess of the mind, an experience of life instead of the meaning of life itself.

There is a basic law of physics that states no two things can occupy the same space at the same time. When we let go of fear, we create a space. Rather than believing in nothing, choose to believe in Love. Let your life be anchored in Love.

This may not seem easy at first. You will be correcting erroneous beliefs that have survived thousands of years of conditioning, challenging beliefs that are being modeled for you every day by the masses. Awakening from the dream will take some courage and diligence when fear is so prevalent around you.

> **"I know that life is given us so that we may grow in love. And I believe that God is in me as the sun is in the color and fragrance of the flower. The Light in my darkness, the Voice in my silence."**
>
> —Helen Keller

Love vs. Fear

Love is what we are. Fear is what we learn. Just as you get rid of darkness by turning on the light, you grow past fear by choosing love, by being love, by letting your life be anchored in love.

A Course in Miracles teaches that love is what is real, everything else is an illusion, a story…a creation of the mind. And every moment, and everything that happens to us, is an opportunity to choose Love. Like tuning the dials on a radio, we choose to tune into, and therefore look for, love's presence—or we choose to tune into fear and start to see proof of its existence everywhere. We see what we look for.

In his book, *Love is Letting Go of Fear,* Gerald Jampolski shares that the way back to love, back to an awareness of the truth of who we are, is to let go of the fear that has blinded us—to release all thoughts that are not of love. Only then can we return to that awe-filled, in-love-with-the-world reality we experienced as children, before we bought into the collective dream the rest of the world was having.

Unconditional love is the doorway. No matter what the situation or circumstance, no matter what the current condition of our lives, no matter what the question, the answer is love. The answer is always love. Otherwise, we are merely managing our misery, working on the level of effect, rather than looking at the cause. When we focus on our problems and lose touch with our innate ability to love, our lives no longer seem to work.

Love is everywhere, within me, with you…within everyone. And when we peel away the layers of fear and guilt and shame with which we have been saddled, we return to our natural essence, which is pure innocence…pure love. In truth we are just like the innocent, lovable babies and little children we so adore. When we realize that our relationship with life, with spirit, is our relationship with ourselves, the question becomes less about how can I fix this, and more about how can I love more? Now, the work is not about self-improvement. We are not here to fix ourselves, for there is nothing to fix. The journey is about waking up from the dream, and remembering the truth of who we are.

Returning to Love

Meditation is a quieting of the mind, where we enter into the space between our thoughts, where we create more and more of that space, and enjoy the simple silence. In that silence, so much corrects itself…reveals itself. As challenging as meditation may seem for the untrained mind, it is the doorway back to ourselves. It is a return to the simple "I Am" presence that we are.

"Love is within us. It cannot be destroyed, but can only be hidden."
—Marianne Williamson

"We are all born for love. It is the principle of existence, and its only end."
— Benjamin Disraeli

A connection with this presence requires the letting go of anything that blocks our awareness of that which is already there. Any thoughts, any desire to pinpoint and isolate this energy, puts it outside of our grasp. Awareness can only come when we get out of our analytical, thinking minds.

This is why meditation is so valuable. It trains the mind. It pulls us out of the story line and re-connects us to our Higher Self. It creates a space within us…a silence. We meet ourselves in that silence, free of the boundaries of our physical body, free of the illusion, free of fear. We have access to—we can feel—our connection to everything.

This is why seasoned meditators seem so peaceful. They have slain the proverbial dragon. They have made peace with their own minds. They have met themselves in the silence and freed themselves of the fear of what was down in there. They are no longer afraid of themselves and their own inner nature.

> **EXERCISE:** Find a quiet place, where you will not be interrupted. Turn off the phone, eliminate anything that could be a distraction. Then, sit quietly and close your eyes. For a few moments, simply breathe, and feel yourself settling into the moment. Feel your body relax around the breath as your breathing gets deeper, becomes steadier… rhythmic even. Begin by relaxing your toes, and as your awareness travels slowly up your body, relax every part of you. All the while, breathing deeply. Finally, bring your awareness to that space between your eyebrows and back about and inch. Focus your awareness here, very gently and without any effort or strain. Simply notice how deep and vast that space is. And feel yourself going beyond the thinking mind, beyond the need to understand, to a place of pure space, pure consciousness. Let the space between your thoughts lengthen. Meet yourself there, in that space. Become reacquainted with yourself here. Starting now, reestablish a deep, honest, authentic, real relationship with yourself here.

Spend Time Alone

Spend time alone, developing this most important relationship you will ever have…the one you have with yourself. We will never be able to do this, to be comfortable in our own skin, unless we are able to love and accept ourselves—all aspects of ourselves—fully and completely.

Over the years, so many of my new students and clients shift uncomfortably in their seats when we talk about the prospect of spending time alone. Often in my retreats I schedule time for quiet reflection and alone time. While in the beginning this often feels awkward, uncomfortable, and even scary for some, in the end many share it was one of the most powerful experiences for them, and something they had never voluntarily done before. Because in that space, a new burgeoning relationship with themselves develops.

One private coaching client expressed dismay when I shared with her my enjoyment of going to movies alone. So much time and energy had been invested in staying distracted from what felt to her like an out of control beast, a monkey-mind that swung from one thought to the next, with very little break in between. These thoughts were mostly about how stupid she was, how fat she had gotten, how alone she was going to be—and these self-effacing thoughts just kept running in a continuous stream of self-hate. She couldn't imagine spending that much time alone. Her initial response was that meditation sounded like torture…an opportunity for all those negative thoughts to catch up, gaining leverage on her.

Once she started to see the wonderful opportunity to develop a relationship with herself that solitude can be, the idea of spending time alone started to hold more appeal. Going to a movie alone started to sound exciting to her. She went from saying, "Oh my gosh, I could never do that," to "wow, I'm actually looking forward to doing that," all in the span of one session. She had effectively shifted what it meant to be alone with herself from something to be afraid of and avoided at all costs, to realizing the gift it is to become her own best friend, cultivating the most important relationship in her life.

"There is no spot where God is not."
—Anonymous

"Learn to get in touch with the silence within yourself and know that everything in this life has a purpose."
—Elizabeth Kubler-Ross

When I'm unsettled and distracted, looking outside of myself for comfort and satisfaction, that is a sure sign that it's time for me to spend time alone, reestablishing my connection with myself. I know my ability to experience inner peace and security is in direct proportion to the quality of my relationship with myself.

At one of my retreats, a woman was worried that because she could feel herself at times pulling away from the others, putting space between herself, and that it was a sign she was shut down and unable to love or to let others in. Knowing how outgoing and friendly she is, I told her it might be the exact opposite. Perhaps it was her own inner wisdom telling her it was time to spend some time alone loving herself…taking care of her relationship with herself. It's not selfish to spend time taking care of ourselves, loving and honoring ourselves. It is necessary. We cannot offer anything to another that we are unable to give to ourselves. When we spend time alone, we return to our center, strengthening our very core. As with anything else in life, balance is the key.

Beginner yogis often focus first on their extremities, wanting to build strength in their arms and legs as they work their way into the appropriate position, and their core is very nearly forgotten. From a weak center, they focus outward and, as we often do in life, they build the pose from the outside in. Often the last place they bring their awareness, and usually only after consistent reminders from a diligent instructor, is to their core. Living from the inside out means finding and living from our center, and establishing a strong core from which the rest of our life stems.

> **EXERCISE:** In your journal, make a list of ways you can spend quality time alone. Include things you can start doing alone, as you cultivate your relationship with yourself.

Silence the Critic

Most of us grew up with voices of others writing over our experience. Often the voices were critical ones. But somewhere along the way, we grabbed the baton and picked up where others left off, becoming our own worst critic in the process. It's time to silence the voice of the critic.

We tend to be very hard on ourselves, mentally berating ourselves for our perceived failures, intolerant of the challenges we meet along the way, and unwilling to allow for the learning curve. Learn to immediately replace the critical thought with a more loving, accepting one. Retrain your mind to see you and your place in the world differently. Allow for a shift in your thinking and in the way you hold yourself in relationship to the world around you.

As you move through your day, begin to notice your self-talk, the way you berate yourself for perceived mistakes. Even after years of doing this work, my negative self-talk was revealed to me in a loud and clear way during a seven-day silent retreat hidden deep in the Berkshire Mountains. During this meditation retreat I, along with 99 others, participated in sitting and walking meditations from the wee hours of the morning, before the sun came up, until late into the evening. We ate in silence, we cleaned in silence…we did everything in silence. There was no artwork or posters on the walls, no phones, no television, no books to read—we weren't even supposed to bring a journal. There was absolutely nothing to distract me from myself. For seven days it was just me, and my thoughts. Oh, how patterns began to reveal themselves.

Half way into the week I found myself getting more agitated and anxious. At one point in my sitting meditation I thought if I didn't get up and leave I might scream. But I still had 3 ½ days left. In the next sitting meditation I again experienced the agitation and irritability as before. This time I chose to sit with that feeling and contemplated: "what is it that I am so agitated about? Nothing is happening. I'm not interacting with anybody, so it can't be something that was done or said to me, and I don't have to be anywhere else or doing anything else, so what is this agitation about?"

It was at this point in my retreat I started gaining new insight into my own mind. I recognized that some of my discomfort and irritation stemmed from thoughts that I wasn't doing "it" right: I wasn't sitting perfectly still enough; I wasn't keeping my mind clear enough; I wasn't staying in the moment enough. I was convinced everyone else there was doing it better.

How liberating it was to realize the discomfort I was experiencing came from thoughts in my own mind! I was amazed at just how hard I tend to be on myself. And I realized just how often I do it—almost all the time, about everything! And I noticed how much I use food, television, phone calls to friends—anything—as a distraction from my own mind turned against me.

At the end of the seven days we broke silence and began sharing about our experiences. It was validating and comforting to know I wasn't alone in my struggle. Others had brought journals to write in, knowing in advance they'd be too challenged without at least that one outlet. Others had snuck away to the nearest phone booth to make homesick calls to loved ones at home, and there was at least one other that threw in the towel and disappeared somewhere early in the week, leaving her traveling companion to find her own way home.

When it Becomes Dangerous

Sometimes the critic takes on a harsher voice, and extracts a much more severe price. When we have turned on ourselves to the extent that it becomes self-hate, we have truly lost touch with what is pure and innocent and beautiful about us. Self criticism can drain our energy to such an extent we end up depressed or look for coping mechanisms to help numb the pain. In extreme cases, the light inside is very nearly extinguished.

There was a young man that participated in my leadership training program at the homeless shelter. He started a day late because he was found just two nights before in the woods, having attempted suicide by overdosing on pills. Fortunately there weren't enough there to kill him, just enough to make him terribly sick. With no family and a girlfriend that had just broken up with him, he was convinced that he was unlovable and alone and didn't have the fight left in him to go on.

Around that same time I worked with a young homeless woman in her early twenties who was so uncomfortable in her own skin, so convinced that she had no value and was unworthy of love, that she would cut herself, and burn herself with cigarettes. She said it was the only thing that would take some of the pressure off of what she was feeling inside, at least for a little while.

Then there was the abused little boy that grew into the abusive man. In his reality, he was unlovable, his father mirroring that back at him throughout his life while beating and berating him into controllable submission. Now, as a husband and father that doesn't believe he has any intrinsic value or worth, he resorts to the same version of manipulation, domination and control every time he feels rejected, or when he doesn't like the mirror he sees in the faces of those he loves. Still running away from the reflection he sees in other peoples' eyes, his abuse stems from his own self-loathing.

Those who are abusive, suicidal or engage in self-mutilation show us what it looks like when we turn on ourselves, which we all have done to one degree or another. We may not be attacking ourselves with sharp instruments, beating those we love or overdosing on pills, but how many of us have sabotaged our lives by destroying an important relationship, or failing to follow through on a great opportunity? If the underlying belief is that we are unworthy, how can we ever be motivated to claim what life is offering us in a healthy way?

> **EXERCISE: RE-WRITE THE SCRIPT** As if you are creating a role for a character in a movie, journal about what it would look like if you lived your life from a place of self-love and self-acceptance. How would you feel on the inside? Then close your eyes, and bring that vivid scenario into your mind. What would it look like? What would it feel like? See and feel this way of being as if it already were your experience.

> Keep this new script by your bed. Visualize yourself in this new role every night just before you go to sleep. Make room only for those thoughts that support this new way of being. With a relaxed smile on your face, give yourself permission to create this new life for yourself. Let that image reverberate through your mind, penetrating your subconscious on the deepest levels as you drift away.

> *"Watch Your Thoughts; They Become Words*
> *Watch Your Words; They Become Actions*
> *Watch Your Actions; They Become Habits*
> *Watch Your Habits; They Become Your Character*
> *Watch Your Character; It Becomes Your Destiny."*
>
> —*Author Unknown*

Watch Your Language

In my hypnosis training we learned a few rules of the mind, such as: once it is programmed with a belief, it often doesn't matter what you tell the conscious mind; if the subconscious mind is not in agreement, the new thought is rejected. The old programming serves as a filter. Like the guard at the gate, that filter accepts and allows through only that which is familiar, rejecting that which it doesn't recognize. A child who was repeatedly told, or overheard, that she was fat, stupid or ugly until she believed it will always tend to believe that. Anytime that adult woman is told she is beautiful, or intelligent she will never fully receive it, because it doesn't match her deep-seated, underlying belief. Until the plug is pulled on that old programming, she will always experience herself as that fat, stupid, ugly little girl.

A friend's 12-year-old daughter had two older teenage brothers who, while they loved her, didn't realize how rough they could be with her at times—cutting her off, telling her she was stupid and generally making her doubt herself. I once heard her say, "I'm so stupid," as she shook her head in exasperation at herself for a simple mistake she had made. I quickly stopped her, saying, "Be gentle with yourself. Think twice about that kind of self-talk." But her tendency toward self-recrimination was already too ingrained, and a couple of years later would turn into self-abuse as she developed a habit of actually hitting herself out of frustration and anger turned inward.

So how do we correct our most deeply rooted beliefs, such as the one that there is something wrong with us, as erroneous as it may be? We do this through repetition and consistency. This is how we condition the mind.

Notice your self-talk. Are you using words to flog yourself, or are they loving, encouraging and empowering? How would you feel if your friends spoke to you in such a manner? If your words do not honor you, than your thoughts don't either. It's fascinating to me how often I hear adults utter the words, "I was bad" because they did or did not do something, or "I don't know what's wrong with me?" because of a perceived mistake made. Remembering the impact of language on how we think, words carry weight, especially when they follow "I am." Anytime a thought or sentence begins with "I am," the words that follow are powerful. Choose wisely.

> **EXERCISE: JOURNAL** In your journal, start with the words, "I am," and explore some of the chronic ways you have been finishing that sentence? When you're finished, look back over your responses and notice any patterns in your self-talk.

If words can have the power to define us up to this point in our lives, let us use that knowledge to re-write the script. If the old tapes playing in your head are telling you that you are unlovable, or stupid, or fat, or not good enough, record over them with a new, empowering thought. Use "I am" statements, like "I am beautiful inside and out," or "I am deeply loved and loving," or "I am bright and creative." Or how about just "I Am," and don't be afraid to claim your space in the universe. At first the statement may ring false and untrue, but state it anyway, and keep stating it until the feeling you

"Behind every word flows energy."
—Sonia Choquette

"An affirmation is a strong, positive statement that something is already so."
—Shakti Gawain

get inside starts to shift, and this new belief becomes more possible. Continue until you start to own it. Give it at least as much validity as the negative belief you are replacing until you reach that tipping point and the old tape is erased.

One of my favorite mantras (*man* = mind; *tra* = tool) when I feel myself getting caught up in the *maya*, in the illusion of fear, is "Only Love, Only Light, Only Truth." For me, it's like cleaning the smudges off my lenses so I can see clearly again.

Prayer, or affirmation, beads have worked well for me and many of my clients. When I have set an intention to re-claim part of my Truth, I take some time in reflection to get clear about exactly what it is I am ready to reconnect with, write a succinct, positive affirmation or mantra to represent that, and repeat it 108 times, once for each bead on the chain. (The 108 beads are symbolic: the 1 means that there is only one of us here; the 0 represents the cycle of life; and the 8 is for infinity—no beginning and no end.) When I diligently do this twice a day, while also visualizing and imaging what it would feel like to know it was already true, I am always amazed at how quickly my experience starts to change. When working with clients often their beliefs about themselves become apparent in the language they use while they are filling me in on the problem. Usually the mantra that would most benefit them reveals itself to me very early on and very organically, and they are given one to work with to help dismantle an erroneous belief and reclaim their essence.

Initially you may have to overcome some mental inertia, but once you get the energy moving around this new thought, it is easier to maintain it. Like building a fire, once the flame is burning it is easier to stoke to keep it burning bright.

A friend of mine has sticky notes, framed quotes and empowering thoughts distributed throughout her house. Open the pantry door and you are faced with a supportive thought. Grab a towel out of the drawer and be infused with a reminder of your lovability. Look in the bathroom mirror and see a note prompting you to realize you are beautiful. If you have been brainwashed before, by the world around you, why not be brainwashed again by someone who has chosen to love and honor you…yourself.

> *"You, yourself, as much as anyone, deserve your love and affection."*
> —*Buddha*

Choose Love

Students often ask: How do you love yourself when you've had a lifetime of conditioning not to? You love yourself with the choices that you make. See brushing your teeth as an act of self-love. Let eating your breakfast be an act of self-love. Let every breath you take be an act of self-love. We love ourselves with the choices that we make.

A teacher once told me, "never do anything that will lower your self-esteem." He understood that failure to love and honor ourselves creates the disconnection. He understood that we cannot be at peace and in love, we cannot be open and free, if we are not connected to our own loving essence and truth. Failure to love ourselves takes us out of alignment with Life.

I no longer think in terms of right and wrong, as much as in terms of cause and effect. Each moment of every day is filled with choices. Choosing to love yourself is choosing to be happy. Any time you are not at peace, you are not coming from a place of self-love. Get into the habit of asking yourself, *what is the most loving thing I could do for myself right now?* Practice self-love and self-acceptance as a new way of being. Make loving yourself your primary goal every day. Don't wait for it to happen—intend it. Bring it into being through the choices that you make. When faced with a choice, always ask yourself: "What would love do now?" Because when you fail to love and honor yourself, you cut yourself off from your connection to your own loving core. And the possibility of sliding back into the fear-based thinking that has become so habitual can follow. When we lose our connection to ourselves, we lose our connection to spirit, to the flow of life, to the universe.

In his book, *The 7 Habits of Highly Effective People,* Stephen Covey talks about the moment of choice. He says that after every stimulus, there is a response. In between there is a gap, about 2–3

> *"Love has no opposite."*
> —Eckhart Tolle

seconds in length, in which we have a choice. Learn to honor that gap as a place where your power to choose lies, and make the choice that honors you. You are learning to play a new instrument, and the instrument is you. Look at your instrument. Admire the shape, the curves, and all the ways in which it shines. Then practice, practice, practice.

A teacher once told me it takes 40 days for consciousness to realize a truth. It also takes 40 days to develop a habit, 90 days to confirm it, and 120 days until it becomes deeply ingrained. Make loving and honoring yourself and your journey your new habit.

Hold thoughts of unconditional love and self-acceptance in your mind until it is recognized...re-assimilated into your being. Let it be embedded deep in your inner mind. Everything else in your life will flow from that more centered, empowered way of being. A little bit of love goes a long way. Start loving yourself every day. Give yourself as much as you can, starting today. And each day add more.

> *"Love is my religion."*
>
> —*Ziggy Marley*

> **EXERCISE: LOVE LETTER TO YOURSELF** Write a love letter to yourself. As if you were talking about a best friend or lover, write about all of the reasons there are to love you unconditionally, and without restraint. Take your time with this, and don't worry about making the letter too long or too passionate...it's not possible.

Be Gentle

One of the reasons I love yoga, both practicing it and teaching it, is for the perfect opportunity to gain insight into who we are that it provides—not only in our bodies, but by offering a panoramic view of our thought processes. Beginners and seasoned practitioners alike tend to come to the mat with a pre-conceived ideal of where they should be in their practice. I see faces pinched with frustration and self-reproach when balance is lost, or when there is an impatient struggle to touch toes or at least be as good as the person on the adjacent mat.

With tens of thousands of yoga postures to choose from, the journey of a true yogi is never-ending. What is true on the yoga mat is true in life. It is the willingness to embrace the awkwardness, to be okay with how much we don't know, to step outside of our comfort zone that gives us the opportunity to expand into a new way of being, to a place of greater self-confidence, and awareness.

But rarely do we allow ourselves to be in the awkward phase, an integral part of any growth process. The end goal pictured in our minds often pushes us to strain to be where we aren't, causing us to miss out on the subtle messages, all of life's lessons that are found in our experiences along the way.

In your journey back to Love, be gentle with yourself.

> **EXERCISE: GIVE YOURSELF A LOVE BATH** Take a few moments to close your eyes and breathe, and slowly bring your awareness to your body. Rubbing your palms together for a minute or two to create some heat and friction, start to run your hands slowly, lovingly, and acceptingly over your body, starting with your feet. Send love and acceptance to your feet. Thank them for supporting you and for being your foundation. Slowly run your hands along your legs, honoring and acknowledging them for carrying you through life. And slowly continue your way up your body, taking your time with each area—your hips and reproductive organs, stomach and abdominal organs, your back and spine, your chest, heart and lungs, and continue all the way to the top of your head. Take time to experience gratitude for your body, offering extra love and acceptance to those areas you find yourself most wanting to judge and disassociate from—those parts you have been most ashamed of, and perhaps even angry at.

Touch Your Soul

Babies just are. They have no judgments about themselves or others. Unless they are sick, uncomfortable or have an unmet need, they are in awe of everything, including themselves. They can be entertained looking at their own hands and feet. If you stick a mirror before them, they will likely giggle and laugh at their reflection. They have no reason not to.

When was the last time you looked at yourself in the mirror without judgment, without sadness, without a hint of negativity? Try this now. Seeing this as an opportunity to gain some new awareness about your relationship with yourself, choose to observe the thoughts and feelings that move through you—some fleeting, others persistent. Just notice, without judgment. Sometimes the simplest exercises are the hardest to do.

Be aware of your thoughts as you look closely at your face. Notice the shape of your face. Look at your lips, tracing the outline with your eyes. Take in your cheekbones, your nose, the shape of your eyes, the arch of your eyebrows, even your hairline.

Now look into your eyes. Notice the color. Is there only one, or are there nuances, shades and specks of color? Look at the contrast of your pupils against your eye color. Now notice any light reflecting in your eyes. Use words to describe what you are seeing, as if you are trying to share the experience with a blind man, but without any judgment attached to it.

Now see past the shape, past the color, and look deeply into your eyes, into your soul. Notice how you feel. Can you sustain a steady gaze, or do you need to break contact, looking away frequently? Without judgment, become aware of how comfortable you are looking at yourself, looking into your own eyes.

Making a conscious decision to keep eye contact with yourself, look very deeply. Remember that bubble? Wrap yourself in it now. Choose to feel love for yourself now, unconditionally and without hesitation. Breathe deeply and sustain your eye contact until you can access that feeling of self-love that was buried so long ago. Do this every morning until it becomes easy, safe, and feels natural.

> *"Do you know what you are? You are a manuscript of a divine letter. You are a mirror reflecting a noble face. This universe is not outside of you. Look inside yourself, everything that you want you are already that."*
>
> —Rumi

EXERCISE: IT'S ALL THERE IN THE EYES Journal about your experience. When looking into your eyes, were you completely comfortable, or did it feel at all unnatural? Were you always uncomfortable looking into your own eyes, or did something happen? Was there a defining moment, an incident that pulled you away from yourself, convincing you that you were unlovable? Retrace your steps to the moment in time when you turned away from yourself. Now see if there is a way to reframe that moment in your mind and in your heart.

EXERCISE: In one of my original drafts of this chapter, I had one gentleman ask me if I thought it was important for us to love ourselves. I said of course, that was what this chapter was all about. He seemed surprised to hear that so he went back and read it again, and said he still didn't pick up on that message. The original version of this chapter included all of the same language around becoming our own best friend, how every moment of every day is an opportunity to choose love...to honor ourselves with the choices that we make. It also included the exercise on writing a love letter to ourselves, and looking into the mirror to make that connection with that deepest, truest part of ourselves. Yet somehow he still missed it. Even when he was looking for it he missed it. I was flabbergasted, so I asked him, what would loving yourself look like to you? This chapter is too pivotal to the underlying message of this entire book to risk missing it. Take a moment and explore that question for yourself now. What does it mean to you to love yourself? What does that look like? And what are some ways you could start doing that now?

*"Our deepest fear is not that we are inadequate.
Our deepest fear is that we are
powerful beyond measure.
It is our light, not our darkness,
that most frightens us.
We ask ourselves, who am I to be brilliant,
gorgeous, talented, and fabulous?
Actually, who are you not to be?
You are a child of God.
Your playing small doesn't serve the world.
There's nothing enlightened about shrinking so
that other people won't feel insecure around you.
We are all meant to shine, as children do.
We are born to make manifest the glory
of God that is within us.
It's not just in some of us, it's in everyone.
And as we let our own light shine,
we unconsciously give other people
permission to do the same.
As we are liberated from our own fear,
our presence automatically liberates others."*

—Marianne Williamson

An Empath Yoga Perspective

Child's Pose   **Take care of yourself**

In Child's Pose, let your heart open to the sky above, and to the Earth below. And empty your mind as you get grounded. Make a connection with Mother Earth. Take a moment to acknowledge her. Allow any tension you become aware of to simply roll off your back, releasing it to Mother Earth to be transmuted.

This is a very humble pose. It is a wonderful way of taking care of ourselves—when we're feeling stressed, tired, or overwhelmed. Whether within your yoga practice, or within your life, give yourself permission to rest and recover as needed. Honor yourself in this way.

Chapter 3

From I to We

*"It is no measure of health to be well adjusted
to a profoundly sick society."*
—Krishnamurti

We are pure potential: limitless beings housed in a body. We are one with our Creator, one with all of life. But when our true, limitless Self begins to over-identify with the body it's in and buys into the collective dream—the story—a false self takes over. For many, our natural curiosity and connection to all that is was lost, buried under the weight of confusion as we were taught we had to change to be acceptable. Eventually we bought into this idea, an idea which is so incongruous with the deepest, most authentic core truth of who we are, and in our confusion, the ego was born.

The ego served us well for many years. It allowed us to develop a sense of self, to ask for what we needed, to claim our space in the world, and to set boundaries. Ego-strength is considered a positive in many mental health circles, making it possible for us to function as an individual in a world of others. The ego gives us an identity, without which many of us would be lost. But there is a point at which our greatest strength becomes our greatest obstacle.

**"The ego is merely a reference point for me.
If I don't have the ego I will fall apart,
I won't know who I am.
The ego is simply holding me together**

as a reference point for communication with each other, a tool...that's all."
—Dr. Vijai Shankar

ego vs. Ego

It is possible to have an ego, a sense of self and individuality, and live in a world with other egos, and still maintain a sense of harmony. But when the ego (with a little "e") becomes the Ego (with a big "E"), we start to observe the world out there as separate and apart from the world in here. There is a very fine line between the ego and the Ego. With the ego, we have a healthy sense of self. With the Ego, we become adversaries, competing with one another. Suddenly everything is divided into good and bad, right and wrong. Along with the experience of judgment and all of the dividing that it does, a belief that we are separate is born—separate from each other, separate from nature, even separate from God.

In *The 7 Habits of Highly Effective People*, Stephen Covey writes about a maturity continuum. At the low end of the continuum, we are codependent. This is fear-based, believing in separation, and with no healthy ego, or sense of Self. A more mature place on the continuum is one of independence. Here there is a sense of Self, but it too is often motivated by fear, separation, and isolation, believing the way to be effective in this world is through competition. The highest level of maturity comes when we realize, when we remember, our interdependence. An interdependent Self sees our connection, and thinks in terms of harmony and sustainability.

In his *Origin of the Species,* Darwin mentioned survival of the fittest only twice, while he mentions the word Love 95 times. Yet all too many have focused on the competition piece, because that is where humanity has been stuck on the maturity continuum. It is time for us to evolve and recognize our connection to all of life… our interdependence on each other.

> "A human being is a part of the whole...He experiences himself, his thoughts and feelings, as something separated from the rest, a kind of optical delusion of... consciousness. This delusion is a kind of prison for us, restricting us to our personal desires and to affection for a few persons nearest to us."
>
> —Albert Einstein

I once heard that if you took all of the money on the planet and divided it by the number of people on the planet, there would be enough for each of us to have $8 million. There are plenty of resources to sustain us all. But because so many are living in their Egos, in a false reality of separation and scarcity, we have edged out our deep inner knowing that we are all connected, that we are infinitely abundant, and that it would take all of us thinking together and working together as one to bring peace, harmony, and sustainability to the planet.

No matter how much we get caught up in the story, in the drama, in the collective dream, there is a part of us that knows, that never forgot, that we are one. It's even a physiological phenomenon. We have mirror neurons that help explain why we wince when we see another in physical pain, or tear up at another's loss. We are wired for empathy and connection—to feel another's plight as if it were our own.

There is a deep-seated knowing that the other is a brother. And since we are pure Love, pure light, pure energy—since we are God expressing through us, so too is everyone else—even when they, and we, have forgotten this. This is why *A Course in Miracles* calls every interaction a Holy Encounter. We are God meeting God.

> *"If you don't see God
> in the next person that you meet,
> there's no use looking any further."*
>
> —*Gandhi*

The Illusion of Separation

The Ego is what developed as the confusion of judgment and fear was introduced into our experience. A construct was born to help us function within a world of other Egos. While the ego makes observations and uses discernment to make the healthiest choices, the Ego judges, divides, separates, and pits us against each other.

We have inherited a paradigm of guilt and separation, believing now firmly in a world of us versus them. This is the only way we could have taken so unrelentingly and irresponsibly from the Earth, not realizing our intrinsic connection to it. How else could we condone war, killing our own brothers and sisters and feeling justified in doing so?

The essence of our being is Love. And just as it's true about you, it's true about everyone. But just as we have buckled under the weight of the expectations of others, so too has nearly everyone else. So now we look out at the world around us, trying to perfect our social mask so that others cannot see the fear and insecurity hidden beneath our cool facade.

Somewhere deep inside, existing next to the belief that there is something wrong with us, is the belief that if we allowed anyone to know the truth of who we are—to leave ourselves open and vulnerable—we would be rejected, abandoned…alone. So we rage against the machine, the collective dream, fighting back against what we feel inside by pushing against the reflection we see in the eyes of others.

This is the dance of the Ego. Its sole purpose is to divide and separate.

We have been taught to engage in a game of guilt and shame, and anger and blame. We have been pitted against each other, aggressively defending ourselves against attack, and finding value in discovering what we perceive to be the holes in each other and pointing them out. We become vested in being right so that others don't have a chance to remind us of how wrong we feel.

The way back to pure innocence and joy and peace is to free ourselves from that second, most damaging false belief—that we are isolated from each other.

The Nature of Cooperation

In nature, a lion chases a herd of zebra, killing one: killing only what he needs to survive. There is no Ego-based desire to keep taking more and hoarding it just because he can, or because it makes him feel powerful to do so. He satisfies his hunger and can later be found coexisting peacefully only feet away from the rest of the herd.

"Our skin is what stands between us and the world."

—Diane Ackerman

> *"If we have no peace, it is because we have forgotten that we belong to each other."*
>
> —Mother Teresa

Darwin also stated that sympathy is the strongest human emotion, and that contrary to what so many of us have been taught to believe, we are actually driven by a need for connection. We are wired for cooperation, not domination and control. When we have lost our sense of connection, our sympathy, and our desire for cooperation, something has gone wrong.

With the recognition of the "I Am" comes the very necessary ego, a sense of Self. This sense of Self allows us to identify our own body, our Self, as separate and apart from other bodies and other Selves, individuals, independent Selves, that get to make their own choices and have their own unique experiences. The Self allows for cooperation and harmony. We are all individual expressions of spirit…together, we are One Spirit.

Some get overly caught up in this individual sense of Self and forget their innate connection to all of life, believing instead that they are separate and alone, isolated from others. They start to see the world in terms of us versus them. The belief in scarcity and limited resources is born, as is the thought that it's a dog-eat-dog world out there, and we must each fend for ourselves.

Our bodies, these beautiful vessels of our individual, unique expressions of spirit, of One Spirit, build thought structures that see the other as a competition, in severe cases even as the enemy. We've built bigger houses that consume more to create more of a wall of protection around ourselves, often effectively keeping the rest of the physical world out.

With our judgment of right versus wrong, and good versus bad, we further cement this idea of us versus them, and our thoughts condemn, separate, and isolate us from each other.

Perhaps this is why so many people feel alone. They have created distance between themselves and their brothers and sisters in their own minds. They have created distance between themselves and Spirit, the Source from whence they came.

This is the work of the Ego.

> *"By seeing your brother as a stranger, you have lost God in yourself in that moment."*
> —*Unknown*

Look Again

One of the greatest, most unexpected gifts in my life was the time I spent working with the homeless. Unbeknownst to me, it would be the beginning of my own spiritual journey, and the very time and place where I would fall in love with people, because one of the things I really got was that underneath it all—our past, our circumstances, our programming…we are all the same.

I learned that regardless of economic class, what kind of education or job one has, which car one drives, the color of one's skin or religious background, we are all innocent children wanting love, acceptance, and understanding.

Every time, without fail, that I took the time to listen, truly listen without judgment, to their stories and how they got to be where they are, I was humbled and had to admit to myself that, given their same set of circumstances and life experiences, their exact life footprint, I too could be in their shoes.

Like the young man who tried so hard to do the right thing and bring as much responsibility into this life as possible, only to bail in the eleventh hour. Chronically unemployed, he just couldn't seem to bring himself to stay consistent, or to follow through on his best intentions. With hippie parents who put more energy into getting high than being parents, even dropping acid (LSD) with him while he was still in elementary school, he suffered most from a lack of good role models, and a loving, stable home environment in which to develop his own sense of self. And while he was present for the entire 120-hour program being taught at the homeless shelter and added much to the conversations, he disappeared on the day of graduation, unwilling to allow himself to receive any recognition.

> *"Do not search for truth; only cease to hold opinions. Do not remain in the dualistic state; avoid such pursuits carefully. If there is a trace of this and that, the right and wrong, the mind-essence will be lost in confusion."*
> —Sosan

Another man spent much of his adult life in prison for theft and other crimes. Growing up on the streets, and actually living on the streets with a father who taught him how to con others as a way to get by, it was foundational to his survival. And while I could see in his eyes how much he wanted to believe in his own self-worth, his lack of self-esteem and belief in his ability to offer anything of value to this world were shackles to his past.

It was this experience that taught me over and over again that when you strip away the story, the car, the house—all the symbols we use to place ourselves in categories and then judge one as better or worse than the other—when we are our most vulnerable, authentic, naked selves—we are all the same.

> ### *"Wisdom is not judgment;*
> ### *it is the relinquishment of judgment."*
> #### —*A Course in Miracles*

"Develop interest in life as you see it; in people, things, literature, music—the world is so rich, simply throbbing with rich treasures, beautiful souls and interesting people. Forget yourself."

—Henry Miller

But in order to know this, to live this moment to moment in our lives, we must recognize and free ourselves from the Ego.

Everyone is a mirror for us, their behavior showing us aspects of ourselves that we proudly own, and parts of ourselves we can't bring ourselves to see, accept, or admit. It is only fear that causes us to push others away. In reality we are all brothers and sisters to each other. We are all part of the human race, and it is only our fearful perception that has led us to believe that we are separate, that it is a dog-eat-dog world out there, that we must fend for ourselves because nobody else will.

The separation is an illusion we have all bought into, and so we are living a collective dream. Be careful not to over-identify with the illusion—the external reality which is so shaped by our conditioning. The way back to the pure innocence and joy and peace that exists within us all, that is us, is by freeing ourselves from the Ego's clutches. Only then can we remember that we are all connected, brothers and sisters, and that we were never truly separate.

EXERCISE: LETTING GO OF JUDGMENT Sit on a bench in the mall, or in the park, and watch people. Notice the almost automatic tendency to make judgments about them—about their clothes, their hair, their behavior. Feel how you have been trained to judge, to make them wrong somehow, or less than you in some way; or worse, to make them better than you. Notice how your judgment creates a feeling of separation between you and them. Feel how your energy constricts as you categorize them in your mind.

Now peel away the film of judgment and criticism that was there, and look at him, or her, again. Choose to see the innocence in her, regardless of her behavior. Choose to see him as a little boy that was innocent and pure, just like you, who received his own brand of programming and hurtful and confusing messages. Shine the light of compassion on that person, energetically embracing him, seeing him as another innocent soul. Do this with everyone that walks by, regardless of size, shape or color, regardless of behavior, social status, or attitude. Do not feed the illusion of separation, for this creates distance between you and your fellow man, and between you and yourself.

> *""You simply look at the reality of the other... to see the other as he is, just to see the reality—not to project, not to dream, not to create an image, not to try to fix the other according to your image."*
>
> —OSHO

Feel how loving others makes you an open channel, allowing your energy to flow, freely and without inhibition. Only then can we be in true joy, for we have let down our walls, let go of our defenses, and stopped fighting against each other.

> *"See the light, not the lampshade."*
>
> —*Gerald Jampolski*

We Are All Connected

Evolutionists say we are merely animals that share a common ancestry as the ape, and perhaps we are—on a merely physical level. But if our bodies and nature have evolved over time, how could consciousness, our cells, and the very energy that enlivens us not also evolve? I believe it's the part of the mind that wants to believe in the illusion of fear, separation, competition and judgment that makes us mere animals.

We as a species have to change the way we are showing up in this world. Mass consumerism and irresponsible stewardship of the Earth, as well as our treatment of each other, cannot continue on its current trajectory forever. We are on our way to physical extinction, all the while pretending it isn't happening.

Science tells us that matter cannot be created or destroyed, so everything that is now always was and always will be. We may have physically evolved, but every cell that is in you and in me now has always been—long before this physical incarnation, and long after. Life has and continues to change form, but ultimately the very energy that enlivens us has nowhere else to go.

Quantum physics now posits that even beyond the cell, the smallest unit of matter is actually a string. The cosmos, and everything in it, is mostly space connected by an interweaving of strings, and on this level everything really is connected. What happens anywhere happens everywhere, as energy travels along this network of strings like a wave.

So whether you believe that God created us, or that we are a result of the Big Bang, there was a point in time in which we were all intimately connected, and now with string theory, the belief is that we still are, and always have been.

> *"One must begin by knowing that the other person is them."*
>
> —*Author Unknown*

If there is only one of us here, learning to love others is learning to love ourselves. Perhaps, then, the healing of the entire planet calls for the healing of all of us—the Universal One Mind.

The Universal One Mind

If you believe, like I do, that all minds are joined, then the answer to the world's problems already exists.

It is said that when Aboriginals separate and go on walkabout, there is no predetermined time and place for the tribe to come back together. Yet somehow their paths converge, and they reconvene in some unspoken, unplanned way. Could it be that their minds are so uncluttered by cell phones and email communication, billboard ads and TV, that they are so free of the entanglements of technological advancements, so unencumbered by the fear and anxiety spoon-fed to the rest of the world by the media, that their innate wisdom has a chance at being heard, and guides them in ways their thinking mind never could?

We are learning now that there is so much more raw potential in the human mind than ever before realized. Perhaps part of what is left unexamined and unexplored is our own innate inner wisdom. Einstein said, "The problems we face cannot be solved at the level of thinking we were at when we created them." It's time to start thinking outside of the box.

The answer to the problems we face today is not about fighting wars over limited resources, throwing money at a financial system that fell out of balance a long time ago, or shrinking and contracting in fear. What if we, as a species, are simply going through an evolutionary growth spurt and experiencing all of the growing pains that tend to go with that?

We all instinctively realize that there is power in the mind that has been untapped. Now think back to what we can learn from the Aboriginals. If we knew that all minds were joined and that our thoughts would have an impact on the collective conscience, would we choose our thoughts differently?

There is a phenomenon in meditation called the Maharishi Effect, which claims that when 1% of a community practices meditation (specifically Transcendental Meditation), the crime rate in that community is reduced by an average of 16%.

We have been hearing for years about the power of creative visualization, and most of us already know that what we hold in our minds, and back with any kind of emotional intensity, tends to be realized. There is at least some comfort in this, as is evidenced by the popularity of books and movies like "The Secret," "Ask and It is Given," and "What the Bleep Do We Know?" Even quantum physics states that our minds are shaping our very reality.

"When you have a thought; its global."
—The Oneness Movement

We've all had the experience of thinking about a friend we haven't spoken to in some time, only to have that friend call us out of the blue. Thoughts are energy, and they travel faster than the speed of light. And just as we call into our experience a radio show by dialing into a particular channel frequency, we tune into a life experience by choosing a particular frequency of thought.

I am convinced one of the lessons we are all learning is that it's time to let go of the competitive us versus them mentality, and begin to realize that we are all in this together. Every thought we think, every action we take, has an affect not only on the people around us, but on the world as a whole. We all know that what goes up must come down, and for every action there is a reaction. For every cause, there is an effect. This is universal law. This is Karma.

Perhaps now one of the most powerful ways we can participate in the healing of the planet is to recognize that we are all part of the Universal One Mind. The more we focus on Love, the more we help our fellow man and ourselves. The Universal One Mind is affected by the thoughts we choose. If you want to save the world, choose your thoughts carefully and intentionally. If enough of us hold thoughts of Love, we will eventually reach a critical mass, and once that tipping point is reached, perhaps the momentum will pull us all forward.

> **EXERCISE:** Try this on for size for one week and see what happens: Go on a media fast. Stop exposing yourself to every fear-based, anxiety-producing movement of the world. Enough already. Turn off the news. Go for a walk. Join in a yoga class. Read something inspiring.

> **EXERCISE:** In your journal, write about some of the times you've experienced the Universal One Mind. When you were thinking about something only to have it materialize unexpectedly. Or when a friend you haven't thought about in years suddenly popped into your mind in a strong way, and then shortly afterward you bumped into each other or he called out of the blue. Start looking for signs of the

connection. Start noticing when it happens. The more you open up your channel, freeing your mind of the fear and self-doubt and thoughts of separation that cause us to contract and disconnect from ourselves and each other, that connection gets even stronger, and these types of experiences happen even more frequently. Start noticing.

Unconditional Love

While it may be hard to choose loving thoughts while so much fear is bubbling to the surface, we must remember it is the only way out of this maze we have found our way into. Generations of failure to listen and love each other, as well as ourselves—lifetimes of disconnection from the very Truth of who we are—has led us down a dead-end path.

The way out of darkness is not to chase the darkness away, but rather to turn on the light. Turn the light of Love on every interaction, every person you meet, every situation you encounter. Love is always the answer.

We make love to the world by the choices that we make. Every moment of every day we get to choose what we are going to tune into. Like adjusting the dial on a radio, we can choose to tune into Love, and see and experience the world through the eyes of Love, or we can tune into the fear that is so prevalent, and experience that as our reality.

Loving others makes you an open channel, allowing your energy to flow freely and without inhibition. Only then can we be in true joy, for we have let down our walls, let go of our defenses, and stopped fighting against each other.

Learning to love others is learning to love ourselves. If we relearn to see the world through the eyes of love, choosing that as the basic foundation of our experience in this life, we let go of anything that is not that. Fall in love with Life as you excavate down through the layers of the story you've been told and return to what is real.

EXERCISE: Meditate on Love and Light. If we are connected to the Universal One Mind, this is all we need to do. Believe it or not, Light is much stronger than dark, and our thoughts entrain with those around us, unless we choose our thoughts with enough intention that our thoughts have the ripple effect.

"I believe...that the borders of our mind are ever shifting, and that many minds can flow into one another, as it were, and create or reveal a single mind, a single energy...and that our memories are part of one great memory, the memory of Nature herself."

—W.B. Yeats

An Empath Yoga Perspective

Cat — **Move around inside your body**

Take a few breaths, and move around inside of Cat and Cow, not only forward and back but also from side to side. Move the hips around, the shoulders, the rib cage, exploring what's happening in your body. See if there's any new information, some new awareness, to be gained here....

An Empath Yoga Perspective

Cow — Move around inside your body

…Feel what's happening in your own body, and develop a deeper relationship with it—with your own self. There's no wrong way to do this; this is just a gentle exploration. Enjoy what it feels like to be in your body, and in your life

Chapter 4

The Internal Compass

"A journey without a purpose is still meaningless; even when it is over it seems to make no sense."

—A Course in Miracles

Each and every one of us is a drop in the ocean, a part of a greater world soul. And just as drops in the ocean don't work at being what they are, our value is intrinsic, lying inherently in what we are, not in what we do. Still, our lives matter, and every choice we make has a ripple effect on the world around us. Just as our bodies rely on the healthy functioning of each and every cell to be vibrant and alive, so too do our individual lives matter. On a physical level it takes all of us working together to change our collective human experience.

Life is not linear, and our interconnectedness not only relates to nature now, and those that walk this Earth with us today. We are inextricably linked to our ancestors, and the contributions we make build on those that came before. Just as they could never comprehend the impact their choices would have on the lives of those that followed, and therefore the world, we may never know the ultimate role we play. A certain level of responsibility comes with the knowledge that we leave a mark, an indelible impression—the choices that we make impacting the world around us, and the lives that follow.

Whether you choose to live consciously and responsibly, making love to the world by the choices that you make, or live in denial of just how important and powerful and valuable you are, you still have made a choice. When cells in the body stop functioning and forget their job, the result is cancer. But miraculous healing happens every day. The body, and nature, is always moving toward homeo-

"One individual who lives and vibrates to the energy of pure love and reverence for all life will counterbalance the negativity of 750,000 individuals who calibrate at the lower weakening levels."

—Dr. Wayne Dyer

stasis. Life's natural tendency is to correct itself and find balance. Our opportunity now is to become a part of the solution, rather than a part of the problem.

> **EXERCISE:** Get comfortably seated, and take a few moments to establish long, deep breathing. And then empty your mind. Now, take a moment to find your center, and orient yourself in relationship to the world around you. Spend the next 10 minutes, or more, meditating on the ripple effects of your life on the world, on nature, on mankind. When that feels complete, journal, listing all of the ways you can make a difference by the choices that you make.

"I cannot believe that the purpose of life is to be happy. I think the purpose of life is to be useful, to be responsible, to be compassionate. It is, above all to matter, to count, to stand for something, to have made some difference that you lived at all."

—Leo Rosten

You Have a Purpose

We are all born programmed with our own intrinsic gifts. These are those talents and abilities that come naturally—with little to no effort on our part. It is those talents and abilities that, when we engage in them, make us feel most alive and energized, because there's a feeling of being in alignment with something larger than ourselves. When we decide to live our lives from this place of inner alignment, being fully expressed—a living example of the gifts with which we have been endowed—we are fortified and strengthened, imbued with the ability to not only survive, but stay enthusiastic about what the future holds. This is what it means to live life on purpose. In spite of the disappointments, heartbreak and tragedy that are part of the human experience, our light keeps on shining.

"Joy can be real only if people look upon their lives as a service and have a definite objective in life outside themselves and their own happiness."

—Leo Tolstoy

> ***"He who has a why to live for
> can bear almost any how."***
>
> —*Nietzsche*

In *Man's Search for Meaning,* Viktor Frankl, a psychiatrist and survivor of four different Nazi death camps from 1942 to 1945, wrote that "man's search for meaning is the primary motivation in his life." He goes on to say, "There is nothing in this world…that would so effectively help one survive even the worst conditions as the knowledge there is a meaning in one's life." Sharing the story of two men on the verge of suicide, he says: "In both cases it was a question of getting them to realize that life was still expecting something from them." For one, it was remaining alive for his child who was waiting for him in another country. The other, a scientist and author, determined it was a series of books that still needed to be finished. "I told my comrades (who lay motionless, although occasionally a sigh could be heard) that human life, under any circumstances, never ceases to have meaning. The purpose of my words was to find a full meaning in our life, then and there, in that hut and practically hopeless situation."

Both in and out of the concentration camp, he found that many "lack the awareness of a meaning worth living for. They are haunted by the experience of their inner emptiness, a void within themselves; they are caught in that situation which I have called the 'existential vacuum.'"

Viktor found, in spite of the fact that he lost his parents, his brother, and his pregnant wife, that his purpose was to help his comrades survive the experience, and to dedicate the rest of his life to sharing his discoveries about man and his search for meaning with others. And this he did until his death in 1997. He served as a visiting professor and lecturer at Harvard and Stanford Universities, and there are more than 12 million copies of his book in print worldwide.

While most of us have never experienced anything as horrid as a death camp and the loss of our entire family, we will all, at one point or another, be faced with loss, death, disappointment and

> *"It is within my power either to serve God or not to serve him. Serving him, I add to my own good and the good of the whole world. Not serving him, I forfeit my own good and deprive the world of that good, which was in my power to create."*
>
> —Leo Tolstoy

heartbreak. These are, at the very least, opportunities to dig deeper, moving beyond the superficial wants of the ego, and discovering what it is our lives are really about.

Your purpose is your intention for how you are going to use this life you have been given in order to affect the whole. Whether you don a clown suit to make people laugh, inspire others through your art, or ensure that everybody with whom you come into contact gets eye contact and a smile, your life matters.

You can also start right now and create your own opening within which to do this work. By discovering and bringing together your dreams, gifts, and values, there is an opportunity in this very moment to begin seeking the answer to arguably one of the most important questions you will ever ask: "What's my purpose in this life?"

> *"It's not enough to have lived. We should be determined to live for something. May I suggest that it be creating joy for others, sharing what we have for the betterment of personkind, bringing hope to the lost and love to the lonely."*
>
> —Leo F. Buscaglia

Dreams

When I was a little girl I always dreamed of being a dancer, and while I was never allowed to take a class, I spent many evenings alone in my room stretching and imaging what it would be like to move like a dancer. Perhaps this is what influenced me to make a life and career involving yoga.

I also remember riding in the back seat of my parents' car on long road trips as a chronic fantasy worked its way unbidden into my mind, without any conscious creation on my part. It was an image of me standing in front of a group of people; but I wasn't singing—I was talking. Even as a little girl, I remember thinking that was odd. I had no idea what I was saying or why, but the image returned often, as if waiting for me to fill in the blanks. Another early dream was to become a writer. At that tender age, I had no idea what I would be writing about, but I used to draw book covers and fantasize about what it would be like to be published. As if being driven from a deep, unconscious place, a series of events have led me to exactly that place—writing articles and books like the one you are reading now, and teaching yoga and personal development workshops to groups of all sizes. It's no wonder my dreams were so topically vague when I was a girl…how could I even begin to imag-

"Adults are always asking kids what they want to be when they grow up, because they are looking for ideas."

—Paula Poundstone

ine I would be speaking and writing about living an authentic life? I didn't even know what that was yet!

It wasn't until my work with the homeless that I gained the experience, and the knowledge, to begin filling in the blanks surrounding those early childhood images. I'll never forget the day I was teaching about trusting that there is a position for each of us to fill in the world, that all of our experiences up to this point in our lives have been preparing us to ultimately step into our station—that ultimately we are always moving toward a divinely guided purpose. As I said the words, I suddenly felt like I was floating, and in the periphery of my vision, I saw a bright light radiating. Although I had this experience, I thought it was mine alone, until two students approached me after class, separately, to tell me that I was glowing… that they never knew what an "aura" was until they witnessed me teaching that day.

I believe that when a person is alive with a purpose—combining their individual life experiences with their unique intrinsic gifts—that is when they begin to vibrate, radiating a light that others at the very least feel, even if they don't see it.

"At the center of your being you have the answer. You know who you are and you know what you want."

—Lao-tzu

My friend, John Strelecky, must have shared similar childhood dreams, which show up in his bestselling book, *The Why Café*. In the story, one of the critical characters comments on the question, Why am I here? "Once you ask the question, seeking the answer will become part of your being. You will find yourself waking up with the question first thing in the morning, and having it constantly flash through your mind during the day. Although you may not remember it, you will be thinking about it while you sleep, too. It's a little like a getaway. Once you open it, it beckons you…"

> **EXERCISE: JOURNAL**
>
> **1.** What kinds of activities did you love as a kid? Think back to your childhood daydreams. In those dreams, what were you doing? Was there a recurrent theme? What was the feeling you had inside when you were lost in those dreams?
>
> **2.** What do you now most love to do? What are your gifts—those talents and abilities that come naturally to you?
>
> **3.** Is there some connection between your childhood dreams, and those talents and abilities with which you seem to have been gifted?

Values

A client once came to me for yoga therapy and life coaching. He explained that at first he was just feeling unhappy with his life and unsure why or what to do about it. Then came anxiety, and eventually full-blown panic attacks that gripped him in the clutches of fear in the middle of the night. He took his doctor's advice and began using antidepressants, but was clear he didn't want to live on them for rest of his life. That was when he found me. Together we embarked on a journey to find answers. With yoga, he began to move his body and establish a healthier relationship with his breath. Through journaling he was able to reestablish a relationship with himself that he felt he had lost a long time ago. After years devoting all of his time and energy to building what is now a very successful career, he has finally been able to slow down only to discover that he feels "empty inside." The real work began when I asked him, "What do you want now?" He looked at me and shrugged… "I don't know."

It is such a blessing to know what you want. Without a clear understanding of who and what we are and what we want for our lives, we run the risk of getting stuck in a place of indecision, or beginning a journey down one path only to forget why we embarked on it to begin with. It's amazing to me how many

> *"You've got to get up every morning with determination if you're going to go to bed with satisfaction."*
>
> —George Horace Lorimer

individuals I come across in a given week that are bored, lost, and unsure of what they want to do with their lives. Until we have done our work, diligently defining what our true passion and purpose and mission is, there will be an unsettled place inside of us, constantly pushing us toward fulfillment.

> **EXERCISE:** In your journal, reflect on the following questions:
>
> 1. What do I want my life to be about?
> 2. What is the legacy I want to leave behind?
> 3. If I could do anything, and money was not an issue, what would it be?

Another coaching client, fast approaching 50 and a self-made millionaire, sought my guidance after coming to the realization he had invested so much time and energy growing a successful business that he had neglected building a loving relationship with which to enjoy the fruits of all of his labors. He also felt at a loss as to what he wanted to do with the next phase of his life, now that money was no longer an issue or a motivating factor.

In order to make the right choices, you must know what you want. In order to know what you want, you must know what you value. Chances are there is more than one thing that you value. For example, you may value freedom, but you may also value friendship, family, love, security, health, a tranquil home life, loyalty, and more. When crafting your personal mission statement, be careful not to sacrifice some of your values for others. With patience and creativity, it is possible to develop a vision that encompasses it all.

A friend once told me that the thing she valued most in life was freedom. She was clear she didn't want to work for somebody else, and she didn't want to be responsible or accountable to anyone or anything. She saved her money, quit her job, and began to work on some projects that had been calling to her for some time. Unfortunately, a year later, she had stalled. In that period of time she had started several projects, but had not finished any of them. Over time she isolated herself, disappointed friends, was reluctant to start any kind of new relationship for fear that it would require her to sacrifice herself and her goals in some way, and had convinced herself that if she was forced to go back to work for someone else, she would have failed. But without a clear vision of where she wanted to be, what that would look like, and how she was going to get there, she had worked her way deep into a maze that she couldn't seem to find her way out of. She was stuck, and seemed to be waiting for something to happen, so lacking in any kind of personal road map that she couldn't bring herself to take decisive action in any direction.

It's not enough just to have a vague, foggy idea of what we want our lives to be; we must get clarity about what we want to create. We must be able to see it in vivid detail and feel it as if it were already happening. Only then can we put our entire being behind something and believe in it so ardently that we can make the difficult decisions along the way that will allow us to stay on course.

> *"I learned that the real creator was my inner Self, the Shakti... That desire to do something is God inside talking through us."*
> —Michele Shea

EXERCISE:
1. In your journal, list all of the things you value most in life. Be as thorough as possible as you consider all of the things that are important to you. Take your time here.
2. When you feel you have written down every possible value you can think of, go back over the list and put a check mark by the 10 that matter most.
3. Finally, number them in order of priority.

"Don't ask what the world needs.
Ask what makes you come alive,
and go do it. Because what the world needs
is people who have come alive."
—*Howard Thurman*

What Do You Want?

I, too, value freedom above almost all else in my life—personal freedom, creative freedom, financial freedom—freedom on all levels and in all things. Therefore, I wouldn't want to make choices that would limit me, or rob me of that freedom. Sometimes knowing what you don't want can help you get clear on what you do want.

I know I want to put my time and energy into being in service to the world in some way. I know I want to spend my days putting my time and energy into pursuing my own dreams. I know I want a career that allows me to be creative and to continually grow and expand both personally and professionally. I know I want my life to be about helping others, and I want an unlimited income potential.

So the number one most important value for me, I determined, was freedom, and for me that looked like pursuing my own unlimited creative endeavors. I also determined I wanted to be my own boss, that I wanted my work to be creative, that I wanted to be in service to others, and that I wanted to travel and experience the world.

Time and time again I have been tested, offered incredible job opportunities that I would have jumped at several years ago. But knowing myself the way I do now, that would have been out of integrity with the life I have chosen to create for myself. My choices have become easier, driven by my internal compass which showed up only after I did my work, the work of clearly defining who I am, what I value most, and what I want my life to be about. With this level of clarity, it actually becomes a no-brainer.

It looks different for everyone. I remember back in my days as a member of corporate America working with a woman who did not share my same quest for freedom. As a single woman with lots of interests and a yearning to be a mother, she valued security and stability most. With a 9-to-5, undemanding desk job, she knew exactly what was expected of her every day, her free time was hers to do with as she pleased without guilt or explanation to anyone, and her creative outlet was dance and art classes, until she eventually had a child of her own and her free time suddenly became even more valu-

"Your time is limited, so don't waste it living someone else's life. Don't be trapped by dogma, which is living with the results of other people's thinking. Don't let the noise of others' opinions drown out your own inner voice, heart and intuition."

—Steve Jobs

able to her. So freedom, and whatever other values we identify for ourselves, may look different for everyone.

Let your choices be driven by a clear understanding of what you want. Again, this work is pointless unless you are willing to be completely, uncompromisingly honest with yourself.

> **EXERCISE:**
>
> **1.** Journal about what you want. Begin the sentence with "I want..." and keep going until you run out of ways to finish that sentence, then write some more. Try to complete 2-3 pages as you define what you want in detail. When you are finished, read over your responses.
>
> **2.** Now answer the question again, shortening your response to only 2-3 paragraphs. When you are finished, again peruse through what you've written.
>
> **3.** Finally, answer the question again, this time paring the answer down to one direct, succinct paragraph.
>
> **4.** Finally, move beyond the mere wanting stage, and actively create and inspire this new reality into being. Re-write your paragraph in the present tense. Let your sentences begin with "I am..." instead of "I want..."

"We will discover the nature of our particular genius when we stop trying to conform to our own or to other people's models, learn to be ourselves, and allow our natural channel to open."

—Shakti Gawain

"What the mind can conceive, it can achieve."
—W. Clement Stone

Vision

Now that you've gained clarity about what you want for your life, it's time to put yourself behind it. If you can believe in yourself and your mission so completely that the road from here to there is nothing more than a technicality, then you are already successfully creating the life you want.

My friend, Christine, continuously shows me what it looks like to passionately create the life you want every day. When she decided she wanted to travel the world, she made an unbreakable promise to herself to travel out of the country in the late spring of every year. Regardless of her personal circumstances, she is uncompromising in her quest to experience other cultures. Now, almost 10 years later, she has visited over 30 countries. Once she made up her mind that she wanted to teach classes at a local private, prestigious, difficult-to-infiltrate-college, she made the statement out loud using language that implied the wheels were already in motion. I remember her words, "I am going to teach classes at Rollins College some day," while she nodded her head at the powerful image playing on the canvas of her mind.

Only two short weeks later she was contacted by her former professor, who informed her that another staff member was moving on, and he thought she would be perfect to take over the class. Months later, when she found the house she wanted—even though it seemed to be completely out of her league—she steadfastly refused to believe that it was anything but hers. She took a picture and affixed it to her refrigerator; she wrote the address down on a piece of paper and slept with it underneath her pillow. Having watched her create something from nothing but a thought in her mind more times than I can count over the years, I was still amazed as I walked through her newly acquired dream home just a few months later. In her passion and persistence, she had worked out a deal with the seller that would likely never have crossed my mind. It's an amazing thing to behold!

In all of these cases, Christine persistently and passionately talked about what she was manifesting in her life. It never ceases to amaze me how much she believes in herself, the power of her dreams, and her ability to ultimately create exactly what she wants in her life. I have never known anyone to illustrate for me the power of our thoughts and believing in ourselves more than she.

Establish your own vision statement. Refer to it often. Consider beginning each day by reviewing and reaffirming it. Prominently display your powerful mission statement where you will be reminded often of what it is you are choosing for your life. Speak confidently and proudly of this new reality as if it already is.

> *"Become aware of what is in you. Announce it, pronounce it, produce it and give birth to it."*
>
> —Meister Eckhart

> *"The mind is everything; what you think you become."*
>
> —Buddha

It is said that the mind does not know the difference between what is real and what is nothing more than a powerfully held vision. If you can hold an image in your mind, and surround that vision with feelings that are positive and expansive, truly believing in yourself and in your ability to live this vision, than it is just a matter of time before it is a reality. Our job is to get clear on what we want; to create a vivid image in our minds; and to believe in it wholeheartedly and consistently. Then we speak of it often, and keep moving forward in the direction of our dreams based on the choices that we make every day. Those choices become easier once we've identified our values, determined with precision exactly what it is we want, and have established a clear vision and belief in ourselves and our ability to create it. You must believe in your vision, and in yourself, so completely that every time you speak it out loud you gain more and more confidence that the foundation of your dream is already being laid.

> **EXERCISE:** Sit quietly for several minutes. Focus on your breathing and empty your mind. Let go of your thoughts until your mind is a blank canvas. Now, with this new understanding of your values and what it is you want, take some time to creatively visualize the life you desire. Project yourself 10 years into the future, living the life of your dreams. What does your life look like?
>
> Do not see your life as if you are watching yourself in it, but see it through your own eyes, as if it is your current reality. See it in vivid detail. What does it feel like? Have a visceral experience in your body as you energetically plant yourself there.

Co-Creating with Spirit

There also has to be an element of humility involved, and the ability to recognize when it's time to adjust and correct our course. Pilots will tell you that no flight pattern is ever a perfectly straight line. They punch in the coordinates and continually correct their course so they are headed toward the final destination.

Whenever I think back to the times when my life was a struggle, there was always an element of me trying to force something. Either things weren't happening as quickly as I wanted them to according to my time frame, or what was showing up didn't look exactly as I wanted it to, and therefore I couldn't see the value in it.

There is so much talk about *The Secret* and the Law of Attraction these days, yet I think a fundamental element of the process of creation has been glossed over or lost entirely. After my position at the shelter ended, I took almost a passive approach as I waited for the Universe to drop my vision into my lap as my new reality. All I had to do was see it, and it would materialize out of thin air, like a genie granting my wish. I sat and waited for it, simply holding the vision.

And nothing happened.

It wasn't until I started taking action, making decisions based on the vision I was holding in my mind, that life started to respond.

Nobody told me that part.

While it is important to clarify the vision of what we would like to create in our lives, if we are too rigid in our thinking, too specific on the How and the When things are supposed to happen, we create a vacuum that does not allow for Spirit to have its say.

The proverbial next step in my journey always revealed itself when I was humble enough to ask, and then pay attention and wait for the answers…waiting for something that felt right before moving forward. When something didn't feel right, I learned to trust that and often had to go on gut feeling alone, even when the voices of others, and my own ego, were screaming that this was a mistake.

The lives lived with most effortless ease appear to be those that leave room for a commingling of these two energies: our heartfelt vision of the masterpiece we would like to live our way into, while allowing room for divine inspiration to co-create that work of art with us.

I call this *co-creating with Spirit*—seamlessly blending a clearly defined vision mixed with deep listening and an acute awareness of what is showing up.

When we allow Spirit, or whatever you want to call that creative energy that so beautifully orchestrates this Universe in which we dwell, to co-create with us, we end up with something that is so much more beautiful and inspired than anything we could have come up with on our own.

We don't need to get caught up in the details (my friend calls this "Mad How Disease"); we merely listen and pay attention to the signs showing up all around us.

And if something is showing up and you are not yet sure what it means, or if it's a sign designed to take you to the next step in your ever-evolving, organic journey through life, a helpful thought may be, "this or something better." Then allow room for more information to reveal itself. Welcome and pay attention to the signs that are showing up all around you. Then trust. You'll know when you know.

Let your purpose emerge from a cellular-level understanding of who you are. With this clear understanding of your purpose in life, combined with what you value and what you choose to create, when you are faced with a fork in the road—a choice to venture down one path versus another—the ability to make the right decision becomes simplified…easier…efficient. Make it a habit of checking in with yourself frequently, asking the questions: Is this in alignment with my values? Will this bring me closer to my vision? Is this on purpose?

Ultimately remember this: There are no answers to go in search of. Just live your life honestly. What would light you up every day? What would you love to do? What would make you wake up in the morning, passionate about the day ahead? Then practice deep listening, and realize it may be a journey that gets you there. It rarely happens overnight. Just keep moving toward what feels right, purposeful, and meaningful. And check in with yourself frequently. You don't force making a contribution. You simply live your life…honestly and purposefully.

An Empath Yoga Perspective

Boat Pose   **Find Your Core**

Boat Pose is a great opportunity to get stronger at your core. A strong core offers us so much more than just six-pack abs. A strong core translates into a strong core in life—a strong center, the ability to know ourselves, to take care of ourselves, and to meet Life from a very strong, centered, healthy, balanced place. It allows us to come from that strong core so we are not reaching for strength or security or validation from outside of ourselves, but instead it's coming from some place deep inside. Allow yourself to dig deep, in Boat Pose and in life, to find that core strength and feel it getting stronger and stronger.

II

Emotional Empowerment

The Invitation Oriah Mountain Dreamer

It doesn't interest me
what you do for a living.
I want to know
what you ache for
and if you dare to dream
of meeting your heart's longing.

It doesn't interest me
how old you are.
I want to know
if you will risk
looking like a fool
for love
for your dream
for the adventure of being alive.

It doesn't interest me
what planets are
squaring your moon…
I want to know
if you have touched
the centre of your own sorrow
if you have been opened
by life's betrayals
or have become shrivelled and closed
from fear of further pain.

I want to know
if you can sit with pain
mine or your own
without moving to hide it
or fade it
or fix it.

I want to know
if you can be with joy
mine or your own
if you can dance with wildness
and let the ecstasy fill you
to the tips of your fingers and toes
without cautioning us
to be careful
to be realistic
to remember the limitations
of being human.

It doesn't interest me
if the story you are telling me
is true.
I want to know if you can
disappoint another
to be true to yourself.
If you can bear
the accusation of betrayal
and not betray your own soul.
If you can be faithless
and therefore trustworthy.

I want to know if you can see Beauty
even when it is not pretty
every day.
And if you can source your own life
from its presence.

I want to know
if you can live with failure
yours and mine
and still stand at the edge of the lake
and shout to the silver of the full moon,
"Yes."

It doesn't interest me
to know where you live
or how much money you have.
I want to know if you can get up
after the night of grief and despair
weary and bruised to the bone
and do what needs to be done
to feed the children.

It doesn't interest me
who you know
or how you came to be here.
I want to know if you will stand
in the centre of the fire
with me
and not shrink back.

It doesn't interest me
where or what or with whom
you have studied.
I want to know
what sustains you
from the inside
when all else falls away.

I want to know
if you can be alone
with yourself
and if you truly like
the company you keep
in the empty moments.

By Oriah © Mountain Dreaming,
from the book The Invitation
published by HarperONE, San Francisco, 1999 All rights reserved
Presented with permission of the author

Chapter 5

Feel Your Way to Real

*"To know your life
is to know intimately what you are feeling."*

—Stephen Levine

Most of us expend a lot of energy running away from ourselves. Unaware of what we are avoiding or why, we multi-task our way through our days, rarely immersed enough in any one moment to fully feel much of anything. While simultaneously watching the morning news, eating breakfast and reading the cereal box, we are already halfheartedly thinking about the day ahead. With one foot involved in the task of readying ourselves for what lays before us, the other has already stepped into it. The ride to work is often a blur, essentially an unavoidable inconvenience taking away from otherwise productive time that could be spent doing…something. It's no wonder we are exhausted before our day has even begun.

Then there's the mostly numb version of ourselves that navigates the way home on auto-pilot while we review what happened and ponder what's next. At the end of the day, many will find it difficult, if not seemingly impossible, to shut it all off, and the mental chatterbox continues…for many, long into the night, robbing us of much-needed deep, restful, restorative sleep. In fact, insomnia is estimated to affect more than half of the U.S. adult population. According to a survey by the National Sleep Foundation, 58% of adults reported having insomnia at least a few nights a week.

There has developed such a disconnection between our minds and our bodies, many of us have become lost in an endless stream of mental chatter that is so busy, we have become like heads walking around without bodies. We become so lost in the thoughts, the story line, the collective dream we are all having, that we no longer have a relationship with, or even feel, our bodies. Yet it is a connection to what is happening inside our bodies that connects us to our center and grounds us.

Most of us believe we are healthy enough if we spend time and energy focusing on caring for our physical bodies, as well as intellectual pursuits. But very little attention is being paid to our emotional wellness, which is the very energy that fuels us, and it affects the quality of our lives. For many, long after they have cared for the needs of their physical body and stimulated their minds with intellectual pursuits, emotional health is the last frontier. Emotions are felt in our bodies, and in a world where everything has become so intellectualized, it's easy to see why so many are afraid to stop long enough to allow one to register.

We have no practice being with our emotions, and have learned to fear them rather than honor them as the valuable tools for insight into ourselves that they really are. In his bestselling book, *Emotional Intelligence*, Daniel Goleman describes this as "a type of social intelligence that involves the ability to monitor one's own and other's emotions, to discriminate amongst them, and to use them to guide one's thinking and actions." And the first step in the process is to gain self-awareness by observing oneself and recognizing a feeling as it happens.

Our bodies are always communicating with us. The messages usually start out as subtle sensations in the body that we can only truly access when we take the time to feel what is happening inside of us in the present moment. This we cannot do when lost in the maelstrom of thoughts filling every crease and crevice of our minds. Often the bodies' messages, those feelings, do not have a chance to bubble to the surface of our awareness, and simply register as discomfort somewhere in the recess of our mind.

Feel Your Way to Real

Most of us, having never been taught the value of tuning into bodily sensation as an opportunity to gain self-awareness, and therefore a level of emotional intelligence, get real busy in an attempt to run away from and avoid whatever it is that we haven't even taken the time to name or acknowledge.

As books like *Feelings Buried Alive Never Die* and *You Can Heal Your Life* so effectively point out, our feelings always have a message for us. And if we choose to ignore them, our body starts sending louder, more obvious messages which will, if denied long enough, eventually manifest as dis-ease in the body. Denying our feelings is like holding a beach ball under water; it cannot be held down forever, and eventually will push its way to the surface.

Un-Comfortably Numb

We have become a numb society. After years of being told it's not okay to feel anything other than happiness and joy, we have disassociated from the very energy that courses through us, reminding us that we are alive. The guilt and shame connected to our emotions has accumulated over generations, and we've become better and better at denying what we feel, driving that energy deeper into our nervous systems because we've never been taught the value of simply allowing it to pass through us.

We are having to come up with new names to call the physical manifestation of dis-ease in our bodies, as stuck emotional energy eventually wreaks havoc on our nervous and endocrine systems. The nervous system is like our electrical system; the endocrine system is our chemical makeup. When these electrical and chemical systems reach a point of overwhelm and confusion, the rest of the body receives too much, or too little, of something vital to its healthy, normal functioning.

At the first sign of this imbalance, traditional western medicine will usually seek to return the body to homeostasis with drugs, essentially introducing another chemical into the mix. While masking one symptom, another series of side effects are created, and the original source of the problem remains. Over time, if those side effects are enough of a nuisance, one or more other drugs are introduced, and before you know it, you have a chemical cocktail with which to flood your system on a daily basis. And if an organ or other part of the body creates enough problems, aggressive, invasive surgery is often next on the agenda.

Yet while we are busy chasing symptoms, the root of the issue remains unacknowledged, and unaddressed.

For most, our parents, and their parents, and their parents before them, never received true, healthy guidance on how to recognize and manage emotions, and so were ill-equipped to offer us any true emotional support. And over time many stopped questioning…anything.

We have been pulled so far from our center, it's no wonder something as subtle as an emotion is seen as more of a nuisance than anything else. But we are in a new age now, when at least some are starting to question the answers, where a growing number of inquisitive souls are seeking new ways to be in this world. And as we evolve out of thousands of years of being told what to think, we are now ready to learn how to think, and how to feel.

This new level of open, expanded awareness for which we as a species are now ready, includes at its very core emotional intelligence. And we will never reach a level of true intelligence around our emotions without the ability to recognize that we are having one.

No journey of self-discovery can go far without a willingness to recognize what it is we are feeling. In a world with so much mental noise and external distraction vying for our attention, something as subtle as a feeling can be easily ignored. But without a willingness to see, own and understand the subtle energy that moves through our bodies, we can never truly know ourselves.

> ***"Emotion is the body's reaction to the mind."***
> —*Eckhart Tolle*

The Body is the Subconscious Mind

Probably the most valuable thing I learned from my hypnotherapy training is the depth and power of the subconscious mind. We come into this world wide open, and like sponges absorb everything that we see, hear and learn. We don't even to begin to develop a filter for what we take in until at least the age of seven. Unlike the conscious mind, which can only acknowledge about five or six pieces of information at a time, the subconscious mind makes a mental impression of trillions of bits of data in any given moment. It is the storehouse of our past—everything we've ever observed, overheard and been told is filed away in this limitless database.

And *the body is the subconscious mind.* The patterning found in the body—how we hold ourselves posturally, where tension is stored and to what extent, and to a degree how illness manifests—all are a result of the beliefs held in the subconscious mind.

So it, too, is the storehouse of every belief; empowering or disempowering thought; and unresolved, unacknowledged emotional confusion, or even trauma—big or small. It's all sitting as energy in our bodies.

Everything we need to know is in the body.

And *the body doesn't lie.*

The Body Doesn't Lie

Most people wear their past hurts like body armor, their posture revealing so much about their past. The body is the subconscious mind and houses the memories of everything that has ever happened to us. Unless the emotional charge of those memories has been acknowledged and released, that energy remains, showing up as emotional holding patterns.

I've seen lack of self-awareness, esteem, and confidence show up in the slack posture of countless men and women; their lack of inner conviction showing up in the way they hold themselves, and in the way they move. You can see rounded shoulders closing in around the heart to protect it from further pain, or indicating that someone is holding the weight of the world on their shoulders. What starts out as poor posture usually worsens over time, even crippling some after enough years of buckling under the weight of their past.

This shows up differently depending on the conclusions one draws from life events. For example, one rape victim retreats inside of herself, safer residing behind the walls she has created to protect her from the outside world, putting on more and more weight as a way of insulating herself. Another determines she will never be victimized again; her aggressive, forward-tilting posture indicates her willingness to now push her way through obstacles; unstoppable in her strength, her body locked up, muscles and joints hard so nothing can work its way into her without her consent.

Developing a Bodily Sense

Yoga is an integral part of my work with people, because its gets people in their bodies. Rather than getting them further into their heads by exhaustively exploring their life story, I seek to get them out of their heads and into their bodies, where they can start feeling again. Since the body is the subconscious mind, and the subconscious goes so much deeper and is so much stronger than the conscious mind, true healing and liberation must happen on that level. All too often we can get caught up in paralysis by analysis, never really moving beyond an old, outdated story line and returning to the truth of who we are, free of any story.

By moving and breathing slowly and consciously, we rediscover parts of ourselves we disconnected from long ago. Bringing our awareness back into our bodies in a gentle, compassionate, curious way allows so much to be revealed about where energy has gotten stuck; it's those areas that we have difficulty connecting with, or where we are so restricted and tight energy hasn't flowed freely there in years.

Emotions are energy in motion, and show up as physiological sensations in the body, be it stomach flips, heart palpitations, increased adrenaline, sweating or even posture changes. Learning to tune into your body is a powerful way of accessing the nature of the emotional energy moving through you.

In my yoga sessions, because there is such a clear intention to be in the body and connect with it, to reestablish a dialogue with ourselves through the body, it is not uncommon for people to be moved

"Here in this body are the sacred rivers: here are the sun and moon as well as the pilgrimage places... I have not encountered another temple as blissful as my own body."

—Saraha

to laughter, or to tears, as emotional energy that has been hung up for years is finally set free. I guide clients to notice and relax those parts of themselves that are most contracted and closed. Dozens over the years have dissolved into tears as we opened their body up, the stretching and opening allowing stuck emotional energy they didn't even know they were holding to surface.

One man broke down four times in the course of one session, realizing that up until that moment, he had never given himself permission to grieve the loss of his father and his brother. A professional businessman and CEO of a large corporation with lots of responsibility, he had never taken the time to allow feelings to fully register, and so all of the unresolved energy of his life had accumulated up to that point to an overwhelming degree. That energy had made him so restricted and so tight he had already succumbed to two deeply invasive surgeries in order to open up his range of motion and relieve the pain and discomfort associated with that. That day, he discovered how much emotional energy he had been holding in his body, and how the accumulation of that was affecting him physically, mentally and emotionally, and in all areas of his life.

Another man rolled over onto his side at the completion of his session, laughing hysterically and crying at the same time, stunned at what he had been holding onto, unbeknownst to him.

In order to be able to set ourselves free and liberate ourselves from the emotional holding patterns of our past, we must be brave enough to acknowledge that they are there. Yoga is a powerful way of developing that deeper, more honest level of awareness of ourselves and our bodies.

Since the body is the subconscious mind, it is only by creating a space and opening to the moment with curiosity and compassion that we can transform some of the old, outdated programming that no longer serves us.

> **EXERCISE:** Sit comfortably, and close your eyes. Take a few relaxing breaths. Now take a trip through your body and visit its various parts. As you focus on each part, don't try to change anything that you feel, just notice what you find.

Start with your feet. Are they comfortable? How do your toes feel? Then become aware of your legs and your knees. Notice any sensations you feel in your legs—in the muscles in your legs. How do your knees feel? How about your hips and buttocks? Can you feel where your body rests against the seat beneath you? Bring your awareness back down to your abdomen. Do you notice any sensations there? Is anything moving?

Keep scanning all the way up your body. Notice your facial expression and how the muscles in your face feel.

Now notice the quality of your breathing. Do you breathe from the top of your lungs? Are you breathing deep, relaxing breaths, or is it constricted in any way? Is the air moving in and out through your nose, or your mouth? Is your chest tight, or comfortable?

Finally, tune into that place in your body where you feel things. Take a moment and find that spot. When you do, place your hands there and for a few breaths, simply establish a relationship with that part of yourself. Now tune into what's happening there, in that place where you feel things. See how you are in their now.

What happens when you ask yourself, "How am I now? How do I feel?" Think of something that has been bothering you lately. See if you can get the feel of that problem there in that place where you feel things.

Notice as you become aware of feelings and sensations as they bubble up to the surface. Listen intuitively for the word that best describes that sensation. What word or words best describe it? Stay with it until you get a bead on it. You'll know when you've got it because you'll feel a resonance in your body.

Meditation

Meditation is another powerful way to develop a deeper, more honest relationship with ourselves. Here we have an opportunity to discover what is waiting to surface. When we can learn to notice, without judging or acting upon what comes up for us, we then have the opportunity to gain true insight.

I am reminded of some of the wall-sized paintings hanging in museums I have visited around the world. Have you ever stood before an enormous piece of art, be it a painting or a sculpture? The closer you stand to the masterpiece, the harder it is to see it. Only stepping back to give ourselves a more panoramic view of the work of art provides the space to see the story, the details, the very essence of what the artist was trying to say. When you stand too close, you simply can't see it. It is too easy to become overwhelmed by the image and miss the whole point of it.

True intimacy with ourselves is not found in our heads. This is why mind control techniques, without true understanding, are so dangerous—using techniques to reprogram the mind, while the subtle undercurrents are not addressed.

It's like shoving all the clutter and dirty laundry into the closets and under the bed. There is a mess going on behind the scenes we are pretending isn't there, and when others arrive we must strengthen that charade, convincing ourselves enough to be able to convince others. Now a lot of energy must go into avoiding opening those doors, even to the point of pretending the doors aren't there, out of fear of the mess that would come spilling out.

At the very least, this makes us defensive; at an extreme we start to believe our own lie. But everyone feels it on some level; other people sense it in you—your body language, your mannerisms are not as relaxed. Simply becoming more convincing doesn't make the truth less so, and no matter how convincing you may be to the world around you, in the recesses of your own mind you know what's true.

Yoga and meditation allow us that space to step back and observe our own thoughts and feelings long enough to learn something from them. Our feelings always have a message for us, but if we are overwhelmed by them, or denying them altogether, we are missing the point. Only stepping back and becoming the witness allows us to establish a vantage point from which we can observe ourselves.

Another analogy is sitting in a theater watching a movie playing. No matter how the movie may move you, you don't get out of your seat and step onto the screen. You are an observer, in spite of any emotions that get stirred up within you. Stepping back from the composite picture in this way allows us to gain true insight into ourselves, and is the only way we can ever attain any level of true self-mastery or inner peace.

> **EXERCISE: MEDITATION** Sit comfortably once again, and reestablish long, deep breathing. Now empty your mind, letting it become wide open like a blue sky. Let any thoughts or feelings that come up simply float by like clouds in that sky, without attaching to them or getting hooked into a story line. With practice, it will become easier to create more and more space between your thoughts.

Learning to Label Your Feelings

Not only have we not been taught to recognize what we are feeling in any given moment as a tool for self-awareness and a road map leading us to our inner truth, there has been so much guilt and shame around having any feelings that are not pleasant that we learned at a very early age to squelch and deny them. If you grew up in an environment where children were to be seen and not heard, you learned quickly that your fluctuating emotional state was of no interest to adults with much more important things on their minds.

Not only were most of us not given the space to look at our feelings and learn from them, we rarely received guidance as to how to deal with them in a healthy way, even if we did have the capacity to understand them. We've all observed adults that were inept at handling their own emotions in a responsible way, allowing themselves to be overwhelmed rather than empowered by them, and those experiences left an unpleasant taste in many of our mouths around feelings. Some of us decided early on it was better to avoid and deny them than risk losing control.

Learning to recognize a feeling or emotion when you are having one, and then being able to label it, is a huge step toward emotional empowerment. This allows us to know ourselves better and becomes empowering, because it is a choice to be with what is coming up in the moment rather than running away from ourselves or getting lost in a story that only serves to perpetuate the pain and drama.

We do this by learning to label our emotions, getting comfortable with calling them by name. This will require some practice, and like learning any new language, we will become comfortably fluent only by expanding our emotional vocabulary. Often when I ask people how they are feeling, they will respond with a tertiary, "good" or "fine" or even "okay." When I want them to go deeper and get really honest with themselves, I'll ask, "How are you really feeling?" That's when things start to get real, and the deep inner exploration can begin.

For example, perhaps you got a promotion at work. Likely your "good" feelings are an amalgamation of excitement at the opportunities that lie ahead, validation of all the hard work you've been doing, trepidation at what may now be expected of you in your new role, concern around how you will balance your new responsibilities with the other important areas of your life, curiosity around how this may change your relationships with your co-workers, and even sadness at what you like about your old role that you are now leaving behind.

Alternatively, the "bad" feelings that may come up around a painful break-up may be a finely-woven tapestry of disappointment—that in the end, even after all the efforts to work things out, the relationship is still over, confusion over what, if anything, you could have done differently, anger and resentment for the pain you are new left holding, sadness that—in spite of everything—you still love her, and maybe even relief that the conflict is finally over.

Even in those moments we would claim to be feeling nothing, feeling language like indifferent, satisfied, content, or even bored or numb may apply.

Realize too that we are rarely experiencing just one emotion at a time. Usually we are feeling a combination of things. The idea is to get as much of a bead on it as possible. That in and of itself is a huge step toward being empowered by our emotions rather than overwhelmed by them.

In my workshops, I give participants a list of feelings to help them get more comfortable with tuning into whatever emotional undercurrent is moving through them. It is a launching pad, a mere jumping off point to help them get started as they learn to recognize what they are feeling. I have included the list below for your consideration.

Feelings

afraid	cold	embarrassed
aggravated	comfortable	empty
amazed	concerned	energized
ambivalent	confident	enthusiastic
angry	confused	envious
annoyed	content	excited
anxious	crazy	exhausted
apathetic	defeated	fearful
ashamed	defensive	fed up
bashful	delighted	fidgety
bewildered	depressed	flattered
bitchy	detached	foolish
bitter	devastated	forlorn
bored	disappointed	frazzled
brace	disgusted	free
calm	disturbed	friendly
cantankerous	doubtful	frustrated
carefree	ecstatic	furious
cheerful	edgy	glad
cocky	elated	glum

Feel Your Way to Real

grateful	mean	sad
happy	miserable	sentimental
harassed	mixed up	sexy
helpless	mortified	shaky
high	neglected	shocked
hopeful	nervous	shy
horrible	numb	sorry
hostile	optimistic	strong
humiliated	overwhelmed	subdued
hurried	paranoid	surprised
hurt	passionate	suspicious
hysterical	peaceful	tender
impatient	pessimistic	tense
impressed	playful	terrified
inhibited	pleased	threatened
insecure	possessive	tired
interested	pressured	trapped
intimidated	protective	ugly
irritable	puzzled	uneasy
jealous	refreshed	vulnerable
joyful	regretful	warm
lazy	relieved	weak
lonely	resentful	wonderful
loving	restless	worried
lukewarm	ridiculous	
mad	romantic	

The more adept we can become in identifying our emotions honestly and accurately, the more we can befriend them as opposed to avoiding them, for they serve as powerful guideposts leading us back to the thoughts behind them.

Our Feelings as Guideposts

Most of us have a feeling move through us and then search for a thought to explain and even justify that feeling. This makes us reactive, responding to a world that is created largely by what happens out there. We can never truly be at peace until we get in touch with the reality we are creating based on the thoughts we choose to feed. Our thoughts generate feelings. Once we learn to identify our feelings we are empowered to trace them back to the thought, or thoughts, that sponsored them.

Life is a sequence of events, and it is these events which cause us to adopt certain beliefs about the world and our place in it. This belief system has been established over the course of our lifetime, and it generates our thoughts. Therefore, our feelings serve as powerful guideposts to help us navigate our way back to the sponsoring thoughts, and even more importantly the deeply rooted beliefs, behind them. Then we discern between outdated, disempowering beliefs and more current, empowered beliefs that serve us.

The HearthMath Institute has done over 17 years of research on the connection and interactions between the heart and the brain. While it is true that the heart responds to neural signals from the brain, what has only recently been discovered is that the heart actually sends more signals to the brain than the other way around. These signals from the heart to the brain affect perception, cognitive function, and even intuition. So while our thoughts create our feelings, we are now finding that our feelings also influence our thoughts. It's all energy. And it's where we choose to focus our energy that has the greatest impact, and influence, on our lives.

Chapter two introduced two polarized thought systems, and ways of feeling this world: Love versus fear. Emotions are energy in motion, and show up as physiological sensations in the body, be it sweaty palms, heart palpitations, upset stomach, muscle aches and cramps. Every emotion, every feeling, every thought registers. Thoughts based on fear leave us feeling contracted, angry, suspicious, sad, alone, jealous, resentful, powerless. Choosing thoughts of Love allows our energy to expand, feeling connected, light, open, relaxed, trusting and at peace. The long and the short of it is, it is now being proven that feeling love heals.

I see the mind as the sum total of the brain and the heart brought together, and it's either working for us or against us, depending on how much conscious awareness and choice we are willing to engage.

When we deepen and expand our level of emotional intelligence, we gain awareness and insight into ourselves. By learning to recognize that we are even having a feeling, and developing our ability to identify and even name it, we become empowered by our emotions, rather than overwhelmed by them. For then we have the opportunity to trace the feeling back to the thought, however subtle and even subconscious it may be, and only then can we recognize that there is a choice.

This is how we bring subconscious triggers and beliefs into our conscious awareness. This is how we further undo the conditioning that has caused so many to go numb, burying the truth of who they are.

> **EXERCISE: JOURNALING TO GAIN SELF-AWARENESS**
>
> 1. What am I feeling?
> 2. What are the thoughts behind and attached to that feeling?
> 3. Is this coming from my Ego, is it fear-based thinking? Or am I coming from Love?
> 4. If it's based on Fear, is this where I want to be focusing my energy?
> 5. What would happen if I chose to focus on Love instead?

Sometimes labeling the emotion and tracing it back to the sponsoring thought behind it is enough to disarm it and remove the emotional charge. When it's not, we move to the next step in the emotional empowerment process.

An Empath Yoga Perspective

Crescent Moon — Allow energy to move

The hips are a place where we tend to store a lot of emotional energy, especially around relationships. Allow yourself to breathe and let some of that energy begin to move.

As your hips sink toward the Earth, feel them continue to soften and open. At the same time, let your heart soften and open to the sky. Breathe here, and sustain the stretch long enough to feel something happening…to feel your body changing…old holding patterns falling away. As you breathe, allow energy to move, resisting nothing.

Chapter 6

Coming Alive Again

*"Never apologize for showing feeling.
When you do so, you apologize for truth."*
—*Benjamin Disraeli*

We live in a world where so many of us have become numb: overwhelmed by disappointment, burdened by past wounds and grief, stubbornly attached to the stories we have created around our lives. Like a movie continuously replaying in the recesses of our minds, each day is a continuation of the same old story…another chapter…a further installment into the epic drama in which we have become inextricably engaged.

Consider again the number of people that rely on antidepressants to make it through daily life, or who only get a good night's sleep with the help of sleep aids—often immediately followed by some early morning stimulant to reignite the forces that will allow them to get through the long day looming before them. It's a tragedy that, for so many, life has become something to get through, something to endure, rather than a gift to be cherished, embraced, and celebrated.

How did this happen? How did we get so jaded—believing that life is difficult—and that happiness is an elusive, often unobtainable goal, something existing only in the distant future as something to be pursued? And because the space between where we are and where we want to be seems so expansive, the journey to inner peace and happiness appears to be such a long and arduous one. Is it any wonder so many of us doubt if we have the energy and endurance to make it?

So how did we lose our child-like innocence, and the faith and belief in ourselves and the lives we wish to create? When did we lose the enthusiasm we once had in our dreams?

For many, it happens in stages, as we experience disappointments and heartbreak, hitting the inevitable speed bumps and road blocks along the way that eventually add up until the disappointment becomes bigger than our belief that we can overcome them.

Once we realize that, although we may have created a road map to help get us where we want to be, we must allow for detours. There will occasionally be car trouble and breakdowns along the way, but as long as we get back on the road and head in the general direction of our dreams, we will eventually get there. There's no way we can miss as long as we always continue on the journey.

Okay, so what if we realize we've lost some of our motivation and inspiration? How do we get it back? We start by retracing our steps, identifying the wounds that we never healed, and letting go of the self-defeating stories we have created around them.

We've all done this. And since we live in a society that rarely encourages us to have enough self-awareness to recognize what it is that we are feeling, or empowers us to actually allow and experience those emotions, they tend to get stuck, blocking us from the free-flow of creative life force energy that we all experienced as children. Our disappointment, sadness, and anger have accumulated and created an energetic block in our system.

Compulsive Behaviors

This may explain why a new yoga client expressed confusion as to why she couldn't seem to relax in the evening until she had downed a bottle or more of wine. Like many of us, she was so resistant to being in the moment and facing the feelings that rose to the surface that she chose to numb out instead. This became her nightly ritual: the only way she could reach a pseudo-relaxed, peaceful state.

Perhaps it is time for us to start feeling what we need to feel, rather than numb out to it all.

This new approach to an old issue appears to be catching on, as so many are now looking to yoga for support in quitting smoking, losing weight, and dealing with issues of insomnia, anxiety, and depression.

In order to effect any kind of real and lasting change, we must ferret out the root cause of the issue and not just scratch the surface by merely dealing with symptoms. One does not just have an addiction to food or cigarettes; there is an emotional component that is driving that behavior. We can give ourselves permission to feel what we need to feel so we can come out on the other side of it without interrupting this very natural, healthy, empowering process by giving into compulsive, self-destructive behaviors. Doing this only serves to make us feel worse, making us scramble for another quick fix distraction and trapping us in a cycle.

"Endure the pain of growth, or live with the pain of regret."

—Yogi Bhajan

> **EXERCISE: JOURNAL** Take a few moments to journal about some of your compulsive, addictive behaviors. What is it that these behaviors are enabling you to avoid? What would happen if you chose instead to allow yourself to acknowledge what you feel, and then gave yourself permission to deeply experience it?

Right around this point in the conversation is when students and clients express fear that if they allow themselves to feel all of the stuff they have been avoiding for so long, they would be overwhelmed by their emotions. But it is only by moving right into the center of ourselves, and facing whatever is coming up for us in any given moment long enough to come out on the other side of it, that we strengthen our emotional musculature and develop faith and trust in ourselves and in our ability to be with what is.

In the beginning, when we are first learning to explore where that inner muscle is and start flexing it, it can be scary to do it alone. This is one motivation behind the group programs I offer. I know that when we, together as a group, are able to foster and create a safe, open, non-judgmental environment in which to be open and honest about what we are feeling, in a setting where everyone understands the value in doing so, something magical happens. What happens when we have loving, supportive witnesses to our own and other's processes is powerfully transformative to our previously pent-up emotional pain. It is also why support groups are such a great idea, allowing you to surround yourself with others facing similar life questions.

What we resist persists, and just because we aren't giving ourselves permission to consciously feel our lives doesn't mean we have moved past an issue. Emotions are energy in motion, and that energy that we are blocking simply finds its way deeper into our bodies, lodging itself in our organs and in our cells. Some will not be motivated to acknowledge the truth of what's going on inside until life falls apart around them, or the accumulation of that energy results in cancer or some other dis-ease. The gift of our darkest moments is the uncompromising self-honesty they bring. Some of the deepest, most interesting people I know have suffered greatly. But it was their choice to learn and grow from these human experiences rather than shut down out of anger, resentment, or bitterness that has enriched their lives the most.

We cannot numb ourselves to feelings like sadness, disappointment, and anger, and still feel all the happiness, peace, and joy that are available to us. Numb is numb, and to be fully alive means to allow the full spectrum of emotion to move through us. Choosing not to feel it *all* is the problem. Resisting, denying, contracting around and holding onto emotions makes us suffer. It is not that we should never experience sadness, anger, and fear, but that we should not *hold onto* that sadness, anger and fear. But if we are only allowing those emotions that we judge as "good" to flow through us, then when a "bad" emotion arises, our fear, guilt, and denial make us resist, and we contract against the feeling rather than allowing that energy to simply move through us.

Buddhists say all suffering is the result of attachment; this includes the attachment to being only happy. Some on the spiritual path say we should be able to transcend these petty human emotions, but we are spiritual beings having a human experience, and we aren't honoring our spirit if we are denying ourselves the gift of

"True freedom doesn't mean freedom FROM. As long as you are alive, you will never be free from pain. True freedom means freedom AS. True freedom is to feel fully, feeling AS this entire moment."

—David Deida

this human experience. It is not the feelings and emotions that make us suffer, it is our attachment to only certain ones, and resistance and denial to others that make us squirm inside our own skin.

"The spiritual path is about the healing of the heart. Everything else is decoration."
—Michael Jeffreys

Some say the things we fear most have already happened to us. Nothing can truly be suppressed, and the only way to be freed—from fear and the emotional toxins of our past—is to allow ourselves to feel again. Only by being with what is can we come out on the other side of it. Each time we do, we strengthen our emotional capacity.

Breathe

The breath is the quickest, easiest way to make the journey from the head down into the body. In yoga, we learn that the breath is at the very heart of the practice. I often tell my students that, even if we did nothing but breathe deeply and with intention for the entire practice, that would be enough to get us further grounded in our bodies. And throughout the yoga practice, for beginners and advanced yogis alike, our attention is consistently and repeatedly brought back to the breath until, ultimately, our breath is like a continuous stream of conscious energy moving through the body without getting stuck, held, or contracted. This can take years of practice, just as it has taken most of us years to dissociate from our bodies to the extent that many of us have.

> **EXERCISE: LONG DEEP BREATHING** Sit comfortably, with your eyes closed. Closing your eyes will help eliminate at least 95% of the external distractions. Now, allow your breathing to begin deep in your lower belly, and to expand all the way up into your lungs. In yoga, this is often referred to as three-part breathing, because you are breathing into three distinct parts of the body: first into the lower belly; then into the lower lungs; and finally into the upper lungs, neck, and throat area. Allow your whole body to breathe, like a balloon filling from the bottom, all the way up to the top.

> Allow each in-breath to take a full count of eight, hold for two counts at the top, and then exhale to a count of eight. Do this for several minutes. Then lengthen the breath to a count of 10, eventually even counting all the way to 12 or 15.
>
> Breathing deeply this way relaxes us, brings us back to center, and grounds us in the present moment. Long, deep breathing stimulates that part of the nervous system that soothes and relaxes us, making it physiologically impossible to stay in a frantic, stressed state.

In yoga, *pranayama*, or breathing techniques, are powerful tools for moving emotional energy. The quality of our breathing is directly related to our emotional state. In his book *The Sutras on Healing and Enlightenment,* Matthew Brownstein says, "The biggest cause of the blockage of breath…is emotional suppression and denial." He goes on to say that "Within blocked breath energy are mental impressions that house memories, beliefs and emotions."

Shamans and healers have always understood this, which is why they use powerful breathing techniques to release the emotional charge of past memories. Not only is the breath an opportunity to open up our channel and allow energy to flow through us, it is a great analogy for the natural and healthy ebb and flow.

Breathe Into the Center of It

Another powerful way to disperse stuck emotional energy, maybe even the most powerful way, is to breathe right into the center of it. Instead of avoiding, denying or running from an emotion, to choose to recognize and acknowledge it, and then move right into the heart of it and feel it fully, is incredibly freeing. When we face it and feel it, it's no longer something that's looming out there, haunting us.

I remember how truly blessed I felt when I discovered that I was pregnant, and when I had a miscarriage right around the end of my first trimester, I felt heartbroken and disappointed. My way of hon-

> *"The wound is the place where the light enters you."*
>
> —Rumi

oring my experience and the grief I inevitably faced was to allow myself to feel it, to acknowledge it when it came up, and to breathe right into the center of it. I didn't deny it or push it away, nor did I get overly caught up in it. I just allowed myself to feel it and for that energy to move through me. Each time I did, I felt lighter and freer.

I had a client who was dealing with the pain and loss around a breakup, and the news that her ex was already in a new relationship. She expressed frustration that she just couldn't seem to get past it. I encouraged her to close her eyes and take a few moments to get in touch with the feelings she was having around the situation: not the story, but the feeling. When it was clear she had done this, I held the space for her to move right into the center of the sensations, and simply breathe, welcoming and allowing all of it fully. She was shocked and amazed when, after just a few moments, she could feel that energy suddenly start to dissipate, and she felt lighter. "What did you do to me? You're a miracle worker!" were the first words out of her mouth when she opened her eyes.

But I didn't do anything. She did, when she chose to be courageous enough to feel what she needed to so that she could come out on the other side of it. That doesn't necessarily mean she was done with her process around that issue, but she now knew what to do whenever something came up for her concerning it.

> **EXERCISE: BREATHE INTO THE CENTER OF IT**   Take a few moments to close your eyes and quiet your mind. Then think about a situation that has been stirring up feelings inside of you. Take some time getting out of your head and into your body, into that place where you feel. Take a moment to get a bead on it, to become conscious enough of what "it" is to be able to name it. Then move right into the center of it, and simply breathe, without any agenda or expectation. Just simply be with what *is* for you in that moment, and notice what happens.
>
> Then, journal about that experience. When you breathed into the center of that experience, did something happen? Did the energy dissipate? Was there any desire to hold onto

> it for any reason? Take some time to explore your relationship with your emotions. As always, be gentle, and do this without judgment. This is a wonderful opportunity to gain awareness, and strengthen your emotional musculature.

Develop Trust in Yourself

Freedom means not that we no longer feel emotion, but that we feel no need to hold onto these emotions. Every time we honor ourselves by acknowledging what we are feeling, and take care of ourselves in a way that allows life to pass through us, rather than getting stuck, we develop faith in ourselves and in our ability to be in our own skin, and in our own lives, fully and without resistance.

I remember when I first learned that it was okay for me to feel anger. I had been carrying so much of it deep in my body for so long, with so much guilt and defensiveness around it, that when I was told it was okay to feel angry, and was given the space and the permission to do so, I felt liberated. I no longer needed to pretend I wasn't feeling angry, nor did I have to feel guilty because I was. And the moment I started allowing myself to acknowledge and feel it, it started to dissipate, as if all it ever wanted and needed from me was my recognition and acceptance. Like a child tugging at my sleeve, it wasn't going anywhere until I gave it the attention it was seeking.

The liberation I felt when I learned to acknowledge and allow what I was feeling was so beautiful and so freeing, I came alive again in my own life, and for the first time felt joy underneath any other emotions that came up for me. Sadness, fear, insecurity suddenly became feelings I was grateful for, because they made me feel alive. I no longer worried that those feelings would overwhelm me, because I now knew that they were simply fleeting as long as I didn't hold onto them. Now, on those days when I feel sad, that's my signal that it's time to take care of myself, and I'll take a bubble bath, cook myself a healthy, intentional meal, watch a light-hearted inspirational movie, or go for a walk. I take great comfort in knowing that this too shall pass. And because I have witnessed this process within myself enough times now to trust in it, and in myself,

"Only to the extent that we expose ourselves over and over again to annililation can that which is indestructible in us be found."

—Pema Chodron

there is joy floating underneath it all. As my friend Amber says, the Love and joy within us push the sadness, insecurity, and anger we feel to the surface so we can acknowledge and release them.

> **EXERCISE: JOURNAL** Make a list of things you can do for yourself the next time you are feeling low. How can you take care of yourself as the energy of life moves through you?

Emotional Energy as Fuel for Our Lives

If we are to truly choose to become empowered by our emotions rather than overwhelmed by them, we must recognize the powerful gift that they are. Emotions are energy in motion. When we learn to harness and channel that energy, it becomes powerful fuel for our lives.

I remember a friend who felt guilty for feeling so angry and even hateful toward her ex-boyfriend for some of the abusive things he had done to her, and for the ways he was continuing to try to control and manipulate her. She could have denied her anger and turned it inward, ending up severely depressed or even ill. She also might have gotten in touch with that anger, but failed to recognize it as a gift she could use to fuel her life and empower her, causing her to react in ways that were self-destructive or even violent. But without the anger, she may never have found the energy or the strength to do what needed to be done to protect herself, staying in a victim role for as long as he chose to keep her there. When she realized her anger was a gift showing her that something was wrong, she was able to make the choice to redirect that energy and empower herself to take the necessary steps to get him out of her life.

Cathartic Emotional Release

Healthy emotional release means allowing emotional energy to flow and finding another outlet for that energy. Yoga can be one of those outlets. Combining yoga with meditation allows us to not only move energy, but to discover the core belief that drives our behaviors. Sometimes, for really stuck emotional energy, I have clients yell, punch pillows, kick and scream—whatever it takes—until they have the cathartic emotional release they need. When the emotion is discharged, what is left is a sense of relief.

Medical professionals are quick to diagnose depression these days, but depression is not an emotion; it is a result of suppressed emotion. Rather than further suppressing those emotions and having to continue to up the dosage in order to keep us numb, perhaps it's time to reclaim our childlike enthusiasm for life by allowing ourselves to feel what we need to feel so we can finally be free.

Move

In Kundalini Yoga, the mantra is simple: "Keep up." The point is that no matter what happens, no matter what life throws your way, you keep moving…you keep living. No matter what happens, keep the energy moving. Engage in some form of physical exercise and movement every day. We do this not in a compulsive, frenetic way, but in a way that grounds us in our bodies and opens up the channels to allow our energy to keep moving rather than stagnating and lying dormant. If we don't, over time, inertia will begin to weigh us down, pulling us into the undertow of that which has accumulated inside of us.

Go for a walk or a bike ride, which have the added benefit of getting you outside, connecting with nature. Dance in your living room or join a class. Practice yoga, getting into your body in a conscious, gentle, compassionate way that builds strength, increases flexibility, and develops balance. Join a softball league. Take tennis lessons. Do anything that will get you moving in a way that opens up your body, leaving you feeling lighter than you were before you started. Feel yourself getting lighter and lighter every day as you get more active in your own life.

"If all you can do is crawl, start crawling."

—Rumi

Create

> *"We are traditionally rather proud of ourselves for having slipped creative work in there between the domestic chores and obligations. I'm not sure we deserve such big A-pluses for that."*
> —Toni Morrison

We are creative beings. And since our creative potential is so closely linked to emotions, when we numb ourselves to the healthy flow of emotion we distance ourselves from our ability to create the lives we want. Which is why Julia Cameron, author of *The Artist's Way*, recommends daily journaling, a minimum of three pages each morning of stream-of-consciousness journaling, as a way of freeing up our creative pathways by purging ourselves mentally and emotionally of that which has kept us blocked.

"Only creative people are happy."
—OSHO

Within each of us is an artist, a creator craving an outlet for emotions, dreams and visions living within: writing, drawing, painting, cooking, gardening, singing, playing an instrument, dancing—anything that can ground us in the present moment and allow the free-flow of creative energy to move through us. An open creative channel is an open emotional channel, and an open channel means energy is moving through us unimpeded and unencumbered by limiting thoughts, outdated beliefs, and contracted ideas. And we are free.

> **EXERCISE: JOURNAL** Journal about some of the creative outlets you would enjoy. Explore some of the ways you can open up your creative channel, and allow emotional energy to flow freely.

Expanding and Contracting

In yoga, we learn to tune into our breathing and let our bodies expand and contract around the breath. The only way to stay healthy is to allow our breathing to be steady, consistent and natural. If we hold the breath in or out, we cut ourselves off from life force energy. The out-breath must be respected as fully as the in-breath.

We all recognize the value of breathing in—to provide ourselves with oxygen and energy. But how often do we honor the value of the exhale, allowing us to release toxins and purify the blood? This can be likened to spiritual awakening. We love the awakening, the ride up the roller coaster, but often resist the rest of the ride, the unexpected turns and loops that disorient us for a time.

When we go through a spiritual awakening, it's like taking a big breath in. We feel open, clear, and expansive, and often believe that feeling will never end. Gone are the days of fear, doubt, and disillusionment!

And then the need to breathe out arises; it actually cannot be avoided if the organism is going to live. It's being at peace during the exhale, when the body is contracting around the breath, that is the true measure of our growth. How much can we trust in the next breath in?

In life, we grow so much while we are expanding, but often grow even more when in a contracted state—if we allow it. It's resisting that makes us suffer. It's believing that we are no longer subject to that very natural rhythm that leaves us feeling as if we've lost something, and if disillusionment sets in, we can get stuck there much longer than we need to.

Everything in life has a rhythm, from the seasons, to the tides, to the phases of the moon. Everything that expands also contracts, except maybe the Universe itself, as the planets continue to create more and more space between themselves. But the Universe is pure consciousness; it does not have an ego.

We do. If we truly transcend it and are no longer subject to the expanding and contracting that goes with it, we would no longer have a need to be on this Earth. I once heard someone say, "As soon as you reach pure consciousness and truly transcend the ego, you have only seconds left to live," because your body can no longer contain you.

But how beautiful is that, to recognize that if you are still here, it is because there is more still for you to learn? And it's only the resistance of it that causes our suffering. So what would happen if we truly embraced it all: the good, the bad, the ugly…and shone the light of compassion on it all?

"...even to be attached to the idea of enlightenment is to go astray."

—Sosan

If we can accept and allow the joy, bliss, and peace that come from knowing we are spiritual beings having a human experience, as well as the fear, doubt, anger, and disillusionment that is a part of the human experience we are here to have, then we can experience true peace. And perhaps that is the lesson.

When we learn to recognize what we are feeling, accept it, and breathe into it—whatever it is—and we combine this emotional awareness with a clear and focused mind, we have the formula for emotional intelligence. In her book *Radical Acceptance,* Tara Brach suggests that when joy arises, when gratitude arises, when love arises, it's easy to embrace it. The gift is when we can say "and this too" when the anger, sadness, and fear emerge, and accept and embrace them as well.

In his book, *On Anger,* Thich Nhat Hanh says if you injure your hand, you don't push it away and deny its pain. You take it in close; you tend to it, care for it, and nurture it back to health. Your anger is like that wounded hand. Only embracing it and loving that part of you allows the inflammation to subside, the healing to occur.

Carl Jung asked, "Would you rather be whole, or good?" To be whole, we must accept it all—the full spectrum of emotion. Failure to do so results in a splintered self. To be fully whole, we cannot deny any aspect of ourselves.

In her book, *The Dark Side of the Light Chasers,* Debbie Ford says that although most people think the color white is the absence of all color, in truth it is the inclusion of all the colors of the rainbow together. We cannot be light beings if we deny any aspect of ourselves; it all must be acknowledged and loved.

If it is true that what we resist persists, then true healing happens when we bring "it" into the light.

The true lesson is in learning to recognize, accept, and allow the energy of all emotions to move through you without getting stuck there. Just as you cannot breathe in forever, you cannot breathe out forever either; you must expand again. I often encourage my students to tune into that place where the urge to breathe begins, and then notice how good it feels to allow it.

We are freed the moment we stop resisting what is, accept that it has become a part of our experience for a reason, and allow ourselves to be humble enough to learn the lesson we have been given with gratitude. This is true health, balance, and freedom.

*"This being human is a guest-house
Every morning a new arrival.*

*A joy, a depression, a meanness,
Some momentary awareness comes
as an unexpected visitor.*

Welcome and entertain them all!

*Even if they're a crowd of sorrows,
who violently sweep your house
empty of its furniture,
still, treat each guest honorably.*

*He may be clearing you
out for some new delight.*

*The dark thought, the shame, the malice,
meet them at the door laughing,
and invite them in.*

*Be grateful for whoever comes,
because each has been sent
as a guide from beyond."*

—*Rumi, "The Guest House"*
Translated by Coleman Barks with John Moyne.

An Empath Yoga Perspective

Downward Facing Dog   Open Your Channel

Upon exploring your way into your next Downward Facing Dog, breathe deeply, and feel your body expanding and contracting around each full breath. Notice as your spine aligns, and enjoy a healthy stretch there. This is a great asana for opening up your channel, allowing energy to move freely and unencumbered through you as you breathe.

Be sure to move around inside of your downward facing dog. Sway your hips from side to side. Explore what's happening in your body, cultivating an even deeper relationship with your own body. Becoming aware of your rib cage, let your heart expand and open in all directions. With a long and healthy spine, let your breathing be deep and full and rich. Enjoy this full body stretch and feel your body opening—your energy expanding in all directions. Enjoy the way that feels.

An Empath Yoga Perspective

Supported Fish Pose — Open Your Heart

Sometimes, when working with clients, and I know there is an opportunity to open their heart, I'll have them lie on their backs, in Savasana, but with a rolled up yoga mat or bolster behind them, positioned just behind their rib cage so they can relax their arms and shoulders, and their heart can expand and open toward the sky. Try this any time you want to be gentle with yourself, and allow yourself to feel whatever you are ready to feel, so that energy can move through you. Simply relax back, succumbing to gravity, and let your heart softly open and expand as you breathe. With some gentle, soft music on perhaps, allow yourself to rest here for several minutes.

Notice and feel how expansive and open your heart becomes when you accept, surrender, and allow yourself to feel what you need to feel, and how that energy is then free to move on.

Chapter 7

Forgiveness
The Correction of An Error

*"Forgiveness is letting go
of all hopes for a better past."*
—*Gerald Jampolski*

Very few people live in the moment. Most are too busy being stuck in the past, as if reliving the story in their minds, and retelling it, somehow allows them to change what happened. Many can't, or won't, move on out of the belief that holding on can somehow protect them from what has already occurred. I am again reminded of something I once heard: that the things we fear most have already happened to us. Out of a mistaken belief, many tend to guard themselves against that experience and defend themselves so they never have to be a victim again. But all too often this changes the very lens through which we see the world, and can become a self-fulfilling prophecy. The players may change, but the story line is the same.

We can never find peace in the present if we are vested in trying to fix the past. The past does not exist. It is only a memory, a collection of images in our mind and the emotional energy attached to it that still resides in our bodies. It keeps us stuck…in a memory, in an experience that is often rich with gifts and opportunities once we let go of our attachment and resistance to the pain associated with it.

Forgiveness is letting go of all hopes for a better past. Forgiveness releases us, creating space in our bodies and minds for us to live each moment fresh and new. Perhaps one of my favorite references to the power of forgiveness can be found in *A Course in Miracles*, where it says:

> *"What could you want that forgiveness cannot give? Do you want peace? Forgiveness offers it. Do you want happiness, a quiet mind, a certainty of purpose, and a sense of worth and beauty that transcends the world? Do you want care and safety, and the warmth of sure protection always? Do you want a quietness that cannot be disturbed, a gentleness that never can be hurt, a deep, abiding comfort, and a rest so perfect it can never be upset?*
>
> *"All this forgiveness offers you, and more. It sparkles on your eyes as you awake, and gives you joy with which to meet the day. It soothes your forehead while you sleep, and rests upon your eyelids so you see no dreams of fear and evil, malice and attack. And when you wake again, it offers you another day of happiness and peace. All this forgiveness offers you, and more."*

In his book, *Forgiveness: The Greatest Healer of All*, Gerald Jampolski tells the story of his own process of forgiveness, and of his work with dozens of "terminally ill" children whom he met with weekly to help them move from fear back to love, with forgiveness as the doorway. Many of these children had deeply buried their own fears so as not to further upset their parents, along with they had left, since doctors and others within the medical establishment told them there was nothing left to do. As these children were able to open up and acknowledge their fears, feel what they needed to feel, and experience the true shift of forgiveness in their hearts—toward the doctors, towards their parents, towards themselves…even towards God—unexplainable and profound healing took place; healing that baffled the medical establishment. The last I heard, over 30 years later, many of those "terminally ill" children were still alive, a testament to the miracle of forgiveness.

> *"Are you fleeing from Love because of a single humiliation? What do you know of Love except the name?"*
>
> —Rumi

Forgiveness: The Correction of An Error

"When you hold resentment toward another, you are bound to that person or condition by an emotional link that is stronger than steel. Forgiveness is the only way to dissolve that link and get free."

—Catherine Ponder

Love and forgiveness can produce miracles. As one of my teachers used to say, "all healing takes place on the level of forgiveness." But in my years of working with people on this issue, there are some common false beliefs and concerns about what forgiveness means and why it is so scary for so many.

When I taught about forgiveness during an Empath Yoga training in the Philippines, there was a beautiful gentleman who, despite his understanding and appreciation for the value of forgiveness, said he was not willing to forgive his father…that to do so would be like saying that what he did was okay.

Others have feared that to forgive would make them vulnerable again. And still others have a belief somewhere inside of them that people that are forgiving are weak. But to forgive someone does not mean that you must let them back into your life, only that you chose to no longer be imprisoned by your past. Anger and resentment will only get you so far. Let your empowerment be real and lasting. Let the boundaries that you set come from a deep and clear inner knowing of who you are in the present, rather than bitterness over what happened in the past. As Mohandas K. Gandhi said, "The weak cannot forgive. Forgiveness is an attribute of the strong." To forgive and still be able to say no when appropriate is one of the ways we love ourselves.

Besides, all of these reasons we have given ourselves for not forgiving another have no effect on them and are incapable of affecting the past. They only keep us stuck there, the energy of that experience alive and well, wreaking havoc on our bodies and our lives. I once read somewhere, "resentment is like taking poison and waiting for the other person to die." And often we are not just dealing with one person, place, or event, but a lifetime accumulation of anger, sadness and resentment, no matter how suppressed that energy may be.

Effects of Unforgiving Minds

Choosing unforgiving thoughts, over time is like filling up a mental garbage can. The trash is our past anger and resentments which we choose not to look at; instead of consciously processing it, we choose to store it in our subconscious minds. Our subconscious mind is the receptacle. Once the receptacle gets "full," we may choose to push the garbage down, delaying the inevitable, and making room for more trash. Eventually, the bin is full and you cannot push it down any further. If you try, the bag may burst. If you still choose to add to the trash heap, it eventually spills over onto the floor, filling up not only the trash bin, but also making a mess of the entire room.

This could be likened to the unforgiving and unloving thoughts we hold onto because we are not ready to let go and forgive, because we fear that to forgive this other person is as good as telling them that what they did is okay. Or we fear taking out the trash may be a long, laborious task, so we avoid it for as long as possible. Failing to empty our minds of anger and resentment results in a build-up that will ultimately spill over into all of our thoughts and feelings, destroying relationships and making a mess of our lives.

This "mess" can take on less severe forms such as chronic stress, distraction and lack of focus, irritability, and unhappiness. Inevitably we start taking this stress out on others, ultimately creating more and more separation in our lives. In severe cases, insomnia, depression, or even a nervous breakdown may occur. In addition to the mental anguish we experience, we store more and more toxic thoughts and feelings in our bodies. When the body is no longer at peace it becomes dis-eased, with these toxins taking on a physical manifestation in the form of an illness, such as heart disease or cancer.

The reasons to forgive are endless. Unforgiving thoughts bind us, imprison us and steal our peace. Choosing to forgive frees us and returns us to a peaceful, often blissful state. For many of us, the concept that we are carrying around angry, unforgiving thoughts is a new one. These thoughts and feelings having been building up in us from a very early age, and we just were not consciously aware of them. Once we realize this, we have the power to do something about it.

> **EXERCISE: JOURNAL** What are your reasons for not forgiving? What is not forgiving costing you? Consider for a moment what a lifetime of misunderstanding, confusion and pain is blocking you from.

"Your task is not to seek for love, but merely to seek and find all the barriers within yourself that you have built against it."

—Rumi

Forgiveness: The Correction of An Error

Acceptance

I remember a time I felt incredibly betrayed. I just couldn't believe that a person who loved me could betray my trust in such a hurtful way. For a time, I was in shock, disbelief, and even outright denial. The whole time I was in that place of resisting what was, I suffered greatly. It wasn't until I started to accept it that the emotional pain started to lift. With acceptance, I was no longer in conflict with myself and my experience, and since I was no longer in denial, I could then shift my focus to how best to take care of myself moment by moment. A certain level of freedom comes when we stop fighting against the moment, and we accept what is. Only then can we possibly move on to the next step in the forgiveness process: compassion for ourselves, which is so closely tied in with acceptance, and compassion for the other person.

> **EXERCISE: JOURNAL** What experience, disappointment or betrayal do you have yet to accept? Explore if there are any ways that being in resistance and denial around this experience is serving you, and in what ways is it costing you.

Compassion

This is where some balk. Why would we choose to be compassionate toward the one that hurt us? For me, its worse to believe that someone who I know has love for me, someone who is a brother or a sister, would hurt me with the intent to cause me pain rather than to realize that it was more a result of his or her own pain, confusion, fear, and disillusionment that could cause them to make such an error. In our ignorance, we've all hurt another without realizing the karmic boomerang effect of our actions. True compassion means being willing to see things differently. We are all doing the best we can.

The old paradigm of forgiveness, the one taught by some religions and passed down from generate to generation, is that forgiveness is a righteous act, that we should leave vengeance to an angry, judgmental God waiting to dole out an appropriate punishment on judgment day. This only perpetuates the lie that we are all separate from each other—some of us more or less valuable than others, depending on the purity of our lives.

This is not the type of forgiveness I'm talking about here.

Just as we came into this world as pure innocence and Love, so did everyone else. And just as we were exposed to the people, places, and circumstances that shaped our perception of the world, so too was everyone else. True forgiveness means recognizing that in our delirium, in our insanity, we have all been doing the best we can.

We are all doing our best based on our current level of understanding and awareness at any given time. When we let go of the story, we recognize that the wounds of others have been bumping up against our own our whole lives. This is how we learn to recognize that we have them, and can begin our own process of healing. This becomes a much easier, quicker process when we realize that the past does not exist, it is only a memory. Underneath the story we are keeping alive in our minds, behind the level of the cognitive, thinking mind, there is a level upon which nothing really happened.

With the development of the Ego fear was born, and the separation began. We accepted the shared reality of an us versus them mentality, erroneously buying into the belief that we could act out of a lack of love toward another and not have it affect us. In our confusion and fear, in our forgetting the Truth of who we are, we've all behaved in ways that were out of integrity. We've lied, cheated and betrayed another in a misguided attempt to get our own needs met. In our delirium we forget that we are connected, that there is only one of us here, and therefore what we do to another we do to ourselves.

The essence of our being is Love. It's true for us, and it's true for everyone else—even if they don't know it yet, even if they haven't remembered. Underneath it all, we are still that innocent little boy or girl that we were before our attention was diverted elsewhere.

That which is true in another, the pure innocence and Love of another, is never lost. We all have a changeless inner core, a divine truth of love and innocence and connection. We are all drops in the same ocean, brothers and sisters.

> *"Ultimately, to forgive someone means to cancel the debt you feel they owe you."*
> —Katherine Woodward Thomas

Forgiveness: The Correction of An Error

Since there is only, ultimately, one of us here, there is nothing anyone has ever done to us that we have not done too, to a greater or lessor degree. Compassion means recognizing that in our confusion, in our insanity, we have all made the same error in perception—forgetting that we are one.

And while we have been living a collective dream, our individual experiences of it are very personal. While one spirit is born as a woman into an intact family, but with an alcoholic mother and emotionally absentee father, another is a boy who's life journey begins with his abandonment at birth. Even those with a seemingly picture-perfect childhood have their own stories to tell.

When we let go of judgment and allow compassion to bloom in our hearts, we realize we are all doing the best we can. I am reminded of Carl Rogers words on what he called the Directional Tendency:

> *"Biologists, neurophysiologists, and other scientists, including psychologists, have evidence that…there is, in every organism…an underlying flow of movement toward constructive fulfillment of its inherent possibilities. There is a natural tendency toward complete development in man. This actualizing tendency can of course be thwarted, but it cannot be destroyed…*
>
> *I remember in my boyhood the potato bin in which we stored our winter supply of potatoes was in the basement, several feet below a small basement window. The conditions were unfavorable, but the potatoes would seem to sprout—pale white sprouts, so unlike the healthy green shoots they sent up when planted in the soil in the spring. But these sad, spindly sprouts would grow two or three feet in length as they reached toward the distant light of the window. They were, in their bizarre, futile growth, a sort of desperate expression of the directional tendency. They would never become a plant, never mature, never fulfill their real potentiality. But under the most adverse circumstances they were striving to become. Life would not give up, even if it could not flourish In dealing with clients whose lives have been terribly warped, in working*

with men and women on the back ward of state hospitals, I often think of those potato sprouts. So unfavorable have been the conditions in which these people have developed that their lives often seem abnormal, twisted, scarcely human. Yet the directional tendency in them is to be trusted. The clue to understanding their behavior is that they are striving, in the only ways available to them, to move toward growth, toward becoming. To us the results may seem bizarre and futile, but they are life's desperate attempt to become itself..."

When we let go of the judgment—of the right versus wrong, good versus bad, us versus them—and remember that underneath it all we are all the same, we soften in compassion. I think back to my work with the homeless—the crack addicts, prostitutes, and murderers—and every time I took the time to really listen, without judgment, to how they got where they were, I had to admit that I could be capable of doing what they did, and more.

There is a leadership training program that has participants sit inconspicuously in a public place and observe strangers as they walk by. There they practice remembering the innocence and Love that dwells underneath our habits and behaviors. Focusing on one person at a time, they repeat silently to themselves:

Just like me, this person is seeking peace and happiness.

Just like me, this person has made mistakes, and acted out of fear and confusion.

Just like me, this person has experienced heartbreak, disappointment and sadness.

Just like me, this person is doing the best he/she can.

We are all doing the best we can. Healing occurs, liberation dawns, when we recognize that every moment is an opportunity to awaken from the dream and remember the Truth of who we are. Since Love is who and what we really are, when we allow ourselves to loosen our grip and let go of our stories, it becomes clear that forgiveness is the only sane response.

> *"True forgiveness is a correction of the error...
> it's a reminder of our innocence."*
>
> —*A Course in Miracles*

We are spiritual beings having a human experience, and to the spirit this is just a dream we are having. So on the level of spirit, on the level of soul, nothing really happened.

But let us not deny the very human level upon which it did. This is where Forgiveness comes in.

Forgiveness liberates us, correcting our error in perception. For not only have we believed that we could behave in a way toward others without a karmic backlash, so too have others. Not only did we buy into the belief that we are separate, that it's a dog-eat-dog world out there, and we must fend for ourselves—so too has nearly everyone else. In our insanity we have lashed out—in fear, in anger, in grief—at the reflection of ourselves in others.

The road back to Love, Truth, and connection is paved with forgiveness.

Willingness is a Key Ingredient

Over the past decade I have seen hundreds of men and women, from all walks of life, transform their lives through forgiveness, which has become a central tenet of the work I do with others. Many roads will get you there. Whether you have the opportunity to spill it all within the safety of a supportive group, or in a one on one interaction with someone you trust to support you in that process, or if you choose to do it alone, the one essential ingredient is the willingness to forgive.

Usually in my work with others, as soon as their fears around forgiveness are acknowledged, and the desire to be free of the emotional sludge under which they have felt trapped is fully embraced, the next question inevitably becomes: How?

Forgiveness is something we do for ourselves, to free ourselves of the pain and burden of the past, and there is no better time for that process to begin to unfold than right now.

We already know the importance of acknowledging what's true for us, and the value of allowing ourselves to feel again—going right into the center of it so we can come out on the other side. Now, the next step is to cultivate a willingness to forgive everyone and everything that we perceive to have ever caused us pain. But don't go after them all. Start with "the big matza ball," and from there the rest of them tend to crumble on their own, once we have had the felt experience of the freedom that follows.

> **Exercise: Journal**
> 1. Make a list of who & what to you have yet to forgive.
> 2. Pick one (the big matza ball).
> 3. What is not forgiving this person costing you?

Begin a dialogue with your deepest inner self—that part of you behind the thinking mind that is connected to something greater. State who you are now ready to forgive. Acknowledge the feelings that arise when you think about this person. Breathe right into the center of those feelings, and then ask for the willingness to let go—to forgive—fully and completely, and to finally be free of the story. Ask that the cord be cut that has kept you stuck in the past, so you can be free. State that you are ready to be free. Then let it go, and trust that the process has already begun.

Pray. Ask for help in seeing it differently. Say to yourself, and out loud, "I am willing to see things differently."

Create a space within which forgiveness can take place. Light a candle, turn off the phone, give yourself the gift of some time alone. Set the intention for the energy around whatever you are ready to let go of to begin to shift. Meditate on forgiveness, letting Love fill you until there isn't room for anything but that. Then send love to the person you most need to forgive—dead or alive, and make a genuine wish for them to experience peace within their own heart. Remember, the other person is us, so forgiving them is forgiving ourselves.

Write a letter, not necessarily one that you send, expressing all the things you never could say. Give yourself the opportunity to finish the conversation you've been having with this person in your mind all these years.

"Children begin by leaving their parents; after a time they judge them; rarely, if ever, do they forgive them."
—Oscar Wilde

Forgiveness: The Correction of An Error   135

I had a good friend whose mother died when she was a toddler, leaving her with no siblings of her own and a father who quickly remarried, putting his energy into a new family. Now, as an adult woman, married and ready to experience that biological bond she felt had been missing her whole life, she was frustrated and distraught when she herself was unable to get pregnant. Believing some energy might be hung up around her relationship with her mother, I suggested she write her a letter. She really set the stage for the experience, took it seriously, and had a heartfelt experience of communicating her feelings of loss and abandonment to her mother.

What commenced was a powerful grieving process as she removed the lid on the pain she had been holding inside for over 30 years. Days later, her husband called to thank me for helping her, as he could see and feel the difference in his wife. And whether that exercise is responsible for the breakthrough or not, she did end up pregnant and is now the mother of a beautiful little girl.

Consider finding a therapist or support group where you can share openly and honestly about your feelings, in a way that encourages you to move through them rather than merely spinning your wheels in the mud. In my private sessions with people, I use a combination of talk therapy, yoga to help open up the body and move energy, and hypnotherapy to help get at the root hidden deep within the subconscious mind.

Sometimes things seem to get worse before they get better, because like popping the top on a champagne bottle, lots of bubbles come to the surface. These are like the emotions we have been holding inside, finally bursting forth as the pressure of holding them down is released. You may not even realize that forgiveness has taken place until you're in a situation that would normally trigger something and set you off, and you realize later that didn't happen. Often we start noticing the signs after we have completed the process and forgotten about it.

"The moment you commit and quit holding back, all sorts of unforeseen incidences, meetings and material assistance will rise up to meet you. The simplest act of commitment is a powerful magnet for help."

—*Napolean Hill*

Grieving

It seems that often what we refer to as depression is really unresolved grief. When we finally accept what has or is happening, a very natural and healthy grieving process ensues if we allow it. If we don't, we're stuck in the pain and fear and we may never come out of it. This fear causes so many to either avoid grieving or to mislabel it. All too often in our society today, a pill is prescribed in an effort to help us avoid feeling what we must inevitably feel if we are to be whole. It is by being consumed by our grief that the energy is transformed.

I once had a friend call me who was finally letting go of a painful divorce that had held him hostage with false hope for almost a decade. It was heartbreaking, painful, and difficult, as it should be when we are truly letting go of something that has been a part of us for so long. When he called to tell me he wasn't "doing well," that he thought he might be depressed, I asked "is it possible what you're calling depression is actually you finally grieving the end of that relationship, a relationship in which you invested so much of your heart and time and energy?" I encouraged him to be very gentle with himself and allow himself to grieve. He called me a few days later to tell me that, while he wasn't done yet with the grieving process, he was feeling much better and felt confident he was on the right path.

After my miscarriage, I remember a healer friend telling me to let myself be consumed by the grief for a while—instead of trying to get back to work and moving on too quickly, to take some time to give myself over to the sadness, disappointment and grief. It was a wonderful reminder to take the time I needed to really allow this process to complete itself, instead of trying to hurry it along so it wouldn't interfere any more with my life.

I once heard Marianne Williamson tell a story of a woman friend she knew who had gone on antidepressants after life had dealt her a difficult blow. When Marianne asked her why she went on the drugs she responded, "What else could I do, sit in my room and cry for three days?" Marianne responded, "Yes, if that's what you need to do, then sit in your room and cry for three days."

Once we accept whatever has happened, we can then accept our sadness, disappointment, and grief, and this is where we start to integrate our life experiences in a healthy way. Grieving is like the heart sighing; it's a release of pent up energy that must be set free in order for us to be free.

This process takes as long as it takes. There is a difference between wallowing in pain, which means true acceptance hasn't really happened yet, and healthy grieving, which often takes time, depending on the degree of the loss. Often it is most intense at first, and it can take days or weeks before you start to feel a little lighter and freer, as if your heart is getting more oxygen. And then there may be more bubbles of grief that surface when you least expect it, with more and more space existing between those moments until one day, you realize its been gone for a while. Often what's left is wisdom, knowledge, and strength, and maybe even gratitude for the experience, if we allow ourselves to see the gift in it.

Self-Forgiveness

People often say, "I can forgive others, but it's me I have a hard time forgiving." The way we forgive ourselves is by forgiving. As we forgive, we are forgiven. Forgive everyone, for everything. Hold onto no resentment. We give what we most want to receive. Since there is only one of us here, giving and receiving are the same.

I remember a man I worked with at the homeless shelter named Billy. He had spent 17 years in prison for killing another man and, while he was willing to go through the exercise of forgiving his own father for what he put him through, he became stuck when we started talking about self-forgiveness. I could see in his face how desperately he wanted to forgive himself, to believe he was worthy of Love after some of the things he had done.

There comes a point when we have to decide if we have punished ourselves enough. Remembering that we are all connected, that our energy creates a ripple effect on the world around us, and that the healing of the planet begins with the healing of ourselves, may be helpful when we finally find ourselves here knocking on the door of self-forgiveness. We cannot move on in an emotionally healthy way until we free ourselves fully. Forgiveness is not a partial process—we either forgive completely, or we do not forgive at all.

I know a woman that was in a marriage with a man that never fully loved or embraced her, and she knew it. After years of doing everything she could to get his attention to no avail, her craving for emotional intimacy led her right into the arms of another man. It was intoxicating to feel seen and heard for the first time in years, and the desire to experience more of that was like a magnet whose force she couldn't resist. Ultimately destroying her marriage to a man she genuinely loved, she spent years punishing herself and sabotaging every relationship with the baggage she was carrying from her marriage. It wasn't until she could finally forgive herself that she was able to move on in a healthy way. In this way, healing ourselves is healing the world. It always begins with us.

Ultimately we find ourselves at a crossroads where it comes down to forgiving ourselves for ever having forgotten who we are, for ever being seduced by the Ego, for being lured into a reality that pits us against one another. In the end, we must forgive ourselves for ever having perceived a lack of Love, and acting from a lack of Love.

A Story of Forgiveness

There was a time when my relationship with my father was strained and superficial at best. A lifetime of drama, years of things done and said, and engagement in our own version of not-so-subtle warfare resulted in us being distant friends, not sure how to cross over the gulf between us. It wasn't until I stopped to acknowledge how much of him I saw in myself that I was able to soften towards him.

But the real movement happened during a forgiveness role-playing exercise, when I was encouraged to say all the things that were left unsaid between us. My father was not present for this exercise; it was for my benefit. It was an opportunity for me to acknowledge the deeply buried feelings that existed around my own personal experience of him, with him; for me to open up the gates to all the feelings and emotions I had suppressed for so long; for me to become deeply, uncompromisingly honest with myself about what lived between us all those years.

When I gave myself that permission—to acknowledge and allow our story and all those feelings to surface—I felt a rainbow of emotions: guilt for admitting just how much distance had existed between us before that lifted, revealing anger and even hatred at the things he had done and said that made me believe there was something wrong with me; sadness and grief at the loss of all those years; and finally compassion, as I began to wonder what must have happened in his life for him to allow that to happen between us.

When I allowed myself to fully feel all of what was coming up for me, one by one those feelings lifted, until finally, very organically, I drew a deep breath in and all that was left was gratitude and Love. For I realized, once all the sadness, anger, and grief were gone, that there was and always had been tremendous love inside of him for me.

In that moment, because I had been willing and able to acknowledge and feel all of what was there, I was able to come out on the other side, and all that was left was forgiveness. Love flowed from me toward him, and he hadn't changed a bit. This exercise was for me. The error was corrected in my own mind.

That was when I realized just how much I, and my Ego, had bought into a story with him. The next day I sat alone in silence as my life flashed before my eyes, image after image showing me what I couldn't see before. And with my new perspective I could see all the ways I had played along with that story line between us; how I had kept it alive.

I felt liberated, free of a weight I had been carrying around for longer than I could remember. I suddenly had so much energy, as the dense guilt, anger, and resentment dissipated, giving way to the light, expansive energy of Love that was waiting there beneath the surface all along.

And yet there were still more epiphanies to be had, as I sat alone in my room to assimilate what had just happened. They say when you die, your life flashes before your eyes. The same was true for me that day; as an old paradigm fell away, an erroneous belief died, replaced by the truth.

I realized the pain my father still carried from his own childhood, and how—in the only way he knew—he was trying to protect me. I saw how, just as he had passed some of his pain down to me, his mother had passed on her own share of inherited familial guilt and fear. As I healed myself of some of my burden that day, I wondered just how long that pain had been passed down through the lineage, and realized healing myself was healing my ancestors, and would lighten the load for my children, and generations to come. The buck stops here with me, I thought, and vowed to make Love and forgiveness a central theme of my life.

In the end it came down to me forgiving *me* for ever having believed any of it to begin with: that he did not love me; that I was not lovable.

Suddenly I could apply that same understanding that, just as with my Dad and me, everyone else is doing the best they can. Perceived conflicts and misunderstandings, both big and small, with anyone and everyone in my life, began to crumble as this realization sank in.

And so another layer of the veil of illusion was lifted away, allowing me to really see and feel again, perhaps more clearly than since I was a little girl, standing there holding that ladybug in my hand.

The love that bubbled up inside of me became almost overwhelming, for as I pulled the plug on the greatest source of my fear and disconnection, I felt the freedom and inner peace that provided. I could no longer hold onto any story, thought, or feeling that would rob me of the fullness of the sense of love and joy I now felt.

We are all loving beings, but we have all been hallucinating, and when we unplug from the collective dream we have been having, Love, inner peace, and oneness are ours once again. Love, peace, and connection is our birthright.

For some, the Ego is too deeply ingrained, too much in control, and they will not allow themselves to remember this Truth until they are on their deathbed, when the Ego is no longer needed and only Truth is left. I have felt incredibly grateful to have remembered, to have pulled myself out of that matrix, while I was still alive to enjoy it.

When the construct created by the Ego crumbles, only Love remains—for ourselves, for our fellow brothers and sisters, for nature—for we remember that we are all connected…that we are all one.

It is the most liberating, joyous, expansive feeling we will ever have—to be realigned with our Truth, to be realigned with ourselves, with each other; to realize that we are never alone, and the only thing that ever separated us was a thought. Everyone is a brother and a sister, even if they don't remember that yet. It's like falling in love. It *is* falling in love—with Life again, for we are reunited with the incredible gift that is Life.

> *"Forgiveness literally transforms vision, and lets you see the real world reaching quietly and gently across the chaos, removing all illusions that had twisted your perception and fixed it on the past."*
>
> —*A Course in Miracles*

My World Breaks Open

The darkness was so heavy
I could feel it in my heart

I was alone in an angry world
afraid of my smallness

My voice was never heard
my soul cried out to be seen

Often I could feel the downward spiral
into a pit of endless despair

To feel so alone, so fragmented,
incomplete

The pain and the burden felt too thick to bear
my soul cried out to be loved

In my darkest hour, gentle hands reached down inside of me
and held my heart in safety and love

Lifting me from the torturous nothingness
releasing me into completeness

That is when the sky broke open,
exposing all of the beauty and wholeness of life

My heart was healed, my soul was seen
and my voice became sweet music

Now as I ascend through the colors and the joy,
my heart aches in a new way

For I cannot take it all in

Sometimes the fullness is so profound
I find it difficult to breathe

As my world breaks open
I see no end to the journey

Floating through the beauty that surrounds me
I carry with me strength, courage and knowledge

Always I feel protected and connected
to a power much greater than me

In this moment I know what it feels to be free

An Empath Yoga Perspective

Triangle — Allow Yourself to Have An Experience

With Triangle, as with all other asanas, see what new information can you gain about yourself and about how you are showing up in your own body—about how you are caring for your own body. Can you be gentle, kind, and compassionate with yourself as you embark on this journey of self-discovery? Are you pushing yourself to be somewhere further along than you are, or are your willing to honor your process, allowing something to open and invite you deeper? Are you aggressive with yourself, or are you gentle and compassionate? Are you judgmental, or are you loving and accepting?

In all asanas, as in life, it's not about achieving perfection, it's about allowing ourselves to have an experience.

Chapter 8

Letting Go

*"We cannot let go
of anything we cannot accept."*

—Stephen Levine

Clearing the Clutter

There is a concept in Feng Shui called *Clearing the Clutter*. The idea is that rooms and closets cluttered with stuff create stress and anxiety in the recesses of our minds and block the flow of energy. Feng Shui is very much about the flow of energy through your living space, and how that is representative of your mental and emotional states. Feng Shui experts know that clearing clutter is a very emotional process that feels like therapy, and it takes emotional stamina to go through it. Clearing the clutter is about letting go of that which no longer serves you, is simply taking up space in your world, and keeping you tied energetically to the past.

I once stayed at a friend's home who was a bit of a collector. She collected and held onto everything. All space was used to store books, knickknacks, collectors' items—things she had picked up in her 50+ years of life. Every room, including the spare, was stacked high with items purchased at yard sales, given to her along the way, handed down from family members—even her house had been in her family for generations; each item had a story of its own and carried with it the energy of the previous owner and every other person that touched it.

In the movie *The Red Violin*, the story spans three centuries and five countries as it follows the journey of a red violin as it makes its way through the lives of its many owners. Made by an artist as a way of remembering his beloved, painted with a stain containing her blood and a brush made with her hair, the red violin passes hands from one individual to the next in its life-long journey. This unknowingly passes the woman's energy onto the many whose lives the violin touches, as well as absorbing all of their energy as it passes through the hands of one to the next, just as the energy of all the items cluttering a home carries the accumulation of countless others—during good times and bad, sadness and joy, health and illness.

This could explain why I never slept well at my friends' house, nor even could fully relax there. There was very little space, as every crease and crevice was filled with things with a story of their own to tell, and I was usually anxious and overwhelmed while I was there, unable to quiet my mind amidst the energetic chaos surrounding me.

Another friend went through a divorce and major life changes over the span of a few years. When she finally decided to go through her home and clear the clutter room by room, it was an emotional experience. As she rifled through boxes she came face to face with memories that were buried not only in her closet, but in the recesses of her mind and body, and by the force of her emotional responses to them, she realized just how much she had been holding onto the past. With every bag of goods donated and disposed of, she felt herself getting lighter and freer, each emotional release providing a letting go she knew was way overdue.

"Stand up and walk out of your history."
—*Phil McGraw*

Just as our physical spaces get cluttered with the past, so too do our minds become filled to overflowing with memories of the past and worries of the future, so much so that it is a challenge to even identify where the present moment exists within it all.

The monkey-mind that results from a mind out of control blocks our ability to tap into and receive intuitive guidance, and like a record caught in a groove, can keep us stuck in a perspective, making it hard to fall asleep at night or relax during our waking hours. And the clutter in the mind shows up in our bodies, as memories stored there. Yogis know these as *Samskaras*, which are imprinted holding patterns, making the body a map of our current internal state, and of our past.

I recently watched as a young girl who appeared to be about 14 alight from a school bus on her way home. She was tall, with a few extra pounds, but the most striking thing about her was her energy. Her expression was flat and lifeless. Her posture slouched, as if she didn't even have the energy or the will to stand up straight. The energy I felt radiating from her didn't feel current, like the way one feels when they've simply had a bad day. I could feel her depression, her sadness, and I couldn't help but wonder when it happened: when the radiant, playful little girl she once was gave way to the sad, lonely-looking young lady I watched shuffling home that day.

As children, our subconscious minds are wide open, and like sponges, we absorb everything we see, hear, and experience. We don't even begin to develop a filter to help sift through the barrage of incoming stimuli until at least the age of seven. This becomes a part of our subconscious programming, until something in our adult lives triggers that old memory, and the beliefs attached to it. Those are our greatest opportunities to gain awareness and to learn and grow. But most of us lack the mental discipline to notice and observe the responses happening inside of us without becoming reactive and getting sucked into an old habit pattern, replaying the past in our present lives.

Then there's the story we have bought into, in which a role is created for us, and we effectively step into it. At some point along the way, we fill in the blanks, creating the story to support the role we have adopted. For most of us, our lives have become about creating, living, and defending our stories. We attract or create experiences that support our stories, that solidify our belief in and attachment to them. Our perception of reality is created by our stories, and we tend to acknowledge, see, and believe only that which reaffirms our story.

"If a person believes a story, it becomes a truth—for them. That's why history and spoken word are such a subjective bee's nest. It's difficult to determine what happened as opposed to what people thought happened, wanted to happen, and felt should have happened. The slant, the spin, is what you must remember."

—Eric Van Lustbadder

If a woman grows up in a household where abusive relationships were modeled for her by the very people she idolized and trusted, and she herself was a victim of that abuse, a deep-seated belief about what loving relationships looks like is born. Once that perceptual framework takes hold, she only gravitates toward those relationships that look and feel familiar, resembling that which was modeled for her at a very young age. In this scenario, the role of abused woman was created and illustrated for her, but it only became her story when she bought into it. Not only will she live it, as all of her choices and behavior become guided by it, she will tell it, over and over again—each time further weaving it into the tapestry of her life.

In this way, not only is a story written, but a self-fulfilling prophecy is created.

Like the man whose broken home was further torn apart as his mother cycled through her bi-polar life, leaving her two boys to fend for themselves from the earliest age as they floated in and out of foster homes. How unsafe the world must have seemed from the earliest age. And when, in early adolescence, the only mother you ever know removes herself from your life by taking her own, what kind of defining moment does that become? Imagine the decisions you would make in that moment out of self-preservation, in attempt to never feel that kind of pain and abandonment again.

Along with that decision comes a reshaping of reality, and then everything is filtered through that new lens so that what we are defending against becomes all that we see.

Meditation is the most effective and powerful way to clear mental and emotional clutter, like pulling the weeds from the otherwise fertile soil-bed of the mind. The weeds are the past…the old programming and outdated beliefs.

I know one woman who so bought into the belief that she was powerless that she not only allowed others to step all over her, she expected it. Because of this, she loses any battle before it even begins. In fact, she doesn't even bother to put up a fight.

By contrast, another woman, when faced with a very similar situation, had a defining moment in which she knew that if she didn't fight for what she wanted, she would lose her self, her dreams, and her power to be and do what she wanted. Almost the exact same stimulus resulted in a completely different outcome. Her belief that she needed to defend herself from attack, and then fight for what she wanted, became her story.

But, as happens when we over-identify with any one person, place, or situation, her fighter instincts never subsided, and her reality became one in which the world was a harsh and difficult place, and she lived her life always posturing for the next fight. Whether the situation warranted the fight or not, she could always find validation for a full-frontal attack. It wasn't until she realized the story she had created around her life that she recognized her ability to choose differently. What a relief it was when she realized she could stop fighting!

What's Your Story?

In my work with clients and in my workshops I encourage participants to create a time line of life events, beginning with their birth, and all the way up to the present and beyond. Then I instruct them to mark on their time line all of the significant, defining moments of their lives. The first pass usually brings up the more obvious memories, like moves, graduations, deaths, and other major life changes. Then I invite them to go through the time line again, and with a little more time spent strolling down memory lane, to record the other events that happened in between the major, more obvious ones. This is when they begin to dig a little deeper and allow things to surface that they haven't thought about for some time. Finally, I encourage at least one more pass, taking some time to allow more subtle memories to emerge. Some have opted to spend a week or more returning to their time line, jotting down memories that are unearthed after a little more time and space is allowed for them to surface.

This is, in essence, our life story, and looking back over this visual representation of our lives reveals so much about defining moments—when a younger self made a decision about what something meant, an interpretation of some sort that often solidified into a belief (erroneous or not) that carried forth into the rest of our lives.

"Giving up doesn't always mean you are weak; sometimes it means you're strong enough to let go."

—Unknown

The time line is also a wonderful opportunity to notice patterns that play out in our lives over and over again, with minor variations, but the overall themes are the same.

One woman was stunned to see, staring back at her, an obvious pattern of playing the victim in her life, and how she kept attracting new people that would allow her to stay in her old, familiar role. The time line exercise offers an opportunity to accept full responsibility for our lives, and is most effective for those that are ready to do this. When I first did it myself, over a decade ago, I realized a pattern within myself of pushing people away using anger to keep them from seeing—and to protect myself from feeling—my own perceived inferiority. The time line is a powerful tool for awareness, and so much information can be gleaned from it, if used appropriately.

Then there comes a point when the next important question is: Who am I without my story? I remember a young homeless woman who, when given an opportunity to stand and share her story before a room of interested, compassionate peers, got so caught up in telling the story it was as if she were describing somebody else's life. I could tell this was a story she had told many times before, each time the story getting better as she told it more eloquently than the last, and she was the star of her own show. There comes a point when the story only serves to hold us back, anchored to the past. Once we've gotten really honest with ourselves, and realized what we can learn from the patterns in our lives, it's important to remember, *we are not our past*.

Again, meditation helps us to step back from the story and see it for what it is—which is usually the Ego chewing on something. We don't always need to know *why* something happened. There is an opportunity to observe the monkey-mind as it searches for the next tree limb to grab onto, trying a different angle to pull us into the same old narrative. Meditation allows us to step back and become the witness, observing our thoughts without hooking into them. With practice, we can strengthen our mental muscle by letting go of the story, of the drama, of the need to know. This is the Ego's allure—wanting to understand, to analyze, to pick apart, to be right.

You know you have let go of your story when you no longer feel the need to tell it. It's the retelling of it over and over again that keeps it alive. We no longer need to tell it when we no longer identify with it.

"Don't hold on to any self-image, because self-image is from the past."

—Mooji

> **EXERCISE:** Create your own time line of life events. Looking back, what patterns do you notice? What were your most defining moments? In what ways did those moments define you? What do you tell yourself to validate your behavior?

"When I let go of what I am, I become what I might be."

—*Lao Tzu*

"We only need to understand a problem if we are planning on having it again."
—Hale Dwoskin

There is a point at which it's time to let go of the need to know. The need to figure it out is often what keeps us stuck in a loop in our minds. We don't need to understand why something happened in order to accept that it did. We can let go and trust there is a gift inherent in everything that has ever happened through us. And in time, this information will reveal itself to us without us having to go in search of it. The key is to stay open and receptive.

Life doesn't happen *to* us, it happens *through* us. And even though we can't always know why, or what will be the pearl of wisdom from an experience until enough time has passed, we can let go and trust that all will be revealed to us. We can let go and enjoy living in the mystery, allowing life to unfold while staying in awe of each moment free of the need to figure anything out, liberated from the temptation to try to make sense of the past, or control the future—as if we ever could. Letting go allows us to live more authentic lives, grounded in the Truth of the present moment.

"If you are to advance, all fixed ideas must go."
—Joseph Campbell

Everything that happens through us is an opportunity to develop our emotional musculature. But our cultural indoctrination that has taught us to deny and avoid what we feel has left us with atrophied muscle. Life will continue to challenge us; we will continue to attract and create by the choices that we make, giving us opportunities to strengthen our emotional muscle in exactly the ways we need it most. As with the client who couldn't understand why she kept being attracted back to an ex-husband who left her feeling mentally and emotionally battered, with her self-esteem in ruins, these experiences bring to our awareness a muscle that needs developing. Like cross-training for the physical body, life is cross-training for our mental and emotional bodies.

What Are You Addicted To?

It can be easy to get stuck in a loop with our thinking, but we also get addicted to certain feelings. If you were raised in an environment where you felt a lot of guilt, anger or sadness, a certain chemical reaction happens in the body to which we, over time, can become addicted. Then the body starts to crave more of that particular chemical and we tend to subconsciously create situations in our lives that will allow us to experience that feeling and have our chemical fix.

Have you ever been addicted to anything? Most of us have, whether we realize it or not. I, for example, have spent a good portion of my life hooked on sugar. I was raised on it (in a family with a history of diabetes), and as an adult there were times that no matter how full I was, I didn't feel satisfied until I had my sugar fix (usually chocolate). I would daydream about it, look for opportunities to indulge in it, and even go out of my way to find it. Then, when I got it, the satisfaction (even euphoria) would last only briefly before I was left wanting more. An embarrassingly high volume of my energy has been expended in my life in search of the chocolate fix.

I also used to be a pack-a-day smoker. This was well over 20 years ago, and while they say an addiction to nicotine can be harder to break than an addiction to heroin, it can and is done every day. But it wasn't nicotine withdrawals I most had to overcome, it was recognizing the moment of choice and choosing a better quality of life for me. The picture in my mind of myself being healthy, happy and free became stronger than any momentary cravings. I put the energy I had previously been giving over to smoking into riding my bike, exercising, and becoming more active all around. Shortly after that, I found yoga.

In the same way we become addicted to certain behaviors, we can become addicted to certain feelings. A person who experienced a lot of anger growing up may walk through life with their energetic "dukes up," looking for their next justification to be angry. If you are familiar with feeling victimized and powerless, eventually you may subconsciously look for, and even create, more situations to allow those same victimized, powerless feelings.

A good friend went through a rough few years in which she was violently attacked, her son nearly killed in a car accident, and she was being aggressively sued by her ex-husband for custody of her daughter. The bombardment of one major stressor after another left her feeling emotionally strung out. When it was finally all over, her life back in order, she found herself still carrying the stress and anxiety with her, and caught herself looking for something in her present life to attach it to. It was as if her body had become so used to the chemicals of fear, there was some unconscious part of her that craved something to be anxious about. Luckily, she had enough awareness to realize what was happening, and chose to let her body process out those chemicals, like detoxing from a drug, rather than attracting another drama to feed the body's addiction.

In his book, *A New Earth,* Eckhart Tolle refers to this as the *pain body*, and says its job is to seek out and create more of the same. It can be like feeding a hungry beast. This is also illustrated so nicely in the movie "What the Bleep Do We Know."

The mind, left to its own devices, will always find a justification, a way to rationalize why we should be feeling those feelings yet again. This pulls us back into that loop until we choose to break that cycle with awareness by strengthening our faith in ourselves and in our ability to choose.

> *"You gain or lose power…*
> *according to the choices that you make."*
>
> *Gary Zukav*

My friend knew thinking and analyzing wasn't going to bring her peace. This is why I often tell my students that the next time someone tells them they are out of their mind, thank them for the compliment. Peace of mind happens when we get out of our heads and into our hearts. Behind the level of thought we can feel the truth, and when we get out of our own way, the energy is able to leave us with one last, big shudder.

Whether we are talking about an addiction to a person, a habit like smoking, an emotion like anger, or a thought like "I'm not good enough," awareness is the key. Once you know, you are one step closer to a position of power. Next time, instead of allowing your feelings to overwhelm you, let this new level of awareness empower you to put those feelings into perspective, so that you are holding them, instead of them holding you. Then you can gain some leverage on that which has been so sticky and simply *let it go*, unclenching that part of you that has been holding on so dogmatically for so long.

Find a quarter, and hold onto it tightly. Squeeze it really tight. Realize that no matter how tightly you grip that quarter, no matter how firm your hold, that quarter will never be a part of you. It's just something you are holding onto. You can let go of it the moment you decide to open your hand and release your grip.

> *"The greatness of a man's power is the measure of his surrender."*
> —William Booth

Creating Space

Once a year I engage in a cleanse—ingesting only fresh, organic, raw fruits and vegetables. The first few days are the toughest, as my body detoxes from all of the accumulated toxins that have built up in my tissues. Things often get worse before they get better. When a space is created by eliminating dead, cooked foods and stimulants like caffeine, sugar and alcohol, the cravings initially can be nearly overwhelming, and I've taken to observing my mind during those times and marveling at just how compulsive and reactionary it can be. But if I stick to it, eventually I experience what is known as a cleansing crisis.

Minus the need to break down newly ingested processed foods and stimulants, the body ultimately releases that which has been stored back into circulation to be expelled. The cleansing crisis can bring with it headaches, fatigue, and other flu-like symptoms. Usually this only lasts a few days, but when I come out on the other side I feel lighter, cleaner, clearer. I have more energy, sleep better, and feel more natural, relaxed, and at ease. My eyes are whiter, my skin brighter, my mind clearer. I feel more efficient mentally and physically.

> *"The intelligent person does not cling to the dead past, does not carry any corpses."*
>
> —OSHO

Along with my physical cleanse, I engage in a mental and emotional cleanse. I stay away from television and the news, watching and reading only that which is inspirational. I observe my thoughts, and steadfastly refuse to engage in disempowering ones. Habitual thinking patterns start to be revealed, giving me an opportunity to gain new insight, and cleanse myself of those fear-based thought patterns that do not serve me. I stay away from people and places that would have any kind of a negative impact on me, and spend as much time in nature as possible. Without food, television, gossip and other distractions, which I might at other times use to avoid recognizing and feeling my emotions, I start to acknowledge and feel things that have been as yet undealt with, using gentle yoga and walks in nature to allow that energy to move through me. Without acting on anything that comes up for me, I simply sit with it and allow the information that those emotions have for me to be revealed and assimilated.

At the end of this physical, mental, and emotional cleanse, I feel as if I have pressed the reset button on my life, and slowly start to reintroduce foods and activities from a much higher level of awareness and conscious choice. This is always one of the most empowering things I do every year, and has become something that I look forward to, knowing it will be a beautiful, empowering, enlightening experience.

> *"I am not a victim of the world I see."*
>
> —*A Course in Miracles*

Feeling Stuck?

If you're not feeling ready to let go of something you know does not serve you, consider for a moment what the payoffs are that keep you stuck. Is it really necessary to put yourself through more suffering? Will punishing yourself really serve you or the world? If you have not already done so, go back and re-read the beginning of this book. Rinse and repeat as needed. Once you recognize and free yourself from the programming to which we have all been subject, decide to no longer buy into it, and choose to remember the Love that is inherent in us all. Realize that there is only one of us here and our greatest responsibility is to be a beacon of Love and Light, and give yourself permission to acknowledge and feel what you need to feel so you can come out on the other side of it. Forgive yourself and everyone else for everything. There is no reason to hold onto anything that is robbing you of your sense of peace, of your quality of life. Where are you not yet complete? Go back and spend more time there. If necessary, hire a coach to help you navigate your way through those areas where you feel stuck.

> **AN EXERCISE FOR WHEN YOU'RE FEELING STUCK**
> In your journal, spend some time answering this question: What are the payoffs that are keeping me stuck? Is it really worth it?

Letting go creates a space within which we can either consciously create something new, or unconsciously fall back into old familiar patterns that just look a little different—as when someone quits smoking and starts gaining weight, or at the loss of a relationship or job, one starts drinking to fill the sudden space in their lives. Whenever we think we've pulled the plug on an old, outdated belief that no longer serves us, Life just sends us smarter people. We will be tested, each time given another opportunity to further strengthen and develop that muscle. Physical exercise and intellectual pursuits are both things we know we must continue to engage in if we are to stay youthful, alert and alive. Why would we expect it to be any different when it comes to our emotional health? The best way to remain emotionally strong is to stay honest with ourselves.

Re-direct your energy in a way that expands you, allowing you to break out of the previously limiting mold. Learn a new skill, take up a hobby, channel that newfound energy in a conscious and rewarding way.

For me, when my biological clock started ticking, creating a sense of urgency within me that robbed me of my sense of peace and ability to relax into and enjoy the present moment, I chose to redirect that energy into developing Empath Yoga. And at the end of a relationship I had invested time and energy into, I redirected my newfound energy into writing this book, something I had allowed myself to be distracted from for some time. My friend who survived the attack and other stressors in her life redirected her energy, when things finally did settle back down, into violin lessons. I know one man who took up running after his divorce. And many women have gone back to school or started a small business of their own after their children grew up and moved out, leaving them with an "empty nest."

> *"We must be willing to let go
> of the life we have planned,
> so as to accept the life that is waiting for us."*
> —*Joseph Campbell*

> **EXERCISE:** Make a list of all the things you always thought you'd like to do someday. As you start letting go, consider what you are now ready to channel that energy into.

Everything is a lesson, an opportunity, a chance to be reminded of the truth of who we are. Let go of the story, of the belief that you or anyone else is anything other than that same pure innocence and loving energy that we always were. Learn the lesson, and let the rest go.

There is Beauty in Death

They say if you dig deep enough, the fear that underlies all others is the fear of death. I recently had a coaching client in his early thirties tell me this was true for him, and how much of his time and energy was spent fearing it and getting his affairs in order to prepare for it. He also went on to share the anxiety he experiences, even full-blown panic, and the medication he has resorted to using in order to manage his fear. And he's not alone.

Which reminds me of something a friend of mine says: "Why do we spend so much time and energy caring for the one thing we know will fail us—our bodies?"

We are not our bodies, which are nothing more than a collection of cells consisting mostly of space, and held together by consciousness. If you were to put our bodies under a giant telescope, what you would see is mostly space. There is space between our cells and space within our cells. Even the cells themselves are not ours as they die off and regenerate. Over the span of seven years, every cell in our body will have turned over and been replaced. Our bodies are amazing, wondrous vehicles within which we get to travel through this life, but we are not our bodies. It is an oversimplified, superficial attachment to this bag of skin we live in that has so many of us stuck.

Our bodies are homes—temporary homes—for our spirit. And just like we care for our homes as a way of honoring ourselves and the people within it, we care for our bodies as a way of honoring our spirit. But just as with any attachment, an attachment to our bodies pulls us away from an awareness of who and what we really are, and we get caught up in the external world—the illusion—of separation, scarcity, and lack, and suffering surely follows.

While I often say to students of yoga that the *asanas* are a great way to get out of our heads and into our bodies, it is the space between the asanas that is most rich. Because there we experience a sense of timelessness, and even if for just a moment, we feel our connection with everything. There is beauty in the void. Within that void is pure consciousness.

In that space of pure consciousness lies the awareness of the truth of who we are. An image of a baby comes to mind. One of the reasons we love babies, small children, puppies, and kittens is because of the pure and innocent expression of life and love that they are. They remind us of what is real. Not only is it real for them, it is real for everyone. We too came into this world as a pure and innocent expression of life and love. And regardless of what may have happened along the way in the human journey, we still are.

"Death is beautiful if you can accept, if you can open the door with a welcoming heart... suddenly you are deathless: the body is dying, you are not dying. You can see now: only the clothes are dropping, not you; only the cover, the container, not the content."

—OSHO

"You don't have a soul. You are a soul. You have a body."

—C.S. Lewis

Letting Go   159

But many will not remember the truth of who they are until they are dying, for that is when superficial wants and needs dissolve, and only love remains. Which is why near-death experiences and life-threatening illnesses often bring with them the life-changing gift of new insight.

Death is so respected and revered within yogic philosophy that every yoga class ends in it. The practice culminates with us laying on our backs so we may practice surrendering and letting go…so fully…so completely, it's like dying. And while *Savasana*, which literally translated means "corpse pose," or "pose of the dead man," is the simplest asana (or posture) in yoga, for some it is the most challenging, because here we are asked to do nothing. There is no self and no doing. The more fully and completely one gives themselves over to Savasana, the more deeply they integrate the benefits of their practice. It is here where old constructs, stuck issues, and rigid holding patterns really dissolve…if we allow it.

There is beauty in death. I once had a healer tell me I was so good at being strong that I now needed to learn how to fall apart, and that it was the holding it all together that was keeping me from integrating some valuable life lessons. Which reminds me of a friend of mine who spent much of his life going from relationship to relationship, merely segueing from one to the next without ever integrating the lessons learned and the growth inherent in them. When he finally had enough, he stopped, not because there was no longer anyone new and interesting out there, but because he was ready to let an old pattern die, and knew that he had not yet fully integrated that yet.

It is one of the most beautiful moments in life when the Ego gives way. Old constructs dismantle, outdated beliefs and habit patterns unravel. Like Marianne Williamson says, "breakdowns are highly underrated."

> **Exercise:** Write about what is beautiful about death.

We are not our minds either. If you cut into the human brain, you will not find the mind. We are energy. We are consciousness. This energy, this consciousness, is the glue that holds it all together in a body so we can live the human adventure and have a vessel through which to explore our particular expression of this life. The mind is a tool for harnessing and focusing that energy.

In nature there is a life cycle inherent in all living things; we are no exception to this. But long after we transcend the need for our physical bodies, the energy that is in you, and in me, lives on. There's nowhere else for it to go.

If it's true that matter cannot be created or destroyed, then every cell that is within you and within me has always been and always will be. When we die, does that energy that is us cease to exist? Or like a magnet that has lost its charge, are we just no longer coalescing into one confined vessel? Just because a light bulb no longer turns on doesn't mean there is no longer any light.

> *"Do not stand at my grave and weep;*
> *I am not there. I do not sleep.*
> *I am a thousand winds that blow.*
> *I am the diamond's gilt on snow.*
> *I am the sunlight on ripened grain.*
> *I am the gentle autumn's rain.*
> *When you awaken in the morning's hush.*
> *I am the swift uplifting rush*
> *of quiet birds in circled flight.*
> *I am the soft stars that shine at night.*
> *Do not stand at my grave and cry;*
> *I am not there, I did not die."*
>
> —*Mary Elizabeth Frye*

Even on a cellular level, dying is as valuable as birth, and must happen in order for new life to occur. Death is nothing more than a shedding of the body, and of the ego, and we are returned to pure consciousness, pure potential, pure energy. A basic law of physics states that no two things can occupy the same space at the same time. What are you ready to let die in order to let the truth live? With every ending there is a new beginning. What is waiting to be called forth into your life as soon as you make room for it—as soon as you let go of what is blocking it?

Death takes us beyond the self, to a place of no-selfness—a state referred to in yoga philosophy as *Anatta*. Here, we remember our connection with everyone and everything, because there is no Ego, no body, no thoughts fooling us into believing that we are separate.

I was once with a woman when she received the news that her husband had died. I stayed with her for weeks while she fell apart completely, going deep into the grieving process as she let go of her husband's physical presence in her life. Never had I seen her look more beautiful—those were such real, honest moments. While she has since moved on, and years later remarried, the energy of him lives on in her, his children, and in everything that he touched while he was alive.

Another man, at the loss of his mother, put her passing into perspective when he said, "Now I get to talk to her all the time, no matter where I am."

Let us not so buy into this bag of skin we are in that we fail to remember that it is a mere vehicle within which we travel. And let us learn to recognize the thoughts of judgment that only serve to perpetuate the belief that we are all separate—from each other, from nature, from Life—and start remembering the truth of who we are.

There is a principal of Attitudinal Healing that says *since love is eternal, death need not be viewed as fearful*. Rather than fearing death, we can choose to embrace life. If we were to recognize the gift of this human journey, without attachment to it, we could simply relax and enjoy what we have been given.

Nobody else gets to be you or me. There will never again be another collection of cells held together by our particular expression of consciousness ever again. Like a snowflake, we are uniquely perfect and beautiful. And what a beautiful gift and opportunity that is, to live fully expressed in this life.

*"I've told my children that when I die,.
to release balloons in the sky
to celebrate that I graduated.
For me, death is a graduation."*
—Elizabeth Kubler-Ross

> **EXERCISE:** Write your own eulogy. Then take it a step further, and design the ceremony that will celebrate your life.

*"We're all going to die.
Some people are scared of dying.
Never be afraid to die.
Because you're born to die."*
—Walter Breuning

An Empath Yoga Perspective

Savasana **Practice dying**

Savasana, Corpse Pose, is where every yoga practice dies. And it's where we practice dying. The idea is to let go so fully, so completely, it's like dying into the moment so we can come out on the other side refreshed, renewed, unencumbered by the past.

Surrender and let go. Let go of your stories, of old holding patterns, of any agenda. Release any desire to change or control or manipulate anything. Let go of all resistance to what is, and give yourself over to the moment fully, holding nothing back.

III

Being in Relationship

On Love
Kahlil Gibran

When love beckons to you, follow him,
Though his ways are hard and steep.
And when his wings enfold you yield to him,
Though the sword hidden among his pinions may wound you.
And when he speaks to you believe in him,
Though his voice may shatter your dreams
as the north wind lays waste the garden.

For even as love crowns you so shall he crucify you.
Even as he is for your growth so is he for your pruning.
Even as he ascends to your height and caresses your tenderest
branches that quiver in the sun,
So shall he descend to your roots and shake them in their clinging
to the earth.

Like sheaves of corn he gathers you unto himself.
He threshes you to make you naked.
He sifts you to free you from your husks.
He grinds you to whiteness.
He kneads you until you are pliant;
And then he assigns you to his sacred fire, that you may become
sacred bread for God's sacred feast.

All these things shall love do unto you that you may know the
secrets of your heart, and in that knowledge become a fragment of
Life's heart.

But if in your fear you would seek only love's peace
and love's pleasure,
Then it is better for you that you cover your nakedness and pass
out of love's threshing-floor,
Into the seasonless world where you shall laugh, but not all of your
laughter, and weep, but not all of your tears.
Love gives naught but itself and takes naught but from itself.
Love possesses not nor would it be possessed;
For love is sufficient unto love.

When you love you should not say, "God is in my heart," but rather, "I am in the heart of God."
And think not you can direct the course of love, for love, if it finds you worthy, directs your course.

Love has no other desire but to fulfill itself.
But if you love and must needs have desires, let these be your desires:
To melt and be like a running brook that sings its melody to the night.
To know the pain of too much tenderness.
To be wounded by your own understanding of love;
And to bleed willingly and joyfully.
To wake at dawn with a winged heart and give thanks for another day of loving;
To rest at the noon hour and meditate love's ecstasy;
To return home at eventide with gratitude;
And then to sleep with a prayer for the beloved in your heart and a song of praise upon your lips.

Chapter 9

Deep Listening

*"Deep listening is like dying...
a relinquishing of control,
a giving over into the art of what comes.
Without such an opening, conditioning stays intact,
and natural innocence disappears into an arrogance
which knows it has an answer for everything."*

—*Tom Lutes*

While pursuing my degree in Communication, one of our required courses was a semester-long class on Listening. I remember thinking, "this will be an easy A." Yet it ended up being the most enlightening, inspiring, relationship-transforming class of my entire college training. It was fascinating for me, and for my classmates, to discover how little we really understood about what it means to listen, to really listen, and how often our own agendas and expectations got in the way.

Prior to his death, USC professor Leo Buscaglia conducted research proving that in all relationships the most important need is the ability to communicate with each other.. In one survey, marriage counselors identified "failure to take the other's perspective when listening," as one of the most frequent communication problems in the couples with whom they worked. In another study, when asked what communication skills were most important in family and social settings, listening was ranked first. In the same study, listening was also found to be one of the most important on-the-job communication skills.

"Listening is a form of accepting."

—Stella Terrill Mann

I, like most people, have spent my fair share of time ignoring, pretending, or practicing selective listening. But I now strive to, at the very least, listen attentively, which statistics show most of us do only 25% of the time, leaving a huge gap in our communication, and in our relationships.

> ***"The first step to wisdom is silence, the second is listening."***
>
> —*Author Unknown*

Imagine as a child in today's world what it would be like to come home to a mother or father who is completely available, willing and able to listen to you completely. This caring adult listens to you attentively with interest as you give an account of your day; the conflicts you encountered, the successes and failures you experienced, and how you feel about yourself at the end of the day as a result. Imagine being given the opportunity to share anything that comes up for you with an open-minded, non-judgmental, unconditionally accepting adult that holds the space for you while you process difficult emotions, confusing thoughts, and frustrating feelings with which you struggle. Afterward you would feel fully received and seen by that person, validated, understood, and valued. You could then shed much of the frustration from the day and move on in an emotionally healthy way. This is an ideal picture, but for most of our children, it is not the reality.

Unfortunately, we have become a society that does not listen to each other. This results in many people feeling alone, misunderstood, and insignificant. Imagine the thoughts going through the minds of our children when they have emotions and feelings going on inside of them that they don't know how to cope with. Today's children have much more complicated, heavy-duty issues to sift through than we ever did. And we are failing miserably at giving them the tools to effectively deal with them. Often Mom and Dad are too busy with work and other stressors to be fully present for them, and other adults, be it family or neighbors, are often too wrapped up in their own dramas to put forth the effort.

This results in our children not feeling seen, heard, or understood. Could this be the reason school violence has become so common? Is it possible these children are giving a cry for help? Could they be feeling confused and scared, not knowing how to deal with the difficult thoughts and feelings going on inside of them, and believe that there is nobody around who really seems to care anyway?

Many children today have learned to get their acceptance, validation, and importance through interaction with friends, who are often going through the same internal conflicts as they are, and together they find distractions to free their minds of the frustration, confusion, and fear that they carry within them. These distractions can be alcohol, drugs, gangs, or other unhealthy and antisocial behavior. This scene is played out all too often in our society today, and little is being done to break this cycle.

This cycle affects us in our adult lives as well. Our failure to listen effectively has resulted in a disconnected society. As a result of poor communication skills relationships suffer or fall apart completely, an alarmingly high number of marriages end in divorce, our children choose less healthy outlets to cope, and society in general has become more separated, as we isolate ourselves from each other and adopt an attitude that "it's a dog-eat-dog world out there" and we have to look out for ourselves. Neighbors stay strangers, drivers have become defensive and aggressive, and people in general have become rude with each other. In our fear and in our anger we have perpetuated an illusion of separateness.

Because of our emotional isolation from each other and lack of caring individuals that know how to listen and be there for us unconditionally and non-judgmentally, many adults also end up seeking their own distractions in food, alcohol, sex, drugs, or other addictions. The use of antidepressants is at an all-time high, with a number of adults relying on them to get through daily life. Others take a more proactive approach and seek counseling, in essence paying for someone to listen to them. The counselor then becomes an outlet allowing them to process difficult thoughts, emotions, and feelings. This pattern, although it happens all too often, does not have to continue. We can break the cycle by learning to listen, to really listen, to others.

> *"The biggest disease today is not leprosy or tuberculosis, but rather the feeling of being unwanted, uncared for and deserted by everybody."*
>
> —Mother Teresa

"The real friend is one who does not advise you, but helps you to become more alert, more aware, more conscious of life—its problems, its challenges, its mysteries, and helps you go on your own voyage, gives you courage to experiment, gives you courage to seek and search, gives you courage to commit many mistakes...because one who is not ready to commit to mistakes will never learn anyting at all."

—OSHO

Listening empathically is the greatest gift you can give to another. When you are ready to listen with empathy this means you are making a commitment to understand the other person, not to offer advice or to criticize. Empathic listening provides the space for an individual to process out loud what they are thinking and feeling. Giving unsolicited advice, problem-solving, or "fixing" will only contribute to their insecurities and fears, making them feel powerless over their situation. As an anonymous author wrote about listening, "you can help, not with answers but with questions…not with advice or solutions but with hope…not with protection but with assurance." Often, just being there and holding the space is all that is needed.

Many times people are not even aware of what they are feeling because they are so caught up in the mental thoughts they are having about a situation or event. When you help guide them to their feelings, that is when they gain a new level of insight into what is really going on inside of them, and it is then that they can get to a point of discovering their own answers.

Practice this and you'll witness all of your relationships transform and deepen. Although it takes effort to create a safe space for others to be fully present without letting our own perception and judgments get in the way, like working an atrophied muscle, flexing your listening skills will, over time, yield great results. When you see how appreciative your loved ones are when they know they have been received, understood, and validated by you, you will want to start offering that gift to others. People will gravitate to you, knowing they can be themselves without fear of judgment or disapproval. Personally, it will make all of your relationships stronger and healthier; professionally, it will allow for open and honest communication with an increased respect and trust level. This gift allows others to unfold, open up, and show themselves. Imagine what it must be like to feel "seen" for the first time when you have felt invisible for so long.

I remember a time many years ago, during the time of my Listening class, when I was sitting in the car with my then seven-year-old niece, Lauren. Her mother had run into the store for something, and while Lauren was talking away in the backseat, I was flipping through a magazine. Only partially paying attention, I allowed her chatter about her friends at school to be mostly that…chatter.

Then I remembered what I was learning and decided to put the magazine down, turn around in my seat, and really listen to her. Instead of the half-hearted listening and vacant responses I had been offering, I gave her my full attention, and starting asking questions to encourage her to open up. What was floating around, just waiting to be acknowledged, was her sadness for a friend whose parents had recently divorced and now the father lived far away. And what surfaced next was her own fear that the same thing would happen to her family. That was a huge illustration for me of the difference between hearing and listening, how much my ability to be present made all the difference in the world for her, and allowed her to feel acknowledged, understood and supported.

> *"The most basic need of all human beings is the need to understand and be understood."*
>
> —*Ralph Nichols*

Deep Listening to each other requires getting out of our heads, and the mind that wants to judge, analyze, fix. The heart just feels. And when we are able to *feel* another person, we have access to their truth. Why would we want to relate to the world in any other way—unless we have an agenda and are trying to figure out a way to manipulate in order to get our way? But this pulls us back into an Ego-centric world, and we already know what that offers. If that were enough for us, we wouldn't have gotten this far in this book.

Deep Listening to another means listening to the message beyond the message, the meta-message. There are the words being used to communicate a thought; then there's the essence of the message, the deeper truth, that must be felt, and that can only be done when your heart has the ability to be open.

Most of us, when we are most wanting to be heard and seen and understood, are essentially saying, "Please hear what I am not saying. Please pick up on what I am having difficulty putting into words, either because I am not even clear yet about what it is, or because I'm not sure its safe to be that vulnerable with you."

> *"People will forget what you said and what you did...but they will never forget the way you made them feel."*
>
> —Maya Angelou

I love and appreciate those people in my life who know my heart so well, and are such good listeners, that they know how to hold the space for me so compassionately, non-judgmentally, and lovingly that I am able to get to my own truth. They do not feel the need to boost their own self worth or feed their Ego by believing they could somehow know the answers to which only I could possibly have access. In her book, *You Already Know What to Do,* Sharon Franquemont makes the point that all of the answers are already within us; we just have to clear a space so we can find them.

When we listen deeply, without agenda, we hold the space for others to find their answers.

> "When I ask you to listen,
> and you start giving advice,
> you have not done what I have asked.
> When I ask you to listen,
> and you begin to tell me
> why I shouldn't feel the way that I feel,
> you are trampling on my feelings.
> When I ask you to listen,
> and you feel you have to do something
> to solve my problems, you have failed me,
> strange as it may seem. Listen!
> All I as is that you listen.
> Not talk nor "do." Just hear me.
> When you do something for me
> I can and need to do for myself,
> you contribute to my fear and inadequacy.
> I can do for myself; I am not helpless.
> Maybe discouraged and faltering, but not helpless.
> But when you accept as a simple fact
> that I feel what I feel (no matter how irrational),
> then I can quit trying to convince you,
> and I can move towards understanding
> what is behind the irrational feeling.
> And when that is clear,
> I will see the truth for myself,
> and I won't need advice. "
>
> —*Anonymous*

My workshops and retreats rarely fail to be a powerful, enlightening, bonding experience. Lives are transformed, not so much because of the material being presented, although I know that's helpful, but more as a result that we set the conscious intention, right at the beginning, to create a place of safety within which we can each explore and look at things we've never been willing or able to look at before, sometimes stuff that has been following us around doggedly for years, nipping at our heals maybe even for a lifetime. Because such a safe space is created, void of judgment, advice-giving, or agenda, we are able to look at and explore those things we have not been able to acknowledge. And when those parts of ourselves are brought into the light—the guilt, the shame, the fear, the sadness, the regret—and they do not bump up against judgment, attack, reproach—they tend to dissolve into thin air, and our load lightens.

Holding the space for others empowers them. Rather than figuring them out or giving in to a temptation to fix them out of an arrogance that believes it has all the answers, we can best support others by holding the image of who they really are, even when they forget it for a time. And who they are is the same as us. Don't get caught up in the story—hold the light. Underneath behaviors, personality traits and idiosyncracies, they, too, are pure Love and innocence, also subject to the confusion and programming; although their life-print may look different than ours, the ultimate essence of who we are is always the same. That can make it easier to hold the image of who they are, regardless of the current emotional state they may be in.

A supportive, loving mirror—reflecting only love and truth back at us, allows us to get back into alignment with our own truth. Then we can receive our own answers, and are further empowered. The same is true for everyone else.

A Lesson in Listening

When I first took the job at the homeless shelter, and was to create the leadership program for homeless adults, I called my college professor. He is the only one I've stayed in touch with because he had such a profound impact on me. It was because of seeds he planted that I was on the path I was on. Only two classes I took with him, but the one on Listening was the one that changed me the most, and he was a beautiful example of what a listener was.

When I shared with him what I was going to be doing with these men and women, he said, "just remember, it's about them, not about you." He was reminding me to keep my Ego out of the equation. I took his words to heart, and as a result I fell in love with people through my work with the homeless. As my judgments fell away, I was able to truly see and hear the truths of others, and I discovered that underneath it all, everyone is beautiful. I never would have realized this if I was caught up in saving them, showing them much I know (thereby implying how much they don't).

One of my first big lessons in listening came early on. A young woman at the shelter had just joined my class, and her thinking seemed to be erratic. She was very intent on talking to me about her problems, not doing a very good job of paying attention and staying present. Frustrated by the distraction she was, I asked her to meet with me so I could try to get her more engaged in the process. She just kept going on and on about her ex-boyfriend who dealt drugs, and how her 15-month-old son was taken away from her; it was a big, convoluted story I couldn't seem to get my mind around, nor did I want to, frankly.

The manager of the shelter walked in and asked what was going on, so I filled her in as best I could with a certain amount of exasperation in my voice, frustrated at the thought I wasn't getting anywhere with this woman. But the manger clued right in, asked the young woman a few questions of her own, and said, "So, call and find out what's going on with her son." I was surprised, never expecting I was supposed to actually listen to what the young woman had been saying. I saw her as a situation to handle, a slightly crazy woman that was talking gibberish. I never really listened to her until my manager said to make the call. Why had that not dawned on me?

I thought I had been doing a good job at listening, but apparently only if it happened within the context of the classroom setting. So in a way, even with my intention not to, I was letting it be more about me and my agenda than about my students.

I am reminded of one of Stephen Covey's *7 Habits of Highly Effective People:* seek first to understand, then to be understood— and also of a saying a friend of mine shared with me: people don't care how much you know, until they know how much you care.

From that moment on I saw that young woman differently, and learned how to listen, to really listen, on a much deeper level. I did get on the phone that day, discovered the whereabouts of her son, asked about the visitation process, then drove her there myself to see him at a place well over an hour away. Suddenly I saw her heart, her humanity, and realized she was a sister in pain, doing the best she could, finding it hard to focus on anything else when her baby felt so far away.

From that point on, she wanted to listen to everything I said, and became a model student. Often she would be the first one waiting at the door of the classroom when I arrived. But it was clear to me that the greatest impact I had was through teaching by example, as I taught her how to really listen, just as she and my manager had taught me.

It takes humility to remember that just as we have all of the answers within us, so too does everyone else. Nothing is more disheartening and isolating than to explore openly and honestly your feelings with another, only to have them analyze you, make you wrong for feeling the way you do, or to feed their own ego by believing they have your answers.

Deep Listening does not mean counseling. It means holding the space with love and gentleness within which another can move around and explore themselves, their lives, their truth, and find their own answers. Often just expressing a fear out loud is enough to allow us to hold it differently, or allows some energy to shift around it.

If we share a fear, and then have to defend why we feel that way, that energy may only get stuck. When we are able to speak it and we know *we* are being received, not the fear that we have shared,

"Our worst sin towards our fellow creatures is not to hate them, but to be indifferent to them."

—George Bernard Shaw

it is easier for that energy to transform. You may not see or feel the results of that immediately. Sometimes its just the beginning of a shift. Trust this process.

Over-Empathizing

In his bestselling book, *Emotional Intelligence,* Daniel Goleman defines this as a type of social intelligence that includes the ability to distinguish between our own and others' emotions. This means not taking on another's baggage.

It's a powerful gift when we put ourselves in another's shoes in order to truly understand what they are feeling and be compassionate for their process and their journey. But to be so open that we absorb their energy is a disservice to everyone involved. By taking on their pain for them, we rob them of the ability to learn the lesson that experience is offering, and deny them the opportunity to transform that energy into fuel for their lives. This is actually disempowering. We also put ourselves through an experience that was never ours be begin with, and create confusion for ourselves around which energy is ours and which is theirs.

This was a lesson it took me a while to learn, but it became obvious when a friend of mine was involved in an emotionally abusive relationship. She would call me, almost daily, in frustration and anger because of another altercation with her boyfriend. Having known her for years prior to that relationship, it was painful for me to witness her going through that. I didn't realize just how much I was taking on her stuff until I got off the phone with her one evening and realized how angry I was, and it took me a few minutes to shake it off. That's when I realized I was taking on a healthy, daily dose of it and that I wasn't doing me, or her, any favors by doing that.

Empaths are known for being so sensitive they can walk into a room and feel the energetic undercurrent in it, and it can be so exhausting to then distinguish between what is theirs and what is not that often crowds can be a challenge for them. Better to learn how to set appropriate boundaries for ourselves while still being open and compassionate listeners. It helps to remember that they, and we, are still Light underneath all the pain, and not get overly caught up in the story. We do this by realizing this is an experience they are having in order to learn some lessons their soul is ready to integrate into their life. The choices that need to be made must come from them. As their listener we can choose to trust, on their behalf, in the perfection of the experience and be grateful for the gifts that are hidden in the mud.

> *"Stop talking and thinking, and there is nothing you will not be able to know."*
> —Zen Master, Sosan

> **EXERCISE: JOURNAL:** What are the risks of over-empathizing? How do you know if you are doing that? How can you listen with Empathy and still maintain the healthy boundary between what is yours and what is theirs?

Deep Listening to Ourselves

I had been learning and teaching about the Universal One Mind, and how listening to our feelings allows us to be more intuitive, when the Universe sent me a lesson that solidified that for me.

> *"The heart's message cannot be delivered in words."*
> —**Mu-mon Gensen**

I have had so many lessons teaching me to honor my inner voice since first being turned on to the power of intuition that I no longer question its validity. But the one that really brought this home for me happened several years ago while playing games at a baby shower I attended with family and friends. For this particular game, the hostess brought out a large jar of peanut M&M's. The instructions were simple: whoever guessed closest to the actual number of M&M's in the jar would win the jar and all of the candy inside.

Instantly interested, I started to pick a number randomly from the air. Then I remembered what I had been learning and teaching about how we know intuitively so much more than we realize, and I stopped, closed my eyes and said silently to myself, "Erica, you know you have access to this information." Clearing my mind, I asked the question and then trusted the first image that came into my mind: a chalkboard, with the number 364 written clearly in white.

Deep Listening

> *"Intuition is only right 100% of the time."*
>
> —Lester Levenson

The image was so vivid, so clear, that I immediately put my pen to paper and wrote the 3 and the 6. Just before writing the last number, the hostess spoke up and told the group there were probably more M&M's in there than we realized, so whatever number we were thinking of, we should aim higher. With that I second-guessed myself, and my vision, and scribbled through my entry before writing another number on the paper.

I was both shocked and delighted to learn the correct number was exactly 364. I didn't care about the M&M's at this point; I was just so stunned at the accuracy of my intuition. That day I received the lesson loud and clear and vowed never to doubt myself again. I can't say that I have been entirely successful at that, but I've certainly learned to check in and trust myself more often than not.

> **"The truth is inside you.**
> **To see it you must open the inner eye."**
>
> —*Buddha*

While this was not a life-altering moment, it did drive home for me the access that we have to information, wisdom and Truth if we can get out of our own way enough to access it. Deep Listening to ourselves is deep listening to life.

It was the same deep listening that led me to find, very organically, what I believe to be my true calling. Whenever I'm not sure what's next, whenever I'm unclear about the next step to take, I pray about it and ask for guidance, opening up a dialogue between me and Spirit, and then I listen…and pay attention.

It can become all too easy to become lost in the *maya*, lost in the world of illusion, when there are story lines being played out all around us, by everyone. Deep listening is the way we find the truth, our truth, in the midst of confusion and chaos. This requires the ability to get quiet, to listen to the still, small voice inside. This is hard to do if we have not yet developed that deep, honest relationship with ourselves, if we do not have the ability to listen to our own heart above all other voices.

Without the ability to listen deeply and access our truth, we become all too easily led—eager, and even relieved that there's someone else out there with more conviction and belief in something than we ourselves have. This is why so many people finally recognize and lift the veil of illusion, fear, and programming that is religion, and end up replacing it with some other dogmatic belief system. We all have access to the same information; we are the Universal One Mind. When we learn to listen to the voice of Truth, rather than the voice of the Ego, we align ourselves with Spirit, with each other, with Life. When we listen to the voice of the Ego, we become splintered, separated from our Source—a source of divine guidance and energy and wisdom, and we enter back into the world of fear and illusion.

The more we listen to the Truth, our Truth, the easier that voice becomes to hear. It speaks to us through our feelings, which is why it is so necessary to tune into and acknowledge what it is that we feel.

> *"What I am actually saying is that we need to be willing to let our intuition guide us, and then be willing to follow that guidance directly and fearlessly."*
>
> —Shakti Gawain

Wise Decisions Don't Come From Your Head

Living a truly authentic life means being guided from an intuitive place within. This is the only way to ensure we are not merely playing out some old programming that no longer serves us. Living an inspired, full life sometimes means dancing to the beat of a different drum. Asking for advice or following some formulaic decision-making process does not allow our life to be an organic, continuously evolving experience. We tap into our Truth, our greatest source of divine guidance and direction, by checking in with ourselves and feeling for the next right answer…and "right" is entirely subjective. Nobody else can give you that.

Consider a current decision you've been mulling over. You can have your truest, most authentic answer right now. First, be honest with yourself about what your choices are, then play them out in your mind one at a time and notice how each possible scenario feels in your body. Those feelings are your spirit, your truth, communicating with you. When you have felt your way to the right answer to the question, you will know…you will feel it in your body. The more you choose to listen from that place, the more quickly and efficiently that guidance will come. It was actually there all along. And the more you practice this level of deep listening and self-honesty, the more efficient you will become at noticing when something is out of alignment.

Positive thinking alone without a resonant belief in the body results in a splintered self. To be an integrated whole, our feelings must be acknowledged. Our emotions always have a message for us, and if the energy moving through our bodies is not in agreement with the thoughts with which we fill our heads, we put our minds and our bodies at odds with each other.

The strongest emotion always wins, so if we are envisioning something we want to attract or move toward that elicits fear inside, but our desire to move beyond the fear is stronger, the thoughts in our mind and the energy in our bodies can align, and we have a free-flow of creative, powerful energy through our channel.

If there is a fear and it exists on a deeper level than the desire, and we ignore or deny that, we are not being honest with ourselves, and to act anyway would take us out of integrity with ourselves. That doesn't mean we let the fear win. But there is some deeper, honest work that needs to be done if we want to live as an integrated whole. If we stay in communication with our bodies, and keep the dialogue open between our minds and our bodies, that is a much healthier, honest, enlightened way of being than using mind control techniques to bend reality to our will.

I have done this. Wanting something in my mind, I ignored my body's message that we weren't ready. My body sent me warning signs in all kinds of creative ways, including insomnia and anxiety attacks as fear gripped my insides. I followed another's urging to do it anyway…to just go for it. But, regardless of the images of what I wanted to move toward, on a deeper level I knew it would be a *journey* that would get me there, not an abrupt, aggressive jump that would throw my system into panic mode.

I ultimately had to regroup and re-evaluate my approach. In the end, I did get where I wanted to go, but by practicing deep listening I kept the journey real, for me, as I stayed honest with myself and respected the messages my body was sending.

While expanding our comfort zone is healthy and empowering, blind leaps without the deep, inner honesty is a recipe for unnecessary stress. This is why only you can know what's right for you, and honoring your process requires engaging your mind and its ability to create and influence your body, while also letting your body, your subconscious, weigh in. Get all parts of you present at the table, give each member on the team a chance to weigh in, get them all aligned, and them move forward in a way that respects and empowers them all.

This is why I have always been attracted to the shamanic way. Shamanism is rooted in having a relationship with the Earth, and practicing deep listening—to ourselves, to nature, to the signs Life uses as a means of communicating with us. It is a much more grounded, real, honest, receptive approach. Here we aren't trying to sell ourselves, or Life, on an idea. A respectful relationship between the mind and the body requires open communication, and deep listening.

Deep listening requires being grounded and centered in your own Self, so you know how to hold yourself in relationship to the world around you. Recognize the difference between when to push and when to allow. This is the dance. Some dances are made beautiful when we move forward with respectful intention. Sometimes the next right move is to allow. Someone once posed the question: what is stronger, the rock, or the wave that splashes against it? The rock is hard, unmoving, dense. The water flexes and flows, adjusting itself around that which is less supple.

In yoga, I encourage students to develop a relationship with their own bodies, to think less about what their practice looks like, and more about what it feels like. Close your eyes and be in your body, and feel what that feels like. Explore this vessel you are in. What messages does it have for you? What new awareness can you gain from being in your body with such presence?

> *"Children begin early to value information over wisdom. Facts over feeling. Mind over heart. They begin to depend on external sources to inform them, and they don't realize how much there is inside of themselves to tap for their own growth."*
>
> —Merna Hecht

"Listen to your heart above all other voices."

—*Marta Kagan*

Now bring that same level of respect and awareness into your life. How do you choose to be in your life? Will you square your shoulders and brace yourself as you move headlong into the wind? Or will you relax back into your center and feel your way into Life, respecting each gentle breeze as you learn to dance with the beautiful subtleties of Life's energy?

As we get more and more honest with ourselves, practice forgiveness daily, and let go, we open up our channel, allowing us to better receive inner guidance. There is a choice here between listening to the Ego—and you'll always know that it is coming from Ego if it divides, separates, judges, or engenders fear, or any of the emotions that come from fear—or if it is coming from Truth, which brings a resonance of peace in the body, relaxes us, connects us, and returns us to Love.

Deep listening means going beyond the Ego, getting still, and listening to that subtle, softer voice that whispers, waiting for us to get quiet enough to hear.

Deep Listening to Life

Deep listening requires humility. How arrogant it is to believe we know how the Universe works—all the complexities of Life, all the rhythms of Nature. It is with a sense of relief that we realize the world does not revolve around us, and that we are a part of some greater whole, our collective energies moving and joining on levels which we cannot comprehend with our limited human brains. This means knowing there is a level on which we are not in control, and what a relief that is!

Living an authentic life is not about getting our way, but about relinquishing control and practicing deep listening to the messages showing up in our bodies—one of Life's primary ways of communicating with us. Guidance and truth cannot come from a place outside of ourselves. To live a life of true authenticity, we must go within.

The real work is about recognizing the Ego as it attempts the most creative ways to divert us from this awareness, creating instead an illusion of separation and competition. It is worst when we are in our arrogance, competing with nature as if we could possibly have access to answers it cannot provide.

When we forget this and follow instead the Ego's guidance, suffering surely follows. For it is all smoke and mirrors, an illusion, whose job is nothing more than distraction, born in those moments when the world outside of us was teaching us, molding us, guiding us so we could fit into the collective dream the rest of the world was having.

I never felt I had a relationship with God until I let go of every agenda, every preconceived idea and bit of dogma, to communicate from the truest, most honest, most authentic place inside. When Life answered back, it was through my feelings, seemingly chance encounters, and those people and places to which I would naturally gravitate when no longer limited by the boundaries of fear.

Deep listening means questioning the answers, no longer blindly following a teaching, or a teacher, who would rather tell you what to think than inspire you to think for yourself. With deep listening, something inside shifts and opens up. The journey becomes a very personal one as we search for a truth that we can only know when we find it. It resonates in the body, rather than satisfying the rationale of the mind.

As your inner landscape changes, your relationship with the world around you is transformed. No longer do you see through the eyes of fear and separation, but through the eyes of Love and connection. That's the world I want to live in. We fall in Love—with ourselves, with each other…with the magic of Life. As we sift through the seemingly complex layers of our lives with Love as our new filter, we see old constructs dissolve, no longer holding up under the new light we are shining on them.

Perhaps the nature and power of this work would be scary if what we were left with was anything other than a deep and pervasive sense of peace. We can choose to undo the fear-based programming to which we have all been exposed, and return to an awareness that has always been there but was simply forgotten.

"The quieter you become the more you are able to hear."

—Rumi

Deep listening, getting out of our thinking minds, our intellect, allows us to tap into Divine Intelligence, the sea of infinite wisdom of which we all are an inextricable part. The only thing that blocks our access to Truth, to the Universal One Mind, are our own thinking minds, an accumulation of emotional baggage that blocks our ability to receive truth.

Deep Listening allows us to tap into cosmic consciousness. Whenever I am seeking divine guidance, I meditate on it so I can quiet my mind and get out of my own way. I pose the question, then let it go. Then I meditate, emptying my mind so my channel is able to open. When it does, the answer, a divinely inspired answer that always feels right because it is coming from a place of wisdom and intelligence, not intellect or ego, appears. I have to really let go of my desire to figure out the answer, and empty my mind. Then the answer slips into my awareness, and I can tell when I have my answer because there is a resonance in my body, as long as I don't give my Ego-mind the opportunity to question or second-guess it.

Sometimes the answer comes during the meditation, after some time of getting quiet. Other times it comes later in the day, or is delivered most effectively while I sleep, and is waiting for me when I awaken, before my Ego-mind has begun to stir.

> **EXERCISE: MEDITATION TO DEVELOP TRUST IN YOURSELF**
> Consider a life question to which you are seeking an answer. It could be something as simple as a decision you are trying to make, or it could be clarification you seek on a course of action. State your question clearly and succinctly, then release it and let it go from your mind.
>
> Now, find a comfortable, quiet spot in your home where you will not be interrupted. Turn off your phone, television, and radio. Ask to be left alone, and set a timer for 15 minutes. Sit comfortably in a cross-legged position, or upright

in a chair with your feet planted firmly on the ground. With your hands resting comfortably in your lap, sit very tall, with an erect spine, close your eyes, and begin to settle into a quieter place within. Intentionally release any tension in your feet, legs and hips. Relax your shoulders, your jaw, and your eyes. Keep your spine long and straight, but relax everything else.

Now begin to breathe very deeply. For several minutes do nothing but sit and breathe deeply, establishing that deeper connection with yourself.

Now empty your mind of all thoughts. Let your mental landscape be like a wide open blue sky. Let any thoughts that come up simply float by, like clouds in that sky. Allow yourself to look at the sky from a distance as an observer. See what comes up, acknowledge it, then allow it to float by. Regularly, and continually, bring your awareness, very gently, back to the breath. Let your breath be your anchor into the present moment, always returning your awareness to the here and now.

Finally, bring your question back into your conscious awareness. Notice the first answer that comes, the immediate response to the question that arises before the Ego-mind begins to wrestle with it, making you second-guess and doubt yourself. Be aware of any struggle you encounter over trusting that voice of truth inside.

Deep Listening

An Empath Yoga Perspective

Seated Forward Bend — Find your edge

Lengthen forward as far as your comfortably can, going just far enough to feel the edge of the stretch. Then close your eyes and simply breathe. If you sustain the stretch long enough, and simply breathe into it, you'll feel yourself beginning to let go. You'll notice your body and mind releasing, opening, and inviting you deeper into the stretch. It takes a minute or two for the nervous system to get the message that you're ready to let go.

All too often people overdo it, wanting to be somewhere they are not yet. They force themselves into stretches, and situations, that take them beyond their healthy, comfortable edge. So with gentleness, compassion, and patience, simply breathe into the edge of the stretch. Wait and notice how things begin to change. In all of your yoga poses, and in life, explore the edge, breathing into it to allow for growth, but without forcing yourself into something that does not honor you and your own very healthy process.

Chapter 10

Keeping It Real

"Reality is merely an illusion, albeit a very persistent one."

—Albert Einstein

Our thoughts are powerfully creative. Thoughts are energy. And we are creating with this energy all the time, consciously or unconsciously. Every moment of every day we are creating our present experience, and our future. Unfortunately, most of us do this based on old programming, like a computer downloaded with an operating system based on the information that came in long before we even knew how to write our own names.

Now take the raw data that came at us throughout our lifetime, and add to that the interpretations we made, often erroneous, about what really happened. And like an old record stuck in a groove, we can keep replaying a song over and over again, bringing into our current reality recycled experiences of our past. The players may change, but the story line is the same. Everyone else in our life simply becomes a foil for us and all that we have yet to learn. This continues until we finally have our fill of that old story and decide to break out of the pattern of thinking that recreates it over and over again.

There is also unconscious programming that has been passed down through the lineage, from one generation to the next. I remember when my grandmother died, her sister, who I barely knew and had only met maybe a couple of times, came to her funeral. That evening as I walked around the corner into the dining room, I stopped short and took a double-take, as I was sure it was my grandmother sitting there at the table. Her sister was holding her head in the same tilted way my grandmother did when she was listening intently to someone, and her gestures and mannerisms were almost identical. What's more, I realized I engage in the same ones. Somehow, these mannerisms had been passed down through the family tree without any conscious intention. This often makes me wonder, if simple hand gestures and facial expressions could be mimicked and learned so easily and subtly, what other familial beliefs, thought patterns, and behaviors may have been inherited? Could this be why some habits are so deeply ingrained they seem nearly impossible to break?

Then there is *karma* that is passed down from previous lifetimes. While some question the truth of past lives, there is memory in our cells. Science tells us that matter cannot be created or destroyed, it just changes form, so the same energy that is in you and me now has always been in existence. We are dealing with cellular memory that is so deeply ingrained, its in our DNA. I have witnessed more than one past-life regression in hypnosis where someone with a current condition in this lifetime was able to trace it back to an experience from what seemed to be a previous life.

The mind, like a computer, is trained to look for patterns that are familiar, but it is so good at doing this we see them even when they are not there. Even when only pieces of the puzzle are present, we will often fill in the rest with our imagination in order to complete the pattern.

It is from this old programming, deeply ingrained in an operating system that is beyond our conscious awareness, that our interpretation of current events is made. Even with the awareness I have gained of how the subconscious mind works and influences everything about our perception, I still find myself, when I'm not careful, engaging in an old story line.

> **"We don't see things as they are.**
> **We see them as we are."**
>
> —*Anais Nin*

The Frame of Reference

Our perception is the lens through which we see the world. There is no reality out there separate and apart from what's going on inside our own minds. Reality is being altered by the very fact that there is a perceiver. It must be filtered through our own frame of reference.

I heard a story about a young girl who asked her mother why she cut the ends off of the roast before she put it in the pot. The mother stopped to consider this for a moment before responding, "You know, I don't know. It's probably to make it even more tender or something. My mother always did it and she made the best roasts." Not satisfied, the little girl went to her grandmother and asked, "Grandma, how come when you cook a roast you would always cut off the ends of the roast?" Her grandma thought about it for a moment, then laughed and responded with, "That's a good question. I don't know why. Now that you ask, I guess I learned it from my mother; that's what she always did." Still curious, the little girl finally posed the question to her great-grandmother. Her great-grandmother, who was still very sharp, thought about it for a long while and finally responded, "Oh dear. I haven't thought about that in a long time. We were very poor, you see, with a very large family, and the only pot I had to cook the roast in was always too small for its hefty size. So I would cut the ends off in order to make it fit."

We give everything all the meaning it has for us. We start with raw data, and the rest we fill in. The mind wants to think in complete images, so much so that we fill in the gaps, like finishing a sentence that has been left hanging in the air with what we assume was coming next, and it is easy to assume that the reality we've created is the right one.

Things like age, cultural differences, our occupation, the current condition of our health, our religious background, and our current self-esteem affect how we evaluate and interpret people, situations, and events. An 80-year-old woman is likely to experience things differently than a 20-year-old man. A police officer probably has a different viewpoint than a teenage kid. Easterners have different values and ways of seeing than many Westerners. A terminally ill man may have the exact same experience as a healthy young woman, but what they do with those experiences internally could be completely different.

Our perception of reality is resultant of our attitudes, beliefs, and experiences, and is yet another way the past has an influence on our present. This is called our frame of reference.

Police officers experience this phenomenon all the time. There could be seven witnesses to the same crime, resulting in seven different statements. To the frail, elderly woman, the perpetrator was a big, intimidating, scary man. The gruff biker describes him as a scrawny punk. The guy with a thing for watches is the only one who notices he was wearing one, and could even tell you what kind it was.

In the film "What The Bleep Do We Know," they say we are reality-producing machines. There are very few facts in this world; the rest we make up. It can be all too easy to get stuck in a perspective, unable to see beyond those limiting parameters.

> **"In order to see, you have to stop being in the middle of the picture."**
> —*Sri Aurobindo*

Even knowing this, I have still made false interpretations of what someone else's actions, words, and body language meant. This is where humility comes in, and we must be willing to give up the need to be right. More than once my impatience to know how something was going to play out caused me to make assumptions about things based on the limited information available to me at the time. I have jumped the gun, made false interpretations based on where I was in my life and how I was feeling at the time, and in my desire to be in control have nipped an opportunity in the bud because letting it play out just seemed too risky, and thus did not give it the time or space it needed to blossom into its potential, further reenforcing that my initial assumption was correct. This is also known as the self-fulfilling prophecy.

In the book, *The Four Agreements,* one of the agreements inherent in Toltec wisdom is: Do Not Make Assumptions. Remember, the perceiver shapes the very reality being perceived; notice how stubbornly we hold onto ours as the right perception.

> *"'Now' is just what is happening— minus everything you think."*
> —Adyashanti

> *"The world is nothing but my perception of it. I see only through myself. I hear only through the filter of my story."*
> —Byron Katie

This affects relationships all the time. A woman who grew up in a close family that did everything together and was very affectionate with each other might feel clingy and needy to a man who was an only child in a less-affectionate family whose members enjoyed their personal space. As adults, their expectations and perceptions feel right because it is such an inextricable part of their frame of reference. These preconceptions make the other person wrong, and without a new meeting ground for understanding between them, may drive a wedge between them.

We do this not only in our intimate relationships, but in all of them. We know why we do things the way we do, and we cannot understand why others don't see it too. If this is taken to the extreme, without being tempered by the humility of knowing that *it's not right, it's not wrong, it's just different,* the result can be a narcissistic belief that our version of reality is the only right one, and a desire to fit others into a world that we control.

In her book, *The Work,* Byron Katie encourages us to check in with our assumptions and test our perception, by asking "Is it true?" If we can at least acknowledge that our version of reality may not be entirely objective, we can begin to relax into the comfort of knowing that we don't know. This, again, is where getting out of our heads, and moving beyond the Ego to get a felt sense of things in our bodies, is a more accurate way of sensing how best to hold things. A reframing may be all that is necessary when we recognize we are seeing through an outdated lens.

"Many of the truths we cling to depend greatly on our point of view."

—Obi-Wan Kenobi

> **EXERCISE: LOOK AGAIN** Consider a situation in your life that is currently causing you stress. Journal about whether there is another way to hold the situation. If you were seeing through the eyes of love, how would you see things differently? How attached are you to the story, and how important is it for you to be right here? Are you making any assumptions? Stuck in a perspective?

> Pray about it. Ask for help. The prayer is a simple one: "I am ready to see things differently. Please correct my perception." Then let it go, and trust and know that, since thoughts are energy, energy is already reorganizing itself per your request.

> *"When someone truly changes his mind, he has changed the most powerful device that was ever given him for change."*
> —A Course in Miracles

What is Real?

There is no formulaic approach or template to follow when living an authentic life. Authentic living is an art, and requires us to check in with ourselves often. What feels right one day may feel differently the next—one little thing may shift, but it could provide us with enough new information to allow us to hold the whole situation differently in our minds. The trick is to check our perception so our reality is being created consciously, and is not a result of the manipulation of fear-based, egoic thinking that is stuck in the past.

Always take full responsibility for your life. This is the message I've had written on my bathroom mirror as a way of reminding me that I get to choose how I hold my reality. They say life is 10% what happens to us, and 90% what we do with that. So if perception is reality, it is our perception that ultimately shapes our life.

Now go back to where we were at our birth, before we were downloaded with what to think and believe. Nothing has any meaning separate and apart from that which we give to it. But if you believe, as I do, that we are pure energy, then we can choose to write over this human adventure of ours whatever it is we want to experience. What we focus on expands. If we focus on fear, we will look

> *"The trick is on what one emphasizes. We either make ourselves miserable, or we make ourselves strong. The amount of work is the same."*
> —Carlos Castaneda

for, and experience, more fear. If we focus on Love, that becomes our reality. Like turning the dial on a radio, we get to decide if we are going to tune into Love, trusting in that energy, or if we are going to tune into fear.

> *"It is not really our eyes that see, but our minds."*
>
> —Anodea Judith

Choose Love and Truth as your lens. In massage school we were taught the bones first, because once we knew the skeleton, we had something to hang the muscles on in our minds. If we choose Love and Truth as our ultimate reality, we have the framework upon which everything else hangs.

Love is the energy that brought us into this world, and with Love we can let go and trust that everything happens for a reason, without getting caught up in the maya…the illusion. What is the point of feeding energy into the fear-based reality to which we were introduced? Fear is nothing more than an illusion we have bought into.

> *"Love is what we are born with. Fear is something we learned here."*
>
> —Marianne Williamson

This is not to invalidate, deny, or discount the level upon which things do happen. We are spiritual beings having a human experience. It is still much more loving to be compassionate with ourselves and others in those moments when we forget this—when we get caught up in the story. We are here to have this human experience, so let us not do it with disdain or disgust. Life is an adventure. Let us not get caught up in any new-age guilt for the moments we are in our humanness.

I once heard someone say the moment we reach pure enlightenment, we have only seconds left to live, for our bodies could no longer contain our energy. How beautiful is that—to know that if we are still here there is still more for us to learn and experience? With that understanding, our struggles and challenges become nothing more than opportunities to expand on a previously limited perspective. Here we have an opportunity to widen our lens—to broaden our internal landscape.

Fear contracts us, narrows our vision, sucks us back into the illusion…the story. I'm not much on advice, believing as I do that we have all of the answers within us, but perhaps the best we could ever offer another is the simple reminder: don't get caught up in the story.

> *"If the doors of perception were cleansed, everything would appear to man as it is—infinite."*
>
> —William Blake

We are a part of the same rhythmic energy that inspires the phases of the moon, the tides of the ocean, and the cycles of all of life. Whether you call this energy Nature, Life, God, or Love—there is something out there with its arms around all of it. There is too much perfection in nature, too many inherent patterns, to believe otherwise.

In yoga, students learn about *chakras*. These are energy centers where the physical and spiritual bodies meet. *Ajna* is the chakra located between the eyebrows and back about an inch, and is often referred to as the "third eye." Ajna has a twofold purpose: to perceive and to command. It is intuitive and it is creative. It is here where we perceive and filter reality, and it is here that we command (or create) reality based on the thoughts we choose to feed.

The human experience is but a blip on the radar screen of all of existence, so why get overly caught up in the human drama when we can choose to simply be the observer? We can choose to observe through the eyes of Love. Have you ever had a dream where somewhere in the middle of it you realized you could direct the dream? Like the catchy tune goes, "life is but a dream," and we are directing the dream.

A friend once challenged me on my assertion that Love is our ultimate truth. I made all the arguments about how our reality is a product of our perceptual lens, and why not choose a lens that prompts me to look for Love—and therefore find evidence of it everywhere? But there is a level upon which we evolve past perception. Perception is a function of the mind. When we get to a place of "no-mind," Love, connection, and oneness is our only reality.

I'm reminded of a video I watched of an infant lying on the floor, the spirit within looking with fascination at his own fingers, and kicking his legs as his discovered how they made contact with the ground beneath him. As he got used to the body he now found himself in, he rocked it to and fro, learning of his connection to the surface beneath him, and experimented and explored the concept of rolling over onto his belly until he eventually figured out how to do it, and then how to do it efficiently. As I watched this video I witnessed the same open, innocent expression of pure love that we so appreciate about babies, for they are as yet unjaded by the world around them.

We have evolved for thousands of years up to this point. Perhaps we are now experiencing an evolutionary growth spurt that demands we move beyond a mere physical world. Like the Aboriginals who migrate back together without any predetermined plan, as we transcend the perceived limitations of the mind, we remember that we are all connected.

This would certainly explain how I could possibly know how many M&M's were in that jar that day, or how nearly 20 years after my last contact with a friend, she could enter into my mind in such a strong way, only to realize that through the wonders of the internet she was finding me right around the same time she was so heavily on my own mind. Stories like this abound, and I have felt my own connection to All That Is too many times, too clearly and undeniably, to doubt that there is life beyond what the analytical, thinking mind can perceive.

Maybe now we have finally evolved to a place where we have access to a higher intelligence. Without that access, we would be mere animals responding to basic survival needs. I think of the story of *The Lord of the Flies*, and how, when left to their own devices, humans often resort to animalistic behavior. If you look at our tendencies, one would argue that we are herd animals, which is why so many are so easily led, and actually find a sense of relief in it. When something doesn't feel right, we may moan and complain, but how many of us will actually rise above the prominent victim mentality and become leaders of our own self?

The Power of Our Thoughts

It's time to change the way we are showing up in our world. After a lifetime of being taught what to think, rather than how to think, most of us have forgotten, or never even realized, the power of our own minds. Everything about our life, about our experience, is the result of a ripple effect from some original sponsoring thought. Our thoughts give birth to feelings, and those feelings show up in the body as emotions (energy in motion).

Unfortunately, we live in a world where we haven't been taught to acknowledge the gift of these emotions, and feeling anything other than happiness, joy, and bliss has become enshrouded with guilt. After years of not acknowledging and processing our emotions in a healthy way, that energy gets stuck and we, at the very least, feel as if we are spinning our wheels and getting nowhere; in more severe cases it shows up as dis-ease in our bodies.

In order to quiet the monkey-mind with which so many of us are plagued, some turn to alcohol, drugs, food, or sex for a distraction. But quick fixes never last, and often we are left with a bigger mess than we started with, and now must sift through the wreckage we've created.

If this stress has actually taken root in the body as dis-ease, our modern day approach is to attack it as if we are fighting a war, invading our systems with synthetic medications, or cutting into whatever areas are not functioning properly. We essentially go to war with our own bodies, looking for something outside of ourselves that can win out over whatever has gone awry inside.

There is another way. The body is always striving to return to homeostasis, but this requires us to start practicing deep listening to the messages of our own bodies, rather than attacking the messenger.

After a lifetime of not addressing or processing the confusing and life-altering events of our lives, our bodies become like overstuffed closets we've closed the door on with the intention to keep it all "out of sight, out of mind." But that energy accumulates, and eventually we cannot ignore the dialogue our bodies are trying to

> *"Minute by minute, thought by thought, your mind is what shapes your life."*
>
> —*Gurumayi*

have with us for much longer. What started out as stress becomes an eating disorder as we attempt to ground ourselves with food, or insomnia as our minds use that opportunity to try to communicate that with which we keep ourselves too busy to notice throughout the day, or anxiety as the truth of what we have been ignoring stalks us like a puppy nipping at our heels just waiting for the right moment to get our attention.

There is a way to find our way back to ourselves as an integrated whole.

Another one of the reasons I love yoga is that it allows us to stop, breathe, and get into our bodies long enough to acknowledge what's going on inside. The body is the subconscious mind, and everything we want to know, or are trying to avoid, is stored there. Failure to make the connection with our bodies doesn't make that information go away, it just forces it to become subversive, becoming more and more creative in its attempt to communicate with us.

By getting into our bodies and moving in a conscious way, we start to get in touch with that which we have been denying, and all it takes is acknowledgement for that energy to start shifting and moving. With our movements and our breath, we create a pathway for that energy to be released from our body. It's not necessary to go in after it and cut it out.

Combine our awareness of all of that with the power of choice, and the realization that our heads create our world, and we now have a twofold approach toward holistic health and wellness.

Conditioning that has been passed down from generation to generation has taught us what to think, rather than how to think. And now most of us are walking through this life as if we are victims of our environment, our circumstances dictating to us who and what we are.

Our heads create our world, and our thoughts are forming the very reality we perceive. Most of us have never been taught this, and even if we have heard it, we don't have enough faith in ourselves to

"It's not what you look at that matters, it's what you see."

—Henry David Thoreau

be able to practice it consistently enough to make a difference. So we complain, and pray, and wait for something to happen, feeling helpless and out of control.

Just like any muscle that has atrophied, we can strengthen our mental and emotional musculature by starting to recognize that at the very core of our lives, creating our external reality and experience, are the thoughts we choose. Flowing from that are feelings which are interpreted by the body as emotions which have a physiological manifestation in the body.

Recognizing the power of choice is absolutely necessary if anything about our lives is going to change in any kind of a real and lasting way.

We start by noticing our thoughts. Our thoughts have a ripple effect on our bodies, and beyond into our outer reality. Our thoughts come from our beliefs—the beliefs we hold about ourselves, about the world around us, about Life. Our beliefs come largely from what has been modeled for us by the world around us, with negativity being one of the favorite pastimes of Americans. The more we feed those negative thoughts, and surround ourselves with others that buy into those negative thoughts, the denser the energy of those thoughts becomes and, like a maze we've walked into, it can be more challenging to find our way out.

But just like anyone who's ever put on weight during a lazy, unmotivated period in their life, it wasn't until they accessed and drew from someplace deep inside that they were able to make the changes necessary to return to health.

As with any atrophied muscle, it's hardest to overcome the inertia in the beginning, but once we get some momentum going we start to wonder how we ever allowed ourselves to flounder to begin with.

The more we choose to create our reality with conscious intention, the quicker and easier it is to re-program a mind that had simply succumbed, for a time, to some erroneous, outdated programming.

Think For Yourself

"To find yourself, think for yourself."

—Socrates

There was a study conducted by Yale University psychologist Stanley Milgram in the early '60s in an attempt to understand how individuals like Hitler succeed in leading so many to commit atrocious acts on their fellow man. Milgram wanted to measure the willingness of study participants to obey an authority figure who instructed them to perform acts that conflicted with their personal conscience.

Volunteer participants who thought they were participating in a study on the affects of pain on learning were instructed to push a button delivering an electric shock to a bound subject on the other side of a wall. The shocks were to increase in intensity with each wrong answer given. The participants in the study were led to believe that the recipient of the shocks, whom they met briefly just prior to the experiment, were also volunteers, when in actuality they were actors participating in a study on how much personal choice and responsibility people are willing to give up in the presence of authority.

In spite of the plaintive wails coming from the other room, and even pleading from the shock recipient, 65% of the participants knowingly continued increasing the levels of shock all the way to the maximum lethal level of 450 volts. None stopped before delivering 300 volts of electricity to the recipient, nearly 100 volts above the current of electricity delivered to our homes by the power company.

When asked later why they were willing to continue issuing pain even after they were begged to stop, these men and women of all ages said they were just following orders, and while they felt badly about it, weren't taking personal responsibility for their actions.

Organized religion has done a number on the psyche of humanity, and here's why. Historically, to question who and what we are was to question God, a blasphemy punishable by death. Thousands were executed, and even more imprisoned, never to see the light of day again if they dared question this authority. The Spanish Inquisition lasted for 50 years, from 1480–1530. Shortly after that, from about the mid-15th century to the early 18th century, a span of almost 300 years, tens of thousands of women and men were burned at the stake if their beliefs or behavior veered too far off what was acceptable. To doubt what we were taught was not an option. Fear has been used to control the masses for thousands of years, passed down through the evolutionary pipeline unencumbered.

Some argue that we need organized religion, some sort of moral governing body to keep a sense of order and propriety in society, and that without it there would be anarchy. Anarchy actually happens when people fail to think for themselves. Its not that we need to know what to think, it's that we need to know how to think.

I sat at a stop light recently, and noticed that when the light for the other lane turned yellow, people kept going. Even after the light turned red, several drivers continued. I'm imagining the belief or the thought was, "Well the person in front of me is going, so it's okay if I go." If the person behind them also went, it validated their decision to drive through that red light even more. No one was taking personal responsibility for their choices, for their actions. The fact that the light was there didn't stop them. It wasn't until somebody said, "This isn't right, I'm taking advantage of somebody else—somebody else's freedom, somebody else's space," that they stopped. It took that one person to check in with themselves and say, "I need to stop here."

Having mechanisms in place that tell us what to think does not cause us to live together in harmony as loving, connected human beings. Its not that a lack of some sort of organizing religion or governing body would leave us all to act like animals and would leave us in a state of anarchy. It is the inability or unwillingness to think for ourselves that creates that.

We have inherited a world, passed down from generation to generation, that was taught what to think rather than how to think. We live in a system of rules and expectations to which we have all agreed because we didn't know we had a choice. It's time to wake up and realize that we have a choice.

When Does Positive Thinking Become Dangerous?

There is a popular belief that has been misinterpreted, misunderstood, and misused. The mind is a powerful tool, allowing us to co-create with Life; and while the mind is powerfully creative, we do not live in a vacuum. We cannot know what lessons we are here to learn, or to help others learn, and what, through the actions of others, has yet to be revealed to us. This is a soul's journey, and it is only with great compassion and humility that we can walk it with true grace.

We don't control the world. We do create our realities based on the way we choose to interpret and respond to it, but there are much larger forces at play. To believe we control life is dangerously arrogant; at the least it is used as a more insidious way of judging ourselves and others. At the very extreme, it can cause us to cease listening, operating under the belief that if we believe something strongly enough, we can bend life to our will.

How damaging and presumptuous of us to tell a rape victim, or a mother who has lost a child, that they created that experience, somehow inviting it into their lives. Or that the victims of 9/11, and their families, are somehow to blame for their demise. While these men, women, and children may one day be able to find a gift borne out of that experience, it is compassionless to rob one of their right, and their need, to feel and process their experience in order to come out on the other side of it. We are not machines quickly calculating the benefits of every life event without the need to experience any emotional fallout—nor would we want to be.

Life is a much more complex web of interwoven laws and theories, and it seems like a gross oversimplification to say that anything we are experiencing is a result of our thoughts alone. I believe in the Law of Attraction, but I also believe in the Law of Gravity, and no matter how much we tell ourselves we can fly, if we jump off of a building we are going to fall—at least at this stage in our evolutionary journey as human beings.

I'll never forget the lack of compassion I once heard in a fellow yoga teacher's voice as she shared the story of a friend who was murdered. While going through a separation and potential divorce, along with the disappointment and regrouping that kind of change invites one to engage in if they are going to keep their life real, she was attacked and killed by an intruder. I cringed as I heard the storyteller share her suspicions that the victim may have been depressed, which would explain why, in her weakened emotional state, she could attract such a thing into her life. I neither felt, nor heard, any true or genuine compassion in this person's voice as she espoused her newly acquired belief so confidently.

Then there's the new-age guilt this engenders for anyone on the conscious path who is trying hard to create with conscious intent only to realize they have created something else.

It makes light of the human journey, and is most doggedly professed by those who recently found the power of positive thinking, and simply haven't been disillusioned yet. It's a better-dressed form of judgment and blame, almost imperceptible in its new duds. This new-age pop psychology feels like such an improvement over the old victim-mentality, because if you've been walking through life hitting yourself in the head with two hammers, and suddenly you realize what you're doing and drop one of them, it feels like a dramatic improvement—but you're still hitting yourself in the head.

Sometimes the honesty is the work, not the changing of the mind.

If I kept believing that I controlled Life with my thoughts alone, I may have put a lot more time and energy into bending the reality of my experience while I was in the corporate world to fit some ideal in my mind, maybe convincing myself that I loved it when I genuinely didn't. I could have used visualization techniques to manifest more or less of something, almost buying into the belief that I was getting what I truly wanted. And while to a degree I may have been successful, it wouldn't have been in alignment with a deep, inner truth that there was another, richer path for me to take. I would have missed out on the gentle nudges of Spirit—of Life—encouraging me in a new direction. I would have missed out on the wonder and beauty of the last 12 years.

I have come across those in my travels that only see the value in feeling good, and won't stop long enough to be real, even with themselves, out of the belief that the mind is so creative that to allow anything other than bliss is an error. But how real can that really be?

We think an average of 60,000+ thoughts per day, and it would be impossible for us to monitor all of them. But if we can learn to become aware of the energy that is moving through us, to recognize and allow rather than stuff or deny what is happening for us, and then strengthen our ability to let go and transcend our fluctuating emotional state rather than try to deny or control every one of our thoughts, we stay real…we stay honest.

There is no light without shadow. There are those that live in houses where everything you see is neat and in order, but if you look under the bed, or open up their closets, you find a chaotic mess. It's the same new-age "guilters" that would have you believe there is no value to anger, sadness, or grief—some of the emotions with the greatest gifts to share.

Our emotions always have a message for us, and if we tell ourselves there is no true value to certain ones, we are more inclined to pretend we aren't feeling what we're feeling. All of this can lead to completely missing the message.

Author and speaker Marianne Williamson says the Universe is simply here to agree with us. Do we really think we can fool the Universe into believing we are happy and positive because we portray only that to the outside world? True humility means recognizing that Life is at least as smart as we are.

It's Time to Wake Up

As is the case with evolution, it appears that now our survival demands that we outgrow the Ego and recognize the interconnectedness of all of Life—the rhythmic, cyclic perfection, and our oneness with each other, and all that is. Wars would no longer be fathomable in our connected minds. Resources would be shared more responsibly while we, together as one race, one team, one family, discovered healthy, sustainable alternatives.

We can already feel these changes taking place, and it's bringing every fear, doubt and insecurity we have to the surface. Perhaps, like adolescents going through the awkward phase of hormonal changes and identity crises, we as a species are also going through an evolutionary growth spurt. It's awkward and uncomfortable because we are in an in-between place. Like teenagers, who are no longer children and yet not quite adults, could it be that we are growing to a place in human evolution where we are no longer simply animals following the herd, succumbing to a basic survival mentality? Could it be that we are moving toward a place where we let the Ego dissolve, and realize that we are all connected, that we are all one—and that what we do, or do not do, matters to the collective? This would require us to be much more responsible, something the masses may not yet be ready to accept, for it is much easier to play the part of the victim and blame others for the mess in which we now find ourselves.

Biologists and scientists may want to discount this type of thinking, and spiritualists are basing an argument on something intangible, that we can only know for ourselves and do our best to describe. Is it because we just need to believe in something, whether or not that something even exists? Or is it because we believe in the Energy that has its arms around all of life, all of nature, this entire evolutionary journey upon which we have travelled thus far, and find it foolish to believe it ends here? You cannot use the intellect to understand Universal Intelligence.

We are in an awkward, in-between, confusing place. Life on this planet is not going to be the same, but for some the fear of what we know is preferable to the fear of what we don't, and they will cling to a ship that is sinking. In the words of the great Ralph Waldo Emerson, "people only see what they are prepared to see."

For some, this phase of evolution will be too scary, too chaotic, too unknown for them to handle, and they will either go insane, or the effects of their fear-based thoughts will wreak havoc on their bodies, eventually manifesting into dis-ease. Or things will get crazy enough, and frenzied enough, that someone will push the proverbial button. Either way, there will likely be a loss of life on this planet, unless there is a dramatic shift in our thinking—unless we expand our consciousness.

Others have, or will, find a place inside that is quiet enough, intuitive enough, and connected to Life and Nature enough to know we are simply going through an evolutionary growth spurt—quantum growth perhaps, where entire constructs are breaking down to make room for what's next.

Things will likely get worse before they get better; the chaos is not over. But it is the ones who have found that place within themselves that is connected to everything else that will start finding the others. There is already a small but growing army of Light workers on this planet, which simply means that there are those that already get it, that we are but a drop in the ocean of humanity, of Life, and we are the ocean itself. They know the thoughts they choose to feed matter, the words they speak have an impact, and the actions they engage in make a difference. They know that while they need do nothing, they also have a valuable and important role to play—they have a purpose.

I go back to the image of that baby, and the expression of pure Energy, pure Light, pure Love that he radiated from within. And as awkward and scary as this whole evolutionary process may seem, it is actually quite simple. It is a returning to the simple truth, a basic awareness, that we are Love.

Yet another reason why it is important for us to take care of ourselves, to love and honor ourselves—it is a responsibility, really. For how can we be there for our fellow man and be an integral part of this historical, evolutionary event in any kind of a way that matters if we are still stuck on whether or not we are lovable? Why would we want to put any energy into believing we are not? We're past that now. Not only are we lovable, we *are* Love.

An Empath Yoga Perspective

Five-Pointed Star — Live from the inside out

In Five-Pointed Star, and in life, as you reach and expand in all directions, let that expansion come from a strong core. Let your spine be long and strong. Feel your core here—a very strong center. Let this pose grow out from that center. Instead of reaching for life and focusing externally, let your life be sourced from deep within, emerging from your center and expressing out in all directions.

An Empath Yoga Perspective

Warrior I — Confidently, Powerfully Meet Life

Warrior offers us the chance to breathe deeply and tap into that Warrior energy that is within us. Remember a time when you felt really powerful, almost invincible in your life. Remembering what that felt like in your body, bring that energy into your warrior pose, and into your life, now....

Warrior II   **Confidently, Powerfully Meet Life**

…Let Warrior help to develop that part of you that knows it can meet Life—that knows it can keep up with Life. Let yourself be a gentle warrior. This isn't aggressive or forceful, and there's no Ego involved. This is about gently, confidently, powerfully meeting life.

Chapter 11

The Gift of Conflict

"Only that which you are not giving can be lacking in any situation."

—A Course in Miracles

I always say you never really know someone until you've had your first conflict. Because it is then, when our buttons are being pushed, that so much is revealed. Where we have unresolved fear, doubts, insecurities—those are all our weakest spots, and it is in those areas where we have our greatest opportunities for growth. It is for this reason that conflict is a gift. It brings to the surface—for us to see, learn from, and grow through—our blind spots, and those aspects of ourselves we deny, bury and even lie to ourselves about. Without a stimulus strong enough to shake these things loose and bring them to the surface, how else could we see them, acknowledge them and grow?

To see the gift in conflict we must have the courage, a strong enough sense of self, and a willingness to bring our shadows into the light. Without that impetus, those areas most in need of development would remain unconscious pebbles in our shoes, indefinitely robbing us of our full potential in this lifetime.

Taking full responsibility for our lives means knowing that people are only able to push our buttons because we have them. It is in our response to others that so much is revealed. Inner and outer conflict shows us where we have yet to grow—where there is a thought, a belief, some conditioning that is keeping us from the deepest, most honest, authentic relationship with ourselves and with the world around us.

"Happiness and true freedom come only when we assume full responsibility for who and what we are."

—Leo Buscaglia

I'm always amazed at how beautifully creative life is at teaching me how my actions impact the world. There have been countless scenarios where I have engaged in behavior that did not come from my highest self based on fear or judgment or selfishness, only to one day be on the receiving end of strangely similar behavior. Whether you choose to call it Karma or not, when we choose not to give into the Ego's temptation to judge ourselves and others as right or wrong, we can rise above the circumstances and see the gift in conflict. Conflict often reveals to us an area in need of developing.

When we need to develop more of something in order to move closer to our own loving essence, how else would we do that other than finding ourselves in situations that demand exactly that? If lack of humility, or compassion, or self-confidence is keeping us from being able to expand into our own loving truth, we will attract into our experience that which will require more of it from us.

Just as gemstones are put into a tumbler together so that by rubbing up against each other their sharp edges are worn away, it is through our relationships and interactions with others that we smooth out our rough edges. Often it is only when those underdeveloped parts within us bump up against another that so much is revealed. We need each other in order to grow.

> ***"Never find a person who has no difficulties.***
> ***He will not be of any help."***
>
> ***—OSHO***

It is inherent in our growth as individuals, and ultimately in the return to our awareness of the truth of who we are, that we shed the layers of everything that is not Love. This is the gift of conflict, and why it is those that challenge us the most are our greatest teachers. As is encouraged in the book, *Thank You for Being Such a Pain,* we can embrace conflict for the incredible opportunities for growth it provides.

One man told me he was tired of dealing with people and the idiocy of the world, and wanted to go live alone on a mountain top somewhere and meditate all day, every day, so that he would be able to evolve and live in peace. I said, "How would you know? You just removed every outside stimulus."

> *"I have learned silence from the talkative, toleration from the intolerant, and kindness from the unkind; yet, strange, I am ungrateful to those teachers."*
> —Kahlil Gibran

Life is energy, and it—and we—are all connected. If we all came to the playground with this same humble awareness and learned to play nice together—recognizing that the other person is us—everyone would be interesting and of value, as we look upon them and wonder: What do you have to teach me? What new gifts do you bring into my experience today?

When we are able to step back from it all, it is actually fascinating to watch how our minds work and the creative ways we try to avoid the truth, always pointing our finger at the other. Thus, the human drama.

When we indulge the Ego and allow ourselves to engage in avoidance and denial, we are only serving to further strengthen the story, the illusion, from which we are now ready to awaken, and the fear, separation, and isolation that goes hand in hand with that. There is no value in ignoring the elephant in the living room, other than as a delay tactic as we resist going on a journey we cannot ultimately avoid. Even if we effectively convince ourselves that the problem is out there, and like a slippery fish escape the current relationship or experience unscathed, we cannot avoid the inevitable—the truth—forever, and Life will simply send us smarter people, and stickier circumstances.

Any true journey inward requires complete and total honesty. If you are not owning up to a personal truth or are choosing to stay in a place of denial, your journey will be stalled. You will be stuck in the quagmire of your own insecurities. To lie to yourself or stay in denial is the same as choosing self-hatred, for the underlying message is that the truth about who you are is too horrible, too unattractive, too unlovable to accept. A decision to stay in the illusion is created by our Egos in an attempt to try to continue to fool the world around us.

> **EXERCISE:** Reflect on the following questions, and explore them in your journal: What am I lying to myself about? What truth am I not willing to accept? What am I resisting admitting to myself?

> Then sit with each question and relax into it, feeling yourself sift through layers of fear, denial, and resistance until you feel yourself getting closer to the truth. When you get there, simply take a breath and acknowledge it, and notice what happens.

The irony is, even though we may refuse to admit something—some truth—to ourselves and to others, most of the time others have already picked up on it. We have just collectively agreed not to discuss it. Every now and then, however, somebody comes into our lives and feels compelled to point out to us what we are doing, how we are acting, or what we are saying that is not coming from the deepest truth of who we are.

Regardless of how this information is shared with us—whether the approach is loving and kind or confrontational and accusatory—we often go into further denial, and the cycle continues.

Unless we have already gained some level of self-love and acceptance, and a willingness to hear the truth, no matter how painful it may be, we may resent this person for "breaking the agreement" and pointing out that which we are not yet ready to face about ourselves. Then the focus becomes comfortably about the other person and how "wrong" he or she is, rather than about us and whether there may be some truth to what was brought to our attention. After all, everyone we encounter is simply a mirror for us, reflecting back the various aspects of our personalities and ourselves so that we can see them.

"Everything that irritates us about others can lead us to an understanding of ourselves."
—*Carl Gustav Jung*

The Mirror

"What I was hiding deep inside you brought out into the light."

—Rumi

Another gift of relationships is the mirror they provide. It is only through relationships that some of our deepest truths are revealed. We learn about ourselves through how we respond to others, and we learn about ourselves through the way they respond to us. When we walk into a room, do people contract, inwardly moaning and groaning, or do they light up, happy to see us? As author Leo Buscaglia says, "Is it a bummer that you are…or a celebration?"

This mirror allows us insight and a view into who we are that we could not get any other way. This is how we become aware: by recognizing the gift of relationship—whether it is with strangers in line at the grocery store, co-workers we befriend as well as those we don't get along with, close friends, brief acquaintances and, of course, family. We cannot fully know ourselves if we do not have relationships—if we do not relate to others.

Often we get frustrated, angry, and upset, and are unsure exactly why. Usually there is an underlying fear in existence. Rather than get in touch with what that might be, it is easier to blame another for making us feel that fear. However, being proactive also means acknowledging that nobody makes you feel anything. If you are having a reaction to a situation, avoid pointing fingers and making accusations. Being empowered means recognizing that you are responsible for your own experience.

When we judge others and reject them in any way, we are actually rejecting the mirror they hold up for us. It is because we cannot accept what that mirror reveals about us that we push it away. In *The Dark Side of the Light Chasers,* Debbie Ford reveals how it is that which we judge in others that we most identify with and fear in ourselves. In this way, everyone is a teacher for us. Those we feel comfortable around probably mirror those aspects of ourselves we can appreciate. Those we dislike and avoid are probably those that show us aspects of ourselves we do not want to acknowledge. The only way we can recognize traits in others is if we have seen them in ourselves, otherwise we would simply see their behavior as curious and interesting, without any negative judgment attached to it. Our judgment of it reveals our identification with it.

We are limitless potential, so what we judge in another reflects an aspect of ourselves, a *potential* aspect of ourselves. This is yet another way that by loving that which we are tempted to judge in another, we more fully love and accept ourselves.

When we slip into an adversarial stance, the lesson becomes a painful one. We have accepted the Ego's invitation back into a false reality of us versus them, right versus wrong, good versus bad. We have slipped into the habit-forming world of judgment, and all the dividing and separating that offers. Since we create our reality based on the thoughts we choose to feed, feeding thoughts of judgment—of ourselves or others—only serves to strengthen our belief in a world of fear and isolation. That which we judge we lend energy. In this way, that which we defend against we keep alive.

So often we are given a gift of objective insight into ourselves that we reject and ignore because it was not offered in the most loving fashion, or because it is simply just too much for us to be able to accept about ourselves and still maintain the illusion. To start opening our eyes—seeing, admitting, and owning the truth—would compel us to embark on a journey of self-discovery. The more we realize who we have been and acknowledge what we are capable of becoming, the less willing we are to maintain the illusion. Self-denial is self-hate. It keeps us from moving through our blocks to experience the growth, love, peace, and joy we could be experiencing every day of our lives.

So when faced with a conflict, the real question is: *What is this situation asking of me?*

Humility

We must be willing to own our stuff, and can no longer indulge in a victim mentality, blaming another for our experience. The moment we start playing the blame game, we have stepped back into the illusion—the human drama. We are so desperate for excitement and something to remind us that we are alive that any energy is better than none. Which is fine, if you like it there—some people do. Some thrive on the drama, not realizing that living in Love is so much more interesting, exciting, and enjoyable.

"Relationships are not sporting events. Stop wrestling for control. No one ever wins this kind of match..."
—Leo Buscaglia

"Love is the energizing elixir of the universe, the cause and effect of all harmonies."
—Rumi

Self-Love

Sometimes the opportunity is to be so secure in your sense of self, so full of self-love and acceptance, that you can hear the complaints and criticisms of others and be grateful for the information being shared, keeping it in its appropriate place by taking what's useful and discarding the rest. Can you discover and acknowledge areas within you that can use some light shined on them without it making you doubt even for a moment the loving, innocent essence that you are? Nick Ralls said:

> "As we peel the layers of the onion of our consciousness we arrive at the core of our being…our true nature…our essence…the truth of who we really are. The journey inwards can be the most arduous, the most challenging but the most rewarding. As we behold those souls to whom we are attracted…either in a positive or negative way…we see in them a mirror of those aspects of us which need to be extolled and those which need to be healed."

Sometimes Its Not About You

Can you be so clear and confident in your sense of self you are able to recognize when it's not about you? For just as others are powerful mirrors for us, so too are we powerful mirrors for them. Then the opportunity becomes more about holding the space for another with compassion, *free of arrogance*, for the story within which they may be stuck.

> ***"We can choose to see ourselves and others as either giving love, or extending a call for help."***
>
> —*Gerald Jampolski*

Another one of The Four Agreements is: Do Not Take Things Personally. Sometimes it's not about you, it is about the mirror that you are for another. It is what you are bringing up within the other person, and what they are projecting onto you. Here there is an opportunity to stay humble. This isn't about you being right and them being wrong; it's about recognizing there is nothing to defend against. Just as others will project their stuff onto you, you have and likely will again do the same thing. But let this not be an excuse to deflect, deny, or avoid responsibility for how you are showing up in the world, because often there is a message in there for you.

Several years ago I went on a backpacking trip through Europe with three friends. I knew intuitively that with four individuals traveling by planes, trains, and boat, bunking together inexpensively in youth hostels while we covered a lot of ground in a short period of time, the probability of conflict was high. During my entire flight to London I meditated, and visualized myself letting go of the need to be in control and relaxing into the experience, trusting that everything would work out just fine. My personal mantra, no matter what happened, became, *its all just part of the adventure.*

There were times we missed our train by just a minute, showed up too late and the hostel where we had reserved our room was already closed, and at times had to make last-minute adjustments to our plans. Through it all I stayed relaxed and expansive, simply enjoying every single moment of the experience, allowing it to unfold exactly as it was supposed to.

More than halfway through the trip, the stress of it all finally got to one of my friends, and in her fatigue and frustration she vented on us all, sending out little jabs in an attempt to find someone to blame. I observed with fascination her attempts to draw one of us into her personal drama, and while I noticed the desire within me to defend and deny, I did not engage. Instead I watched her without judgment, and realized that there were times in my life that I, too, had behaved that way.

A few hours later, finally settled into our hostel, the others left in a desire to put some space between themselves and her. Realizing she was in pain, that it wasn't about me and that she was suffering, I sat down next to her and just listened, and validated, what she was feeling. I was able to recognize that, in our letting go of so much control, she felt like she was carrying all of the burden of organizing the entire itinerary.

From that point on I became more involved in the decision-making process. When she realized she wasn't going to get a fight, resistance, or judgment, it was amazing to watch how quickly that angry energy started to dissipate, for there was nothing for it to feed off of.

Real growth occurs, for us individually and in our relationships, when we see the opportunity and avoid preparing our attack and defense. This is the difference between being proactive versus reactive. To be proactive means adopting a longer-term, visionary approach to the possibilities in any given situation. It means honoring yourself and the other person, as well as the relationship between you, rather than getting caught up in being right. The moment we indulge in an adversarial attitude, the lesson becomes a painful one.

The Win-Win

Conflict is unavoidable. Whether internally there exist parts of ourselves at odds with each other, or externally in our relationships, there will be moments when we are faced with conflicting needs. This is not necessarily a sign that the relationship is bad or even unhealthy; it has brought to the surface an area that needs attention. It's as simple as that.

We can deny it, avoid it, or come at it with an aggressive, full-frontal attack. But in each of these scenarios the relationship, in the end, surely suffers. Those that run from and avoid conflict usually leave themselves and the other feeling frustrated. No real growth or expansion can occur here, and everybody loses.

Even a more aggressive approach, untempered by respect and a mutual understanding of each others needs, will result in a lose-lose. One walks away with their needs unmet, while the other appears satisfied. While this may appear to be a win-lose, this is where resentment builds. Any time we gain at another's expense, it is a bittersweet victory. We are all in this together, and nobody truly wins if anyone is walking away unsatisfied.

Even a compromise, while a slightly more evolved approach, leaves both parties giving up something that they wanted. Only a win-win satisfies the needs of everyone involved. This is not a compromise, but a better solution that gives everyone involved what they want while still maintaining harmony. A win-win is only useful in those relationships that actually mean something to you—where you actually care about the other person. Since everyone is a brother or a sister, that means every relationship we have.

A win-win requires enough conscious intention to be able to say, "Let's agree to discuss this until we find a solution that satisfies both of our needs." Set some time aside to explore what everyone's needs are. Reflect on what your own personal needs are, and ask yourself if you are coming from Ego and the need to be right, or are you speaking your truth. Take time to find your truth, something that can only be done after we've taken the time to develop a deep, honest relationship with ourselves that is free of social conditioning. If necessary, utilize a journal, or sit in silence and meditate. Then come from that place of truth.

Be willing to listen with an open mind. Is there an area where you can stretch? If you start making the other person wrong in your mind, you run the risk of slipping into an adversarial stance. Stretch your previous limitations. Find new ways to flex. Communicate clearly and respectfully.

The critical step is taking the time to recognize that the other party has needs as well. Practice deep listening with the intention to understand their point of view first. When you feel you can really appreciate their concerns (not in your head, but in your heart), paraphrase back to them, in your own words, your understanding until they know they are being heard and understood. They will feel validated and honored that you took the time to hear them, and this puts them in a much better position to let down their defenses and in turn hear you with an open mind.

Realize that just as you may need some time to gain clarity on exactly what need you have that is going unmet, so, too, may the other person. You can lovingly hold the space for him or her by practicing patience, tolerance, and listening without judgment. Give your partner the opportunity to get to their own truth without feeling interrogated, attacked, or shot down along the way. If the issue being discussed is a recurring one, realize that if it is still coming up it is not yet resolved.

Is it possible to listen on a deeper level? What are the other person's real concerns? If you listen, really listen, to what's being said you will likely find that the concerns being expressed are not frivolous, nor are they an attempt to pick a fight. Rather, they are issues that are not going to simply disappear. If this is the case, perhaps it is time to acknowledge them rather than judge them and push them away.

Practicing conflict resolution proactively will improve the quality of your relationships. Let yourself become the "eye of the storm." Create an intention to grow from conflict and honor your relationships at the same time. This gets easier with practice, until eventually it becomes natural and automatic. As your confidence in yourself and in your ability to handle conflict grows, you will no longer be fearful of it; you will be able to relax. Allow yourself to be empowered by embracing conflict as one of the most potent opportunities for growth that exist.

> **EXERCISE:** Consider an unresolved conflict in which you are engaged. When considering the deeper message, what are the real needs that the other is trying to meet? Are you clear about your own? What might a win-win solution look like? Is there a way to open up a respectful dialogue and explore it?

"In my defenselessness my safety lies."
—*A Course in Miracles*

Become Defenseless

I once had an older, much more conventional friend challenge me very aggressively on a relationship I was in with a man. In that relationship I was choosing to explore being in it without imposing any societal rules upon it. While everyone around me wanted to know what we were doing, we tried to be in the relationship in an organic, spontaneous way for a while. We were letting go of all of the "shoulds" and allowing it to unfold, moment by moment, free from expectation or agenda. This offered me an opportunity to be in a relationship a little differently than I had been in the past—liberated from the pressure of where it was going and what was the "right" way to do things. I wanted to think outside of the box, to see what would happen if we explored the unconventional as I felt out and explored why I hold things the way I do in my mind, and whether there is an area wherein I can stretch.

When I experiment in my life in this way, I sometimes find a more expansive way of being in a world that likes pre-conceived patterns—as outdated as they may be. Other times I realize my original framework is the one that best fits for me, at least at that point in my life. Often this inspires others around me to look at their lives a little differently. Sometimes they expand as a result. Sometimes it stirs up their own fears, which they then project outward. In this case, while I tried to express to my friend that I was consciously exploring this other possible way of being, she kept pressing me on whether I was being honest with myself. I suspected this was probably coming from her own fears about what stepping outside of her comfort zone in such a way would feel like for her. Rather than get defensive, I simply said, "Thank you for inviting me to look at this."

When you know what is real for you, what is true for you, you can allow for differing viewpoints—for your house is not a stack of cards, and your world is secure. You can allow Life to flow through you, not needing to clamp down and contract around an untruth in order to defend yourself against it. It is the defending against something that gives it validity, that makes it real. Otherwise that energy would just move through us, dissipating, or go in search of another to which it can stick.

When we remove the boundaries that are our physical bodies and our Ego-minds, what's left is pure Love, pure Energy. When we recognize that the other person is us, the need to be right or win at another's expense becomes a pointless waste of energy. We can move beyond the level at which our personalities meet, and choose instead to remember that we are all drops in the same ocean, a part of cosmic consciousness, the Universal One Mind. What we do to others we do to ourselves.

Even when we have gotten lost in the story, we are still that pure Love and innocence. Learn to separate the person from the behavior. Remember, we have all been subject to the programming that came with our inhabiting these human bodies, and entering into a social arena. Think beyond the limitations of our temporary human bodies and minds and remember the truth of who we are: that we are one with All-That-Is; that there is only one of us here. Do not buy into the story—about yourself, or about anyone else.

As children, the ego helped us create our self-image. But when we buy into the image that has been created, we lose sight of who we are in any given moment. The Ego-self causes a separation from our true, authentic, inner self. If we are not careful, we can buy into the image created so strongly that we become stuck, no longer able to be flexible and fluid, or rediscover ourselves freshly in each moment. Our authenticity may be lost, as we steadfastly adhere to the picture and ideal of who we think we are.

If our self-created image is threatened, our Ego will push us to emphatically defend it. The more we defend, the more we become stuck, or stale, outdated versions of who we used to be. Growth can only take place when we allow ourselves to choose who we are, and respond authentically, in each moment. This is when life becomes enjoyable and fun again. We no longer have to be vested in protecting anything, and we are set free to truly BE, relaxed and present in each moment. Our center can be found in ourselves, not in a story that has been written over time, binding us to our past. We have to develop a sense of self so that ultimately we can transcend it. When you have nothing to protect, there is nothing to defend.

The Ego also creates a disconnection between ourselves and others, as we mistakenly buy into the belief that somehow their perception and interpretation of us matters. What others think and believe about us only matters if we have given away our power. True power means not being defined by others. Authentic power means realizing we create our own reality. Once we genuinely get this we can hear the criticism and input offered by others—whether it is gently offered or aggressively shared in confrontation—for what it is at its very core. Either there is an element of truth and an opportunity to learn and grow, or it is simply not about us at all, but a creation of the Ego in the other person.

In either case, our sense of self is strong and secure enough that it won't really matter. Without feeling a need to defend, we can take in the useful information and not take offense to the rest. In this way, if there is a chance for us to learn, we can receive the lesson and evolve. If it is not about us, we will be centered and grounded enough in our Self that we can let accusations and attack pass right through us—leaving us unharmed. By not hooking into another's fear and anger, there is nothing for that energy to feed off of, and they will either calm down and let it go, or they will move on and try to find someone else to engage. Only the truly aware, those who aren't choosing to buy into the Ego any longer, will be able to resist its pull and sidestep becoming angry and fearful themselves.

We can return to Love when we recognize the work of the Ego, and when faced with the choice between Love and fear, we make the investment in Love. When we return to Love, we return to ourselves, we become one again with all of Life, including others, recognizing that there is no separation, and we open ourselves up to a connection with All-That-Is. Life…Love…Truth cannot be felt when we are in fear.

> **EXERCISE ON BECOMING DEFENSELESS:** Over the course of the next week, whenever somebody says something to or about you that you would normally be compelled to defend, stop yourself and make a mental note to reflect on what they've said later, when you are alone. Practice saying, "Thank you for bringing that to my attention. I'll have to look at that." Then, using your journal, consider for a moment whether or not there could be any validity to what they've presented you with.

This is where the uncompromising honesty, self-love, and acceptance come in, giving you the ability to own your stuff, and not beat yourself up with it, choosing instead to use the information to grow and become empowered. Remember, awareness is the key to our continued growth and expansion. But we will never be able to gain new awareness of ourselves if we abuse ourselves with each new truth we realize.

Judgment vs. Discernment

One of the hardest lessons for me to learn was the distinction between judgment and discernment. Not too long after I began my own personal journey of self-realization, an older, wiser woman who was much further along on the path of self-discovery warned me to be careful around a certain friend. She felt confident that this friend of mine was so full of darkness that I would be negatively affected by it. I thanked her for her concern but essentially shrugged it off and ignored her warning. After all, everyone is Light, I thought. To reject her would be an act of judgment on my part, and I had made a firm commitment to love and connection in my life.

However, that relationship was toxic, and it took years for me to learn the value of setting appropriate boundaries in order to love and care for myself. I thought anything but open arms was tantamount to rejecting a brother or sister.

It has been a hard lesson, with years of unnecessary pain and struggle, in that relationship and in others, to realize that some people are so deeply embedded in their pain and fear, and have become so comfortable in the dark, that they may never come out—perhaps until the moment of their death when the Ego falls away and all that's left is the truth. Until then, there are those who have buried their Light, and only know a facsimile of Love.

There are those that have chosen to dwell in fear and anger—to live in the dark. I remember one man, a friend, who was so full of anger it had become his home. Any prolonged attempts by me or anyone else to entice him out of it only put us in harm's way. In the end, I had to walk away. Sometimes the only way to practice unconditional love is to take care of ourselves, and honor the choice of another—even if they've chosen to live in the dark. We do this not as a rejection, but as a way of honoring everyone involved. By setting a boundary, we love ourselves and the other person.

A relationship between some friends comes to mind, in which the man is verbally abusive, disrespectful, and condescending. I always felt sympathy for the woman because she seemed so helpless. Stranger still was the fact that it was obvious they both deeply loved each other, and I knew he hated himself for treating her that way. His childhood wounds were being allowed to run amok, and excuses were being made by everyone involved.

One day I realized she was a much stronger woman than she was giving herself permission to express, and I stopped seeing her as a victim. I realized she had made a choice to support him in his wounds; in fact, in some ways, I could see how *she* was doing a disservice to *him*. It couldn't feel good for him to get away with treating her that way, and he was doing it because she was *allowing* it. She was not respecting him by accepting a standard of behavior that couldn't feel good to him either, so in this way, *she* was not honoring *him*.

Setting Boundaries

Sometimes the most loving thing we can do is set a boundary. I remember a retreat participant expressing such relief when she realized she wasn't a bad sister for cutting off her drug-addicted brother. He refused to take responsibility for himself, and after years of trying to help she had finally had enough, and wasn't willing to put herself or her family through the drama any longer. She struggled with her decision, and felt a certain amount of guilt for "abandoning" him, but it was empowering for her to recognize that it was a decision that honored him, too. He may have chosen to live in the dark, but the Light inside of him would never want to be enabled in that way. As I once heard someone way, there is no value in organizing ourselves around the weakest parts of another.

I'm reminded of a friend who had to put a boundary in place between herself and another, and essentially ended the friendship. What was impressive was her ability to do it and still have only love in her heart for him. While her Ego had plenty of material to justify making him wrong and her right, she was able, instead, to recognize that he was simply stuck in his wounds, and that it was healthier for everyone involved for her to love him from afar. Now when she thinks of him, she imagines wrapping him in light and sending him love. This allows her to still have a loving relationship with him, but from a healthy distance.

Enabling another does not honor anyone involved. Transformation and liberation often occurs only after we hit rock bottom, and one never does if there is always somebody there willing to hold them up.

> *"Our finest moments are most likely to occur when we are feeling deeply uncomfortable, unhappy or unfulfilled. For it is only in such moments, propelled by our discomfort, that we are likely to step out of our ruts and start searching for different ways or truer answers."*
>
> —M. Scott Peck

While it is true that we are all one, sometimes the most loving thing we can do is set a boundary, or even leave the relationship altogether. If a choice is necessary to honor one person in the equation, it by default honors everyone involved, even if it means that one or more are left with a fair amount of growth and "healing" to do, for healing is nothing more than a return to Love.

The Ego doesn't want us to hit rock bottom, because in that moment we become humble enough to see the folly in it all. The Ego would much rather have us swim in a sea of misery, which is why some will have to suffer greatly before they are exhausted enough, and fed up enough, to be brought to their knees. The most powerful moment of transformation occurs when the constructs of the Ego give way, and we start the journey back home.

We are not honoring another by enabling them to stay stuck, especially if it requires us to sacrifice ourselves in the process; nobody wins. The Love within them would never want that for us, even though their Ego might. What's truly right for you is, on a deep level, in the best interests of everyone involved.

Compassion

Just as every person that comes into your life does so for a reason, so, too, do you come into theirs for a purpose. The answer is compassion all around, for we're all doing the best we can.

While more and more people are waking up every day, there is a very small percentage of the human population who have taken full responsibility for their lives and are choosing to live in a conscious way. When we do, we expand and evolve. As more and more of us take responsibility and choose to live in Love rather than fear, the energy of that becomes infectious, and the ripple effects are felt into the world around us. When enough of us wake up from this collective dream and remember the truth of who we are, we will eventually reach a critical mass, a tipping point, and it will be easier for us all to live that way here on Earth, in these bodies.

To do this, we cannot be afraid of the dark. The way out of the dark is to turn on the light. Shine the light of Love and compassion on every interaction, especially those that are most emotionally charged. This is the gift of conflict. The fears of ourselves and others are right out there in the open, and what a wonderful opportunity for them to be transformed.

This is where deep listening and conscious perception come in handy again. Be willing to put yourself in the other person's shoes. When another comes to us, or at us, in a way that indicates disharmony, notice when you find yourself posturing for a fight, or becoming defensive. Get your Ego out of it and recognize the gift with which you are being presented.

Most people do not enjoy conflict. Those that do are in a tremendous amount of pain, and they are projecting that pain out on the world because they don't know what else to do with it. If you really listen to another, not from your head but from your heart, free of the constricting confines of judgment, so much is revealed about their internal state.

I once sat behind a man on a plane who was cantankerous and impossible to please, as the flight attendants did everything they could to make him happy. It was as if he was just looking for a fight. While I heard others around me mumbling and judging the man for his behavior, my heart went out to him, for I realized that in order for him to be putting that kind of energy out, he had that kind of energy inside of him, and he probably lived with it every day. I couldn't help but wonder what kind of pain that man was carrying around inside, and realized he probably had no idea what to do with it. All I wanted to do was send him Love, and so I did, silently. Knowing that thoughts are energy, I believe there was a level upon which he received it, and just a little bit of healing happened. Love heals all, because Love is all. The rest we have made up.

We are all going to reach enlightenment some day, but as a friend of mine says, for some it will be immediately followed by death. Many will not be able to see the truth until they are on their deathbed, when the Ego and all of its illusions falls away. Others, like you, are choosing to peel away the veil, layer by layer, now. As you do so with courage and commitment, you will experience greater and greater levels of peace.

> **EXERCISE:** Journal about a current area of conflict in your life. Explore for yourself the question: What is this situation asking of me? What aspects of myself is this giving me the opportunity to develop?

An Empath Yoga Perspective

Plank   Notice how you handle life's challenges

Plank offers us a wonderful opportunity to notice how we face life's challenges. Creating a long line of energy with your body, breathe deeply here; feel yourself getting stronger. Notice your self-talk, and how you respond internally when you are being challenged by Life. Do you push yourself aggressively to meet the challenge? Do you back off and not give yourself enough credit for that which you are truly capable? Or are you meeting the challenge in a healthy way? Are you allowing yourself to grow?

Repeat to yourself silently, "I am getting stronger and stronger, every day, with every breath I take." Let your breathing be deep, rich, full, and consistent. When you are challenged—in Plank, and in life—the breath will get you through it.

Chapter 12

Being Fully Expressed

*"Speak your truth,
even if your voice shakes."*

—*Maggie Kuhn*

We have arrived here, at this final chapter, with what have hopefully been some powerful realizations, the first of which is the realization that we are Love, and that not only is this true of ourselves, it's true of everyone. As we, each and every one of us, were subject to some level of social conditioning, so many of the messages received were in direct conflict with the inherent innocence and Love and perfection that is our Truth. In our confusion, the very necessary ego and the healthy sense of self it provides, has hardened, out of fear, into the Ego. In that moment, we entered into and agreed to a new reality, a reality based on fear, isolation, and separation. And because we have forgotten that we are One, we indulge in anger and blame (seeing the other as wrong), and guilt and shame (seeing ourselves as wrong).

When we entered into the story line of the human drama, a condition of the Ego, we buried and lost touch with our truth. It is my hope that this book helps those who are ready to excavate their way back to the core truth of who they are, and to choose to live from that place.

Here, in this final chapter, we taken an even closer look at how we are showing up in our lives, starting with our relationships.

Becoming Fully Expressed...
In Our Relationships

We see evidence of our alignment or misalignment with Truth in our relationships. The quality of our relationships is a direct reflection of our ability to love. This requires diligent recognition and shedding of the trappings of the Ego, and the Ego is cunning, seeking more and more creative and clever ways to entice us into a disconnect from Love.

Speaking Your Truth

In this chapter, where we introduce the concept of being fully expressed, speaking our truth is at the very center of that. But as we give consideration to why it is so important to speak our truth in our life and in our relationships, we must make sure we are able to distinguish between what is Truth and what is Ego.

When we are engaging in making the other person wrong, we have succumbed to the Ego's allure. When we are feeling victimized by Life, or guilty or shameful, we are indulging in old programming that has little to do with Truth.

If we convince ourselves that we are speaking "truth," when we are really coming from fear, we are merely managing our misery, and attempting to get others, and Life, to agree with our false reality. Unfortunately, it won't be too hard to find others who will, because there are still so many stuck in the illusion. If that is really what you want—to be right, and to be stuck in the story—you will be able to find support in that. It takes real awareness and diligence to ensure we are aligning ourselves with Truth. If it divides and separates, if it makes one wrong and the other right, if it's an attempt to control things, it is likely coming from Ego. If it is sourced from Love, seeks to foster deeper understanding, acceptance, connection, and expansion, it is coming from Truth.

Before speaking your truth, take some time to get in touch, deeply in touch, with what it is. Reflect, journal, meditate—whatever helps you gain clarity and perspective. Allow yourself time and space to sift through the layers of story, reactivity, and any justification your Ego may be chewing on. Clear a pathway within your own mind and find your way home to Truth before you open your mouth and put it into words. In other words, before you speak your truth, make sure you know what it is.

When we are speaking our truth, if we are taking full responsibility for our lives and for how we feel (which means giving up the popular victim mentality entirely) and for how we are interpreting things, we are going to choose "I" language. The moment we approach someone and point our fingers saying, "You make me...," we are giving our power away. But when we come from "I," we are taking responsibility for how we feel, and how we choose to interpret and perceive life. Not only does this keep you centered in your Self and in your power, it makes it easier for the other person to hear you.

If we are coming from Ego, the Ego in another will likely respond. When we come from Love and compassion—for ourselves and the other—they are less likely to be put on the defensive and the Love within them can respond. If we come from Truth and mutual respect, and the Ego in the other still responds, we can rest in the knowledge that we came from Love, and their reaction is not about us. Even while taking care of ourselves, and whatever choices that requires us to make, we can still do so with compassion, love and understanding for the other. Beware what I call the Spiritual Ego, deciding you are better and wiser, and therefore right, because you believe yourself to be more aware and more evolved.

> *"Spiritual awakening*
> *is about waking up from your ego.*
> *It is not about awakening your ego."*
>
> —*Sampo Kaasila*

Finding Center in Self

It's important in all of our relationships that we stay centered in ourselves; that we come from a strong and clear sense of Self, so that we are not reaching for Truth, so that we are not searching for wholeness from someone or some place out there.

"Saying no can be the ultimate self-care."
—Claudia Black

Every healthy relationship with others begins with a healthy relationship with ourselves. Failure to love and honor your Self leads to your own sense of self being lost, your personal power depleted, and your peace of mind and security determined by the actions of others. This leaves you feeling victimized, out of control, reactive, and insecure.

Allowing this slippery slope to occur in your relationships sets you up for disappointment, and the relationship either becomes painfully dysfunctional or dies a slow and agonizing death. In the end, you are left feeling lost, abandoned, and confused, and your self-esteem plummets to an all-time low.

To avoid this relationship pitfall, a healthy relationship requires you to honor You, and to constantly evaluate and re-evaluate who you are and *who you are not* when in relationship. Redefine your relationships and recognize them as incredible opportunities to grow and evolve to higher and higher levels of self-awareness. Set appropriate boundaries, learn to say "no" if something feels uncomfortable and does not honor you, and spend time alone, cultivating the most important relationship you will ever really have—the one you have with yourself. Doing so sets your feet on firmer ground, allowing you to be more centered and balanced in all of your relationships, and less needy, clingy, and dependent.

Making these choices, consciously, increases your feelings of personal power—which will also be felt in other areas of your life. Conscious and healthy choices raise your self-esteem, and cultivate and nourish a sense of inner security that is unaffected by the actions of others.

> *"Every second you spend looking*
> *for something outside yourself is another second*
> *you spend away from your true self."*
>
> —*Michael Jeffreys*

Keep a strong network of friends, continue to grow as an individual both outside of and inside of your relationships, speak your truth and practice deep listening. When we see relationships as the opportunity for personal growth that they really are, we can avoid devaluing ourselves by making somebody else the center of our world. Allow your self to be self-centered—not in a selfish, egotistical way, but in a self-full and self-loving way. Being centered in your Self and coming from Love within is also honoring and loving others, because it allows you to be more grounded, secure, honest, and real. Strive to discover and become your authentic Self in all of your relationships and they will become enjoyable, enduring, and deep.

A result of this deep inner work, and a strong and healthy relationship with ourselves, is an awareness of who we are. Knowing this, every day will be an opportunity to find our voice, to speak our truth, to be fully expressed. Coming from a place of Truth is the strongest place to come from; there is no stronger way to be. Truth is always about Love, for that is the very essence of who we are.

If speaking your Truth is something that those close to you cannot hear, then that's definitely something you need to know. Sometimes the most loving thing you can do is let somebody go so they can continue on their journey of life lessons. This isn't an opportunity for the Ego to buy into a belief that we are somehow better than another. It is simply a choice to surround ourselves with those that will honor and respect us.

We Teach People How to Treat Us.

Our relationship with others is a direct reflection of the quality of our relationship with ourselves. We teach people how to treat us. Everything we do and say, every mannerism, speaks volumes about who and what we are. Every choice we make conveys a message about us. Without even necessarily saying a word, we are communicating with those around us. Consciously or unconsciously, we are always communicating. We cannot not communicate.

The way others treat you is in direct response to the way they see you treating yourself. If you honor and respect yourself in all ways, others will do the same. You set the standard. You create your reality. If you are hard on yourself, beating yourself up for mistakes and blaming yourself when things do not go the way you expected, others may feel comfortable doing the same. In other words, if *you* are willing to blame you when things go awry, they may be willing to blame you as well.

If you are kind and gentle with yourself, honoring and respecting your humanity and remembering that mistakes are what help us grow, others may treat you that way as well. One thing you can be sure of, nobody is going to give you anything you are not willing to give yourself. If they did, you wouldn't be able to receive it anyway.

Self-acceptance and respect sets a standard and creates an expectation. When you love and accept yourself, you are better able to recognize and receive the Love and acceptance of others. And when you love and accept yourself, you are better able to offer love and acceptance to others. If complete and unconditional self-love and acceptance is not easy for you, when it is offered by others you may question their motives, doubt their authenticity, and disbelieve their words and actions. Over time they may get the message that what they thought was the truth about you is inaccurate. Your inability to accept their impressions about you is a subtle rejection. On some level, this may cause them to think twice about being so generous with you again.

One of my coaching clients had such a self-deprecating way of talking about himself, it was nearly impossible to pay him a compliment without it being negated. He would swiftly and deftly take what started out as an acknowledgement of him and turn it into an opportunity to be unworthy. While he did it with a sense of humor, I could feel his negation of my appreciation of him.

One of the first things we worked on was getting him to recognize what he was doing, to interrupt that habit by simply saying "thank you" to a compliment, and to start noticing his own self-talk. Within weeks of that discussion, I noticed a complete shift in his attitude toward himself. He was much gentler on himself, and I found him choosing much softer, more compassionate, kinder language with himself. Not only did his choice of words evolve, he felt bigger, more confident. His self-esteem expanded.

> *"Never do anything
> that will lower your self-esteem."*
> —Matthew Brownstein

As you start to recognize the whole and complete human being that is you, you will be able to recognize it in others as well. When others treat you or respond to you in a way that does not honor you, the self-love and acceptance within you will lovingly speak your truth and clarify their misperceptions. Or you will intuitively know at a very deep level that it's their stuff and not about you at all. In either case, compassion and forgiveness will flow freely from your heart to theirs as you recognize that you are a mirror for them.

Speaking of teaching people how treat us, if we are to take any kind of responsibility for our lives, we must be willing to look at how we are showing up in our relationships. While it is important for us to know our truth, it is equally important to know how to speak it.

Only the truly conscious, and the courageous, have what it takes to show up in their relationships honestly and directly. Assertive communicators are clear about who they are and what they want, while still honoring and respecting the other person. In fact, it is by speaking our truth that we honor the other person, because we know they are strong enough to hear it.

While it is important to address the energetic undercurrent that's taking place within a relationship, being direct does not have to feel like a full-frontal attack. For others who are not yet used to open, honest, and real communication, to be on the receiving end of it can be somewhat disconcerting. We can temper any potential bluntness with tact by coming from respect, compassion, and kindness—for them as well as for ourselves, by honoring them *as well as* ourselves. If they choose to play the victim, beat around the bush, or refuse to acknowledge "the elephant in the living room," that is their prerogative, and their choice.

The Power of Our Words

A Course in Miracles says words are just symbols twice removed from reality. While this may be true, energy organizes itself around our words. They carry meaning and intention; we must remember the power behind them.

> *"Every thought you think,
> and every word you speak,
> is affirming something."*
> —*Louis Hay*

Words carry creative power and potential. Once we speak something, we have affirmed it. I once heard a teacher say words are 10 times more powerful than our thoughts, because once we speak them, we have put them out onto a sound current that travels, carrying that energy into the ethers. Yogis know this, which is why mantra, and chanting, are such a powerful part of their spiritual practice.

Recognize and replace disempowering language, like "I can't" with "I can"; "there's nothing I can do" with "let's look at our alternatives"; and "she makes me so mad" with "I control my own feelings."

This last one is especially important when it comes to our relationships, because it means we are taking full responsibility for our lives and realizing nobody makes us feel anything. Which is why when speaking our truth, "I" language is the most proactive and conscious choice. Instead of the knee-jerk reaction and finger-pointing at the other person, using "I" language empowers us by allowing us to take full responsibility for what we think and feel. Failure to do so fosters a victim mentality.

> *"We must use the power of our words
> constructively."*
> —*Stella-Terril Mann*

A young workshop participant in her twenties was in the midst of a difficult life transition, and was lamenting how scared she was, and her disappointment in what she felt was a lack of sympathy and support from her mother. She said that while she knew her mother loved her, she couldn't remember ever hearing her say the words, and she wasn't one to offer hugs or affection. It was clear my client wanted their relationship to change, so she volunteered for a role-play exercise to help illustrate some of the communication skills we had covered in the workshop, and to help prepare her for a conversation she knew she wanted to have but was completely intimidated by.

I coached her to be proactive when approaching her mother and not wait until they were in the middle of a conflict. She agreed she would request a meeting, letting her mother know she wanted to sit down and have a conversation with her, and together they would choose the best time and place to have the discussion. Then, I encouraged her to recognize the good qualities of her mother; to be accountable for how she, herself, was feeling; and to be aware of her tone and inflection, making sure her nonverbal communication was in alignment with her words. Finally, I asked her to be prepared to make a clear request, by knowing what it was she was ultimately asking for.

Then she was coached to spend some time visualizing a successful interaction between them. When we started, all she could really see and feel was the strife and frustration she felt around their relationship dynamic, so we took some time to get clear on what she really wanted, which she identified as a closer, more loving relationship with her mother that allowed them to evolve their relationship to a true friendship. When given the opportunity to play herself approaching her mother in this role-play, she wasn't even sure where to begin, because she often felt so shot down and cut off that she couldn't speak, or even think clearly. So we started with her playing the part of her mother, and I played her approaching her mother. The conversation went something like this:

"Mom, as you know I'm going through a very difficult time right now. I'm really scared…and I really want to know that I have your support. Not only do I want to know you are there for me, I want us to be closer. I want us to hug. I love you, and I know that you love me. I want us to tell each other that more. Basically, I just really want a closer relationship with you."

"Love people enough to tell them the truth and respect them enough to trust that they can handle it."

—Iyanla Vanzant

When I was done articulating all the things she had identified as her truth, lovingly and honestly, and stopped to give her a chance to respond, as her mother, she looked stupefied. "I have no idea how my mother would respond to that," she said. "I've never communicated with her like that before." She admitted that her mother would probably be able to receive the message if it was presented that way. We then switched roles, and she was able to practice the direct, open, honest, respectful, loving communication she wanted to experience.

In the end she felt prepared, but filled with nervous excitement around her pending discussion with her mother, and we all rooted for her. The following week we were thrilled to hear that the conversation went well, and still months later she said their relationship had never been better. In fact, her mother has asked, "What happened in that workshop? She's like a completely different person."

It is a true testament to the fact that only one person within a relationship needs to change in order for the entire relationship dynamic to shift. Taking full responsibility means knowing we could be that person. This means letting go of blame entirely.

> *"Maturity is the balance between courage and consideration."*
> —Stephen Covey

EXERCISE: Think of a relationship dynamic which you would like to shift. How could you be showing up differently? Is there is a conversation that needs to take place? Take some time to explore what it is you would like to see happen, and what you are willing to do to create that possibility.

Expression is not limited to our words. As much as 93% of the message is nonverbal. It is possible for the words we choose, our inflection, tone of voice, and body language to align for a message that is assertive, clear, and direct, but also respectful and kind. I like to think of it as a strong-but-soft approach.

Being Fully Expressed

> **EXERCISE: JOURNAL/VISUALIZE** What does it mean to be strong but soft? Close your eyes and imagine what it would look like if you were showing up that way in your life. In the beginning, your voice may not be as clear. Imagine you are learning to work with a new instrument. Get your mind aligned with your heart, and your language will automatically reflect that. Your words will flow more effortless, more freely.

Be gentle. Surround yourself with people that will support you in your growth and honor your process.

> *"Surround yourself with people who respect and treat you well."*
> —Claudia Black

BECOMING FULLY EXPRESSED... IN OUR LIVES

Becoming Bigger than the Fear

As soon as we stop playing the role of the victim and recognize the power of our thoughts, our words, and our choices, we're able to create powerfully. We're able to harness and channel the raw, creative energy that flows through us, and that is us, by keeping our channel open and clear, without contracting and closing in fear.

If we let our lives be about managing our fear, the focus quickly becomes what we cannot do and why. We start to contract, living smaller, safer lives, and our spirit mourns. We yearn for more, but allow our Ego-mind to convince us with clever excuses that justify our playing small.

A friend with children allows a desire to put his kids through a posh private school, take their two annual vacations, and add an extension onto the house be his reason for staying at a job he

"Life begins at the edge of your comfort zone."
—Neale Donald Walsch

bemoans every day, while his true dream and passion floats further and further away. I've asked him if "playing by the rules," as he puts it, is really in the best interests of his family. Does he want his daughters to play it safe when they grow up, or does he want them to live their dreams? What kind of energy does he bring home into the house every night? Is it inspired and on purpose, or is he just getting through life? And finally, is this what he wants to be modeling for his children?

We can either choose to play it safe and live our lives in fear (and when we're in fear we contract), or we can choose Love, faith, trust, and courage, and we expand. When we recognize and become aware of our fears, we can choose to expand in the face of them, becoming bigger than the fear.

> *"The things we fear most have already happened to us."*
>
> —*Deepak Chopra*

When you repeat a thought pattern often enough, you create neural pathways in the brain that, over time, can develop into deep grooves of habitual thinking. The deeper those grooves become, the harder it is to change. Many times a habitual thought pattern is born as a result of a powerful stimulus that overrides the system, and when we become overwhelmed in this way there is enough confusion created to cause us to keep thinking about the event, over and over again. As a result of that intense focus, and the strong emotions that usually accompany it, a neural pathway is either born or becomes much more deeply entrenched into our psyche. Suddenly those thoughts become part of the filter through which we see the world.

If a strong enough stimulus can affect us in such a way, why not use this knowledge to our advantage? This is what prompted me one day to stop in my tracks and say out loud, "I am going skydiving." I could hear the surprise in my own voice when I said the words.

I had a full 10 days after booking my jump to allow my head to come up with a creative enough excuse that I could justify changing my mind without losing face. But my motivation was clear: my

> *"Eventually, you get to a place in life where you are moving toward what you want faster than you are away from what you fear."*
>
> —Mark Austin Thomas

skydiving adventure would serve as a microcosm of my whole life, and I would use it to observe my own mind. Would I contract when faced with fear, or expand? Would I allow the fear to be bigger than me, or would I allow myself to become bigger than the fear?

Over the 10 days, I observed the stories my mind started to weave, from, "It's too expensive and I can't afford it right now," and "I'm too busy to take the time off for this," to "what if I end up horribly disfigured or…dead?" But because I intentionally brought into the experience a conscious awareness of all the ways my mind would chew on this, I simply observed my thoughts instead of feeding them. I thought, "That's just fear, Erica. You can choose not to feed it."

Each time, I interrupted the fear-based thought midstream and replaced it with a more empowering thought. I kept visualizing myself standing at the doorway of the plane just before the jump, and knew that in that moment I would have to embrace trust, and then let go. If I could do that in the face of such a powerful stimulus, surely I could parlay that into other areas of my life. It only took a couple of times before I witnessed my mind already creating a new neural pathway. It became easier and easier to recognize the fear and redirect my thoughts.

Because of that intention, fear never got a chance to get a foothold, and each day I could feel my excitement, not my fear, building. And although the jump was truly a rush, it was actually everything I experienced within myself leading up to it that was most memorable. Standing in the doorway of the plane, I didn't feel any fear, only exhilaration, because the fear had already been faced. I was free to just be in the moment and experience the fullness of it. Amazing.

So it is with Life. If we can become conscious enough of our thoughts to notice when fear has begun to surface, we can decide if we want to feed it or not. Do we want to nurture the fear and allow it to overwhelm us and rob us of our freedom, or do we want to expand and become bigger than the fear and feel the liberation that comes with that? What would happen if we started doing that consciously every day? In the beginning it might take some focused effort, but once that thinking takes root and is nurtured a couple of times, this new possibility can blossom into reality.

Stop Making Excuses

Being fully expressed also means recognizing that, whether you believe in reincarnation, or that life ends with the shedding of these bodies, this is the only life we know we get to live. Why not live it to the absolute fullest potential we possibly can? This means no longer making excuses, and choosing instead to make the most of what we have available to us.

My friend whose passion for life may be dying on the vine while he plays it safe and secure at a job may feel comfortable, but not alive. While he's made his choice and works hard to be at peace with it every day, he doesn't seem truly happy or free.

By contrast, another family lives modestly and frugally, home-schooling (or more accurately, world-schooling) their children by taking them to different and exotic locations around the world. These are wise children with a beautifully developing worldview they could never have gotten from within the four walls of a school. They are immersed in other cultures and ways of life and, as a result, have an understanding of Life that most kids, even in expensive private schools, do not. For that matter, they may have a better understanding of Life than a lot of other adults. And while this family's lifestyle comes with its own share of stressors, they are staying true—living the life they want to live without believing they are a part of a system in which they have no control.

This is not to say one family's choices are better or worse than the other's. They are just living the lives that are a product of the choices they have made, and that is either allowing them to be freely and fully expressed in this life, or not.

I, for one, want to suck all the juice out of this experience I call my life, which is why I have chosen to be on purpose with my work and stay true to what I believe to be my life's calling. I have created, through the choices I have made, a life that allows me to touch people's lives and make a difference. I have found, and created, a way to combine this with travel, another of my passions, and have a freedom for which I am eternally grateful.

"You must not let your life run in the ordinary way; do something that nobody else has done, something that will dazzle the world. Show that God's creative principle works in you."

—Swami Yogananda

"...only by stepping without hesitation into the next inch of the unknown can we build confidence in the life we are about to live."

—Blind Frenchman, Jacques Lusseyran.

"Many of us treat life as if it were a novel. We pass from page to page passively, assuming the author will tell us on the last page what it was all about."

—James Hollis

It hasn't always been easy, and it hasn't always been graceful. I have lived out of my car, bounced from one friend's couch to another, and lived like a starving artist and gypsy while I poured all of my energy, resources, and attention into growing my business and writing this book. So when people tell me I'm lucky to be able to live the life I live, only those who know the sacrifices I have made, and the uncompromisingly diligent effort I have put forth to stay true, know that there was little luck involved. Our lives are a consequence of the choices we have made along the way, and it takes courage to stay in integrity with ourselves when things get rough.

> **"The only time you have a chance to show courage is when you are afraid."**
>
> —*Dan Millman*

Which is why I was so disappointed when a friend who I believed understood this sent me an email asking me to stop communicating with her. In her email, she said she felt I was insensitive to the plight of the single mother, which she is.

The irony is, I have wanted a child of my own for years, and part of the driving force behind my efforts was an intention to create a lifestyle that could support me and a child. I've carried a vision of me doing my work and traveling the world, *with* a child, floating around in my mind for years, and wondered if I'd be blessed with such a gift. So when just months before my 40th birthday I discovered I was pregnant, I didn't doubt for a moment how much I wanted it.

I knew that while it wouldn't be *as easy* to travel and experience the world as freely as I had before, I was committed to thinking outside the box to allow me and my child to have our own unique experience of this life, and of this world. I hired a midwife, focused entirely on a natural birthing experience, and vowed I would home and world-school my child by taking her everywhere with me. I felt sure it was a girl and, yes, even had a name picked out for her.

When, right at 12 weeks, I had a miscarriage, to say I was devastated is an understatement. There were a few moments there when the sadness and grief was so great I thought there was no way I would recover. Of course, in the end I had no choice; it was either throw in the proverbial towel and admit defeat, or use every tool I had—the ones I write about in this book—to love myself through the experience.

Ultimately, this gave me an opportunity to choose, once again, to let go and trust in the flow of Life. I am reminded of a line in a movie that has become sort of a personal mantra for me: "Life is right, in any case. As for me…my heart is open."

I realize that, while this might not be the last time I experience loss or disappointment, it could be the last time I doubt life. I can choose to live in the flow, and be as creative as I possibly can in how I interpret my experiences and what meaning I give them. Then I can let go and move on. Like the Kundalini Yoga mantra, so powerful in its simplicity: "Keep Up." No matter what happens, no matter what life throws your way, you just keep going. You keep living. Like the phoenix rising out of the ashes, each moment is an opportunity for re-birth.

I could have used this as an opportunity to adopt the role of the victim. I could have given up and become bitter. I could resent those that have children and blame them for being insensitive to me because I do not. Or, I can choose to trust Life. I can choose to trust that if things are happening the way that they are happening in my life then *there must be a good reason for it*.

While it turns out having a child of my own is not in the cards for me, maybe someday I'll adopt. Maybe I'll be a foster parent to many children, and leave an indelible print on their lives. But whatever happens, it will be beautiful and perfect and right, because I will choose, again and again, to see it that way.

"Where did we get the impression that THIS shouldn't be happening?"

—Michael Jeffreys

Gratitude

One of my favorite places to visit in San Francisco is Café Gratitude, where they say, "We love the expansive feeling we get from cultivating an attitude of Gratitude." Their entire mission is to do exactly that, and to inspire it in others. I love seeing their bumper stickers and t-shirts around town, posing the simple question, "What are you grateful for?" Gratitude asks us to look at what we have, rather than what's missing. While fear contracts, gratitude expands, allowing us to receive more of Life.

> *"Grace isn't a little prayer you chant
> before receiving a meal.
> It's a way to live."*
>
> —Jacqueline Winspear

We can focus on what's missing, on what's "wrong," or we can focus on what's right, and be grateful.

A dear friend found himself shaken to the core when he discovered he had a life-threatening illness. While there was naturally a fair amount of fear that news shook loose and brought to the surface for him, it inspired him to spend time looking at his life, and he discovered he was grateful; grateful for how abundant and full of love his had been. During that time, he began every day with an exercise in gratitude, choosing to focus on the beauty and the blessings. Even now, after having completely recovered and receiving a clean bill of health, he still practices gratitude every day.

When we are being challenged, an attitude of gratitude inspires us to ask: What is life showing me? And what am I going to do with it?

Be the Master Alchemist. You are holding energy in your hands, in your heart, in your mind. How are you going to direct that energy that flows through you, this Divine gift of Life? Life needs You to bring it into manifestation on this material plane, in this physical incarnation you are now in. Do it justice. With immense gratitude in your heart for the gift of this life, *live it*. Live it fully and without fear…without excuses. Be a light onto the world. Emanate Love, for that is what you are. It's all you ever were. And it's all you ever will be.

> *"Love is the way I walk in gratitude."*
>
> —*A Course in Miracles*

> *"Wake at dawn with a winged heart and give thanks for another day of loving.*
>
> —Kahlil Gibran

> **EXERCISE:** Take some time to reflect and journal, answering the question for yourself: What am I grateful for?

It is only fear, and our desire to control things, that makes us suffer, because it puts us at odds with Life. It's a very Buddhist philosophy that our attachments to the way things are and the way things ought to be is what makes us suffer. If we can instead find gratitude for what we have and the way things are, then life opens up for us—life expands.

How often have you heard the story of the woman who couldn't get pregnant, and as soon as she let it go, she did? Not only does it speak directly to the topic of having children, but it is also a great metaphor for any circumstance in life. The same thing is often said to people who are looking for their soulmate. The incessant yearning and searching tends to push it away, keeping what you want just out of reach. As soon as you let go and stop trying, what you were searching for comes to you. Like a magnet, we attract when we trust. Every moment is an opportunity to trust in the natural order of things. We can choose to let go and trust, and make the most powerful choice available to us moment by moment.

How do we choose to interpret life events? How do we choose to interpret a breakup, the loss of a loved one, a miscarriage, the loss of a job? Gratitude gets us looking for the gift…the opportunity…the possibility…Like the mother who loses a child only to channel that energy into pioneering a cause to raise awareness. Or the man who gets cut loose from his job only to turn that loss into an opportunity to finally get clear and on purpose in his life.

Even in the instance of my miscarriage, when nobody would blame me for shutting down and contracting, my heart just opens wider. I open up to Love even more. This is always, always, always, the pathway back to peace. We will never know true and lasting peace until we have this piece. It is our birthright. As my friend Kristen sums up so nicely, "Let Love be your center of gravity." Always return to Love. Find your center in it, because that is who, and what, you are.

"Take your life in your own hands and what happens? A terrible thing; no one to blame."

—Erica Jong

Choice

We are creative beings. We cannot not create. Every thought we think is creating something. The thoughts we choose to feed affect the choices that we make and, ultimately, our lives are a product of those choices. This is why the thoughts we choose to feed are at the very center of our creation process.

It is time to recognize and rid ourselves of the victim mentality that is and has been so popular amongst the masses. There is a reason why there are so few people we can think of who are living a truly inspired life. They are amongst an elite group who have chosen to live their lives their own way. It isn't always graceful. It isn't always easy. But neither is the cookie-cutter existence for which so many have settled.

Nobody is going to give you permission to be who you are capable of being. That permission, full creative license, was already given to you, by Life, when you were born. It is up to you, now, to claim it.

So answer, again, perhaps the most important question you will ever ask: Who am I? Now you get to choose the You that you are living your way into, and you do this by the choices that you make.

Wise decisions don't come from your head. Living a truly authentic life means being guided from an intuitive place within. This is the only way to ensure we are not merely playing out some old outdated programming that no longer serves us, or living uninspired, "safe" lives and simply waiting to die.

> ***"It's not that people make the decision to die; they make the decision to stop living."***
>
> —*Sherry Evans*

Living an inspired, full life sometimes means dancing to the beat of a different drum. Asking for advice or following some formulaic decision-making process does not allow our life to be an organic, continuously evolving experience. We tap into our truth, our greatest source of divine guidance and direction, by checking in with ourselves and feeling for the next right answer… and "right" is entirely subjective. Nobody else can give you that.

"It is not because things are difficult that we do not dare; it is because we do not dare that they are difficult."

—Seneca

> **EXERCISE:** Consider a current decision you have been mulling over. You can have your truest, most authentic answer right now. First, be honest with yourself about what your choices are, then play them out in your mind one at a time and notice how each possible scenario feels in your body. Those feelings are Spirit, your truth, communicating with you.

If you still find yourself waffling, consider to what degree fear is playing a part, and if that's the place from which you want to live your life. What would courageous look and feel like?

If the next right step on your path still is unclear, perhaps the best possible answer needs a little fine-tuning. Consider what would need to happen in order for this to feel right A friend shared with me that she had been experiencing minor symptoms of postpartum depression. It took first being really honest with herself that something wasn't feeling right, and then some reflection and self-honesty for her to realize being a stay-at-home-mom wasn't what she wanted. Once she let go of her own self-judgment around what kind of a mother that made her, she eventually hired a part-time nanny and started freelancing, and now her life is feeling more balanced. Sometimes a little tweaking goes a long way.

You may even want to play out in your mind what would happen if you did nothing, because choosing not to decide is still a choice. How does that one feel in your body? A client struggled with leaving his unfulfilling, stressful, and demanding job out of fear of what the future may hold, yet every day was a physical, mental, and emotional challenge for him just to get through. While it took him a while to get to a place of real clarity, he eventually drew his own conclusion that doing nothing was slowly but surely killing him.

We are all starting to wake up from a collective dream, and cookie-cutter lives are holding less and less appeal. Be willing to look at your perceived limitations. Watch for statements that contain the words "I can't," "I should," or "I shouldn't." For many, now marks a time of beginning to think and live outside of the box.

When you have felt your way into the right answer to the question, you will know—you will feel it in your body. The more you choose to listen from that place, the more quickly and efficiently that guidance will come. It was actually there all along. And the more you practice this level of deep listening and self-honesty, the more efficient you will become at noticing when something is out of alignment.

Courage

There lives within all of us an unlimited range of possibility. Pure potential is what we are—behind the social mask, beneath the personality, beyond the physical self and the material belongings amassed. We are each a drop in the ocean, one potential expression of Spirit. We will return to the Sea of Infinite Possibilities, and in truth were never really separate. We are each one possible expression of All-That-Is—one experience of consciousness exploring itself, expressing itself, through us.

While this experience of You, and of Me, this particular expression of consciousness exploring itself through us, lasts for a limited period of time according to our linear, thinking, human mind, that which is truly us never goes anywhere. We simply return to the sea of cosmic consciousness from which we were never really separate, only, perhaps, to be remanifested into another opportunity of pure potential, expressing another variation of all that is possible through us.

In this life, this experience of pure potentiality, the only thing blocking us from remembering that our life is our canvas, that we are the artists expressing our way through this reality that is our masterpiece, is the mind. The more we align our heads with our hearts, and see the mind as the tool that it is, the more we can remember the truth of who we are, and live this life, this expression of ourselves, with complete and total freedom, joy, and bliss. There is nothing to fear. This world, this life, is our playground. We can frolic in this ocean of pure freedom, potential, and bliss, for there is nothing else for us to be or do.

"Life shrinks or expands in proportion to one's courage."

—Anais Nin

Non-Attachment

Often when we are not at peace in our lives, we will find attachment—to a person, an outcome, or an ideal. Our need to have something be the way we want it shows up as a need to control, dominate, or manipulate. This is what robs us of our inner peace, for it implies that something is not as it should be. It implies that something must be different in order for things to be right.

Practicing acceptance is something we get to do every day. Begin to look at your attachments; notice those moments when you feel yourself contract, and feel the desire to impose your will over a situation. Then notice what happens in your body when you follow that urge to control with a deep breath and a decision to accept the moment exactly as it is, and simply witness it unfolding. See how your body relaxes, be aware of how your mind clears, recognize the expansive shift in your emotional state.

> *"Accept whatever happens*
> *and let your spirit move freely."*
> —*Chuang Tzu*

Trust

All of this becomes easier if we also cultivate trust in the natural order of things. When we can rest in the belief that everything happens exactly as it should, when it should, the need to force things melts away. No longer do we feel the need to exert so much effort and will over things that are ultimately beyond our control. An insistence upon controlling only makes us miserable, and that misery bleeds over into the lives of those we care about most.

Recently a friend struggled with the possibility of losing her daughter in a nasty custody battle to her domineering, abusive, relentless ex-husband. Her attachment to a right outcome, her fear over losing custody of her daughter, was making her physically ill. She wasn't eating, she wasn't sleeping, and her daylight hours were spent emotionally exhausted from the fight.

> *"When you worry you are saying to God/the Universe/Life, 'I don't trust you.'"*
>
> —Michael Jeffreys

It wasn't until she confronted her attachment to the outcome that she was able to shift her experience. By getting in touch with the purity of her love for her daughter, and trusting in the outcome, whatever it might be, that her experience began to change. She wasn't releasing her love for her daughter, or her desire to have her in her life, but she was accepting that whatever happened, she would be okay. She would survive. This required her to recognize what image in her mind she was attached to, to consider all possible alternatives, and begin accepting all of them. Then she put her trust in her love for her daughter and gave the situation over to a power that was greater than her.

In the end she did get her daughter back, and saved herself weeks of useless and unnecessary anguish. If the outcome had been different, as a result of all her inner work she would have already been on her way toward healing, and capable of surviving the blow.

This marked the beginning of a powerful transition in how she was holding a situation that, up to that point, had been torturous. The reality is, there are very few things in life that will actually kill us. Much of what we experience is an opportunity to gain awareness, to practice acceptance, and to trust. Although sometimes the challenge is a big one, like my friend's, and stretches us to our very limits, every day is full of opportunities.

Trust that the same energy that keeps the stars in the sky, the planets in orbit, the rhythm in nature, and the cycle in life also has its arms around your life. This is the human adventure, all of it strengthening us, seasoning us, tenderizing us. Open your eyes each new day with courage, faith, and trust—in wonder and awe of what the new day brings, free of the burdens of the past. Be in the flow of Life. Watch in fascination what shows up. Be open to the experience. When you align your energy with the creative energy of Life, amazing things happen. What is waiting to be born in you? Expressed through you? Be a conduit for Light, for Love, for Truth.

Fill Out Your Spirit

Having never been a performer of any kind growing up, with no musical, dance, or theatrical background, there is a part of me that appreciates those that do. I know a brother and sister who grew up singing, playing music, participating in team sports, and exploring the many different aspects of themselves. They also grew up in a family whose feet were pretty firmly planted on an evolutionary spiritual path. They learned early on that they were beautiful beings of Love and Light, and that anything is possible if they believe.

This wasn't something they were taught to just think, but something that became so deeply ingrained in them from such an early age that they seem to live it with effortless ease. This is not to say they experience no fear, but that they recognize it for what it is and don't give it a chance to get a foothold.

What's most impressive about them is their *presence*. They really fill out their lives—thinking big, believing big, and therefore living big. Not in a way that's about fancy houses, expensive cars, and designer clothing, although they can and do afford these things, but with a confidence in themselves and in the support that Life offers in a myriad of ways. They trust. It is a beautiful thing to behold—what we are capable of when we believe in ourselves rather than in fear.

Some people are hiding in a small corner of their minds. Don't be afraid to fill out your body, your spirit, your life. Claim your space in the world. Know who you are. When you stand tall and fill out your space, your whole aura changes.

In yoga there is an asana I love to use to help students get a feel for how they are showing up in their lives. *Tadasana,* or Mountain Pose, is a simple standing pose, with arms relaxed by our sides, which is designed to help improve posture and bring a heightened level of awareness into all other standing poses. It is here we can gain insight into how we are showing up in our lives. Some slouch down into their hips, unwilling to take up their full height. Others round at the shoulders, as if to duck and hide, while others lean forward into life, as if they can somehow control it. It is usually only with practice and guidance that students are able to relax back into their bodies, stand tall and claim their space. The way we show up in our bodies tends to be the way we show up in life.

There is no better place to be than alive with the truth, and the deep and all-pervading confidence that comes from knowing yourself intimately, and choosing always to honor what is true—what is real for you. To live any other way is to live within a house of cards. It will all come tumbling down eventually.

Once you know your truth, it is up to you to live it. This is your life; nobody else gets to live it for you. It is an intricately woven tapestry made up of all of your choices. Let it be your masterpiece.

> *"Life is a great big canvas;*
> *throw all the paint on it you can."*
>
> —*Danny Kaye*

You are the Channel

Thoughts are energy. Emotions are energy. We are energy. Energy vibrates. It moves. If we want to brighten our light—to raise our vibration—we must allow that energy to move.

Yogic philosophy teaches of awareness, or energy, that lies dormant at the base of the spine, resting like a coiled serpent. We call this *Kundalini* energy. On the path to awakening, that energy must be awakened and allowed to rise, freely and unencumbered, along a central channel—an energetic channel—that runs alongside our spine, all the way up to our crown and beyond.

Along this channel there are energy centers called *chakras*. The energy of the lower chakras is contracted, heavier, denser, and then becomes lighter, freer, and more expansive as it passes through all seven chakras from the lower, earthly energies to the higher, cosmic energies, re-uniting us with cosmic consciousness, returning us to an awareness of the Sea of Infinite Possibilities from whence we came.

In order for this energy, this Kundalini energy, to awaken and rise, the health of these energy centers must be strong and balanced. This is called the Liberating Current—to move from fear and illusion to higher and higher states of consciousness—to move toward, to return to, Love and Light.

We are creative beings. Allowing Life's energy to move through us is to create, is to be alive. If we are not creating, energy is not moving, eventually getting hung up…stuck, and if it is not flowing outward and manifesting into our reality, that energy is being turned inward, driven deeper into the nervous system. If we are not creating and expressing, we eventually collapse in on ourselves—imploding. I know far too many people who are just waiting to die, their lives lacking spark as their internal flame has become so diminished it is nearly extinguished.

Life isn't something to be gotten through, it's something to be celebrated. If we aren't celebrating, more than likely we've stopped creating. The joy is gone.

Your Life is Your Canvas

In yoga there is a another current of energy that moves through us. This one from the heavens above, from Pure Potential, the Sea of Infinite Possibilities—down through that same channel, the channel that is us, into reality. This is called the Manifesting Current. We are a conduit. We are the conduit for that possibility, if we get out of our own way.

Imagine you are the pen, and Spirit is the ink—the energy that flows through, expressing itself onto the canvas that is your life. We honor Life by being a healthy channel and allowing Spirit to use us…to co-create with us. The more open our channel—the more free of fear; unencumbered by the past; ridden of outdated thoughts, beliefs, and emotions—the faster that current of creativity manifests.

From the Sea of Infinite Possibilities a seed of raw potential is planted, and shows up in our mind as an inspired thought. If the mind is open enough to receive it, that thought begins to take shape, formulating as an image in our minds. That image, brought more and more into focus—like fine- tuning the lens on a camera, becomes an inspired vision.

> *"How often—even before we began—have we declared a task 'impossible'? And how often have we constructed a picture of ourselves as being inadequate?...A great deal depends upon the thought patterns we choose and on the persistence with which we affirm them."*
>
> —Piero Ferrucci

If we believe in the vision, and in ourselves enough, we start to put it into words, speaking it into existence in the minds of others, as well as our own. If the audience is chosen wisely, and our vision is supported, the energy around this possibility strengthens, and we start to feel it as a possibility. If our heart is open, and we give ourselves permission to feel it happening, the energy continues to solidify, and we start to take action.

Those who lack heart will not take the steps necessary to call this idea forth into existence, and the energy will fade, the flame dying out. This is where the saying "all talk and no action" comes in. The heart has to be on board, which is why it is so vitally important to love, to consistently return to Love. Then we must be willing to move, to take action, to do what needs to be done, and to have confidence in our ability to do so. This is why it is so important to love ourselves.

> ***"If you don't set a baseline standard for what you'll accept in life, you'll find it's easy to slip into behaviors and attitudes or a quality of life that's far below what you deserve."***
>
> —*Anthony Robbins*

The next stop—or go—in the channel of creation is recognizing our interdependence on each other. We need each other. If we are healthy, open, and aligned, we will attract all the right people, circumstances, and opportunities needed. This is why it's important to love each other.

The health of our life is a direct reflection on, and extension of, the health of our relationships. And the health of our relationships is a direct reflection on, and extension of, our relationship with ourselves. We are all in this together, and nobody has ever accomplished anything great without the love and support of others.

> *"You may be happy enough going along,
> but with others you'll get farther and faster."*
>
> —*Rumi*

Finally, if the energy is still moving, alive around this possibility—and we are grounded and stable, and focused enough to give birth to it—this inspired thought, which was nothing more than an idea that seemingly appeared out of nowhere, is born through us. This is why it's so important to be in our bodies—joyfully, consciously, freely.

> *"If we are really to heal ourselves and our planet,
> we will have to live in our bodies and on our planet,
> rather than constantly looking
> for ways to leave them"*
>
> —*Frank Natale*

Even then, even when it is born through us, we do not own it. We are but a conduit. Let us not be overly attached to our creations. Life, and death, are a natural cycle, a rhythmic indication that energy is continuing to move as it should. As it *must*.

Once we're clear on who and what we are, and what it is we want to create, then we become the chemist, working magic with energy. Energy is available; it flows through us, looking for direction. We direct it with our thoughts; with where we choose to focus; with where we put our attention. It is an invitation to practice deep listening, to have that relationship with Spirit, remembering that life is a co-creation. It's always a co-creation. Again, what is Life showing you, and what are you going to do with it?

We want to make sure we don't loose the humility and the ability to listen on a deep level. At the same time, we don't want to be so humble that we sit back waiting for the Universe to drop it in our laps. We are Master Alchemists; as soon as we learn how to work with this energy, this energy that flows through us. This energy that is us. We are a channel. We are the pen, Spirit is the ink, creating onto this canvas, this beautiful work of art we call Life.

> *"No one awakens...
> Life sees it was
> never bound."*
>
> —Michael Jeffreys

Being Fully Expressed

"A painting is never finished—it simply stops in interesting places."

—Paul Gardner

Let your life be a tribute to the presence that is within you. Get out of your own way so that Spirit can create a beautiful masterpiece through you, and with you.

You can rewrite your story. You can write whatever story you want. Just remember it's still a story. So why not make it big? Why not make it a beautiful, epic adventure and Love story?

Let go of the past. Remember the truth of who you are. Move around inside of this life you have been given. Explore the boundaries. Find your edge. Create. Consciously create. And love. For God's sake, remember to love.

AN EMPATH YOGA PERSPECTIVE

Tadasana — Relax into your body

Tadasana, Mountain Pose, is like standing at attention, but without the tension. Notice how solid, stable, secure, and strong you feel, while at the same time allowing yourself to relax into your own body. Be in your body in a very centered, grounded, present way.

Notice how you show up in the world, how you hold yourself in relationship to the world. Do you lean forward, as if to push your way aggressively into Life in an attempt to make things happen, or do you relax back into your center and allow for a beautiful co-creation with Life? Do your shoulders buckle under the weight of Life, or do you stand tall with your heart open and expansive? Are you trusting Life? Simply notice how you hold yourself in relationship to the world around you.

Now is just the beginning…

www.ingramcontent.com/pod-product-compliance
Lightning Source LLC
Chambersburg PA
CBHW080333170426
43194CB00014B/2550